The Ultimate Greek Cookbook

111 BEST Greek Dishes To Cook Right Now

By

Slavka Bodic

Copyright @2020

All rights reserved. No part of this book may be reproduced in any form without writing permission in writing from the author. Reviewers may quote brief passages in reviews.

No part of this publication may be reproduced or transmitted in any form or by any means, mechanical or electronic, including photocopying or recording, or by any information storage and retrieval system, or transmitted by email without permission in writing from the publisher. While all attempts have been made to verify the information provided in this publication, neither the author nor the publisher assumes any responsibility for errors, omissions or contrary interpretations of the subject matter herein.

This book is for entertainment purposes only. The views expressed are those of the author alone and should not be taken as an expert instruction or command. The reader is responsible for his or her actions. Adherence to all applicable laws and regulations, including international, federal, state and local governing professional licensing, business practices, advertising, and all other aspects of doing business in US, Canada or any other jurisdiction is the sole responsibility of the purchaser or reader.

Neither the author nor the publisher assumes any responsibility or liability whatsoever on the behalf of the purchaser or reader of these materials. Any perceived slight of any individual or organization is purely unintentional. Similarity with already published recipes is possible.

ISBN:

Imprint: Independently published

Please sign up for free Balkan and Mediterranean recipes:
www.balkanfood.org

Table of Contents

WHAT'S THE MOTIVATION FOR THIS COOKBOOK? 1

WHY GREEK FOOD? 2

LUNCH AND DINNER 5

    Moussaka 6

    Greek Lemon Chicken 8

    Slow roasted shoulder of lamb 10

    Greek Thanksgiving Turkey 12

    Greek Beef Over Zucchini 14

    Grilled Mediterranean Chicken 15

    Beef and Onion Stew (*Stifado*) 16

    Zesty Chicken Oregano 17

    Braised Chicken in Aromatic Tomato Sauce (*Pastitsatha*) 18

    Stuffed Grape Leaves (*Dolmades*) 20

    Grilled Octopus With Oregano 22

    Greek Chicken with Olives 23

    Tomato Pilaf 24

    Greek Quesadilla 25

    Chicken Casserole with Olives 26

    Cinnamon Chicken (*Kota Kapama*) 27

    Rice with Feta 29

Shrimps with Feta Cheese (*Garides Me Feta*) 31

Meatballs (*Keftethes*) 32

Athenian Stuffed Peppers 34

Zucchini Pancakes (*Kolokythia Krokettes*) 35

Artichoke and Pea Stew 36

Okra Stew 37

Green Peas with Veal 38

Cabbage Dolmathes (*Lahanodolmathes*) 39

Soutzoukakia 40

Veal with Lemon 41

Fish Plaki 42

Grilled Salmon & Zucchini with Red Capsicum Sauce 43

Herbed Fish Fillets 44

Shrimps with Spinach and Zucchini 45

Tuna Patties 46

Hearty Turkey Stew 47

Lamb and Apricot Hot Pot 48

Baked Potato 49

Artichoke Cod with Tomatoes 50

Pork Souvlaki with Tzatziki 51

Feta-Brined Chicken Breast with Rosemary 53

Lamb En Papilotte (*Arnaki Klephtiko*) 55

Beef and Quince Stew (*Moschari me Kydonia*) 57

Corfiot Veal with Vinegar Sauce (*Sofrito*) 59

Octopus with Ouzo and Olives (*Htapothi me Elies kai Ouzo*) 61

Red Mullet Baked in Grape Leaves (*Barbounia Psita sta Klimatofylla*) 63

Pork Braised with Celery and Leeks (*Hirino me Selina kai Prasa*) 65

Egg Noodles with Warm Tahini-Yogurt Sauce 67

Green Peppers Stuffed with Feta (*Piperies Gemistes me Feta*) 69

Chicken Gyros with Tzatziki 70

Greek Lamb Patties with Tabbouleh 72

SALADS 75

Warm Chickpea and Silver Beet Salad with Sumac 76

Boiled Leafy Greens (*Horta Vrasta*) 77

Greek Salad 79

Cypriot Cracked Wheat Salad 80

Twirls Salad 81

Greek Hot Potato Salad 82

Greek Avocado Salad 83

Goddess Salad 84

Athenian Salad 85

Greek Country Salad (*Horiatiki*) 86

Carrots Sauté 87

Salmon and Pumpkin Salad 88

Mediterranean Grain Salad 90

Pomegranate Orange and Baby Spinach Salad 91

Orange and Olive Salad (*Salata me Portokalia kai Elies*) 92

Roasted Red Pepper Salad With Feta and Herbs (*Piperies Florinis*) 93

Watermelon Feta Salad 94

SOUPS 95

Easter Soup with Avgolemeno Sauce 96

Greek Lentil Soup (*Faki Soupa*) 98

Bean Soup 99

Meat Ball Soup (*Youvarlakia*) 100

Chickpea and Pomegranate Dip 101

Greek White Bean Soup with Garlic and Lemon 102

Greek Fish Soup (*Psarosoupa*) 104

Greek Goat Soup 105

Classic Vegetable Soup (Lahanosoupa) 107

DIPS, PASTRIES AND MORE 109

Tzatziki 110

Skordalia 111

Greek Olive Spread (*Alifi apo Elies*) 112

Greek Fried Cheese (*Saganaki*) 113

Spinach–Cheese Pie (*Spankopita*) 114

Easy Tiropita in Pan 116

Greek Trinity Loaf 117

Saint Basil's Bread (Vasilopeta) 119

Galaktoboureko 120

Haloumi Cheese Pastries 122

Baked Feta Parcels with Thyme-Infused Honey 124

Homemade Phyllo 125

Homemade Greek Yogurt 126

DESSERTS 127

Baklava With Walnuts and Almonds 128

Almond Shortbread (*Kourambiethes*) 130

Greek Diples 131

Kourabiedes 133

Greek Coffee Cake 135

Cheese and Honey Pie (*Melopita*) 136

Greek Butter Biscuits (*Koulourakia Voutirou*) 139

Greek Chocolate Balls 140

Greek Rice Pudding 141

Melomacarona 142

Yogurt Cake 143

Greek Almond Macaroons (*Amigdalota*) 144

Greek Christmas Cookies 145

Zwieback (*Paximadia*) 147

Pistachio and rose semolina cakes 148

Orange Cake in Syrup (*Pontica*) 150

Kataifi with cheese and syrup (*Kunefe*) 151

Nutella Baklava 153

Almond Halva Cake 155

Greek Amaretti Cookies 156

Baked Quince with Yogurt (*Kythoni Psito me Yiaourti*) 157

Figs Poached in Mavrodaphne with Manouri Cheese 159

Honey Soaked Walnut Cake (*Karydopita*) 160

Tahini cake (*Keik apo Tahini*) 162

What's the Motivation For This Cookbook?

I was born in the Balkans and I lived in the former Yugoslavia, but I visited Greece so many times and was enamored by the cuisine. In fact, I've spent several months during every year in this unique country. When I ask my friends from around the globe about positive things about Greece and Greeks, they always mention the amazing food and nice, hospitable people. "I love gyros," or "moussaka is amazing" is something I've heard so many times. I tried to present only recipes that Greek mothers have made for decades, without adding "modern food."

I'm extremely grateful if you'd post a short review on Amazon to promote global foods and a celebration of culture.

Slavka Bodić

Why Greek food?

I guess that some of have Greek backgrounds or once upon a time visited some Greek island or location. You probably know something about great Greek history and its heroes. You've likely seen the movie, *My Big Fat Greek Wedding*, right? At the end of the story, Greece is always a good choice for vacations and spending holidays.

Apart from lovely beaches, history, and people, food is one of key reasons to visit Greece. I know many people who were so surprised how delicious Greek food is and how such a vast variety of dishes exist. "My stomach couldn't have been happier with Greek food" recalled one of my friends, after she visited Greece for the first time.

Luckily, I'm from the Balkan region, where Greece also belongs. I'm presently spending several months during the year in Northern Greece, which allows me to check with local people what needs to be adjusted in recipes that I found on the internet. The same dish is prepared in different way in diverse parts of Greece, while cultures around the globe have their own versions that are also available online.

Moreover, many people are already adjusting some well-known Greek dishes for some needs in the modern world, such as the Mediterranean and Keto diets. I also compile a cookbook of recipes for the Mediterranean diet, and you can find it [HERE](). Also, if you want to learn more about food from other Balkan countries, please check this [Balkan cookbook]() as well.

Greek food has spread its culinary influence throughout the world. It's renowned as some of the best food in Europe! With an age-old tradition, Greek cuisine has been greatly influenced by both the West and the East. Fishes, seafood, fresh vegetables, and cheese play a significant role in the dishes, mostly because of its long coastline; in contrast, meat is treated as less popular.

However, the flavors of Greek food change with the seasons and regional geography.

Lunch and Dinner

Moussaka

Preparation time: 20 minutes
Cook time: 40 minutes

Ingredients
1 pound ground beef or lamb
1 large eggplant
Vegetable oil
2 medium chopped onions
2 minced cloves garlic
2 egg whites
2 tablespoons chopped parsley
1 1/4 cups canned tomatoes
1/2 teaspoon thyme
1/2 teaspoon oregano
1/2 teaspoon nutmeg
1/2 cup bread crumbs
2 tablespoons grated Parmesan cheese
1/2 cup white wine
1 teaspoon salt

Sauce
2 egg yolks
3 tablespoons flour
3 tablespoons butter
1 1/2 cups milk
1/2 teaspoon salt
1/4 teaspoon pepper

Preparation
Pare the eggplant and cut it into 1/2–inch slices. Sprinkle with salt and set aside for 30 minutes. Rinse and dry thoroughly. Brown meat in vegetable oil with onions and garlic. Drain off the fat. Add salt, tomatoes, seasonings, parsley, and wine. Cover and cook slowly for 28-32 minutes. Cool and mix in unbeaten egg whites as well as half of the crumbs.

Brown the eggplant slices in vegetable oil. Sprinkle bottom of a 13x9 inch baking dish with remaining crumbs. Cover with the eggplant. Spoon the meat mixture over the eggplant and pour sauce over this mixture. Top with cheese and bake at 350 F for 42-48 minutes.

Sauce
Melt butter. Add flour slowly, stirring constantly. Remove from the heat and slowly stir in the milk. Return to the heat and stir until the sauce thickens. Beat the egg yolks well and gradually stir the yolks, salt, and pepper into the sauce. Blend well.

Greek Lemon Chicken

Preparation time: 20 minutes
Cook time: 40 minutes

Ingredients
Marinade
1 cup fruity white wine
1/4 cup olive oil
1/4 cup fresh lemon juice
1 teaspoon freshly grated lemon peel
1 teaspoon salt
1 teaspoon freshly ground black pepper
3 cloves garlic, crushed

Chicken
6 whole chicken breasts, boned and skinned
3 tablespoon olive oil
2 tablespoon butter
2 tablespoon all-purpose flour
1/2 teaspoon salt
2 teaspoon prepared mustard
1 cup milk
2 egg yolks
1 freshly grated peel of lemon
1 teaspoon fresh lemon juice
1 teaspoon dried dill weed
1/4 cup fresh minced parsley
1 cup sour cream
1/4 cup melted butter
1/2 cup crumbled feta cheese
1 pound angel hair pasta, cooked al dente, and kept warm
1/2 cup Muenster cheese, shredded

Preparation

In a bowl, combine all marinade ingredients. Pound chicken breasts slightly and place in shallow casserole or in plastic Ziploc bags, and cover with marinade. Refrigerate for up to 11-13 hours. Discard marinade.

Heat the oil in a skillet and sauté the chicken until tender. Slice and set aside. In the saucepan, melt 2 tablespoons butter. Blend in the flour and salt to create a roux. Add the mustard and slowly add the milk, stirring constantly until thick and smooth.

In a small bowl, stir the lemon peel mix, egg yolk, and lemon juice. Whisk a small amount of roux into the egg mixture. Then whisk the egg mixture into a roux and bring to a gentle boil. Remove from the heat and add the dill and parsley.

When the parsley wilts, stir in the sour cream. Add 1/4 cup butter, 3/4 cup of the egg sauce, and feta cheese to cooked pasta and stir well. Place in a greased 9" x 13" casserole and top with sliced chicken, the remaining sauce, and cheese. Broil until the cheese is golden.

Slow roasted shoulder of lamb

Preparation time: 20 minutes
Cook time: 90 minutes

Ingredients
1 lamb
10 cloves garlic
1 red onion
1 carrot
1 stalk of celery
1/2 cup white wine
2 lemons
2 cups of water
Salt & pepper
Oregano or rosemary

Preparation

In the middle of a baking dish, thickly slice an onion into four pieces. Cut the carrot into thick slices and make a celery bed for the shoulder to sit on. Make a few slits in the shoulder and press the garlic in. Leave it rest whole in the pan. Salt & pepper the lamb and place it over the bed. Sprinkle oregano, juice one lemon, and pour over. Slice the other lemon and put in the roasting dish. Place the lamb in a hot oven 180 degrees for about 60 minutes and then reduce to 120 degrees for another 30 mins or more, if needed, and cover with foil.

During cooking, be sure to check if it needs water as it takes a while to cook, and it should evaporate. Spoon the sauce over the lamb occasionally. Once done, take out the shoulder and squash all the veggies in the sauce, push through a sieve to make the sauce. If needed, thicken it with a little corn flour. Serve with lemon roasted potatoes or with tzatziki.

Greek Thanksgiving Turkey

Preparation time: 20 minutes
Cook time: 60 minutes

Ingredients
10-12 pound turkey
2 chopped onions
2 teaspoon chopped fresh parsley
1 chopped stalk of celery
1 teaspoon chopped fresh dill
2 tablespoon butter
3/4 pound peeled roasted chestnuts
1 pound ground beef
Coarsely chopped liver from turkey
1/4 pound finely chopped Pignoli nuts
1/2 cup white raisins
1 pound mild breakfast sausage
1/4 cup white rice
1/2 cup dry red wine
1 cup water
2 tablespoon tomato paste
1 pound white bread crumbs
Salt and pepper to taste

Preparation

Brown the onions and the celery in butter. Add liver, beef, and sausage. Cook until brown and add wine, the tomato paste, and herbs. Simmer until the meat is tender. Add the nuts, raisins, and rice. Stir in water and cook covered, until the rice is done. Mix in the breadcrumbs and season to taste. Stuff loosely into the turkey.

Greek Beef Over Zucchini

Preparation time: 15 minutes
Cook time: 40 minutes

Ingredients
1 1/2 pounds stew meat
1 large chopped onion
Salt and pepper to taste
1 teaspoon cinnamon
3 small cans tomato sauce
12 medium zucchini

Preparation
Slice the zucchini lengthwise and brown in oil. Drain and put onto a large platter. Brown the onion until clear. Add the meat and then brown. Add tomato sauce and spices to simmer until done. If needed, add water. Pour this over zucchini and serve. Sprinkle on just a bit of cinnamon and grate Romano cheese over the top. Instead of zucchini, this may be served over spaghetti.

Grilled Mediterranean Chicken

Preparation time: 30 minutes
Cook time: 40 minutes

Ingredients (12 servings)
12 4 oz chicken breast halves (bone-in, skin removed)
8 cloves finely chopped garlic
4 tablespoon fennel seeds (toasted and crushed)
2 tablespoon fresh ginger root
1 bn cilantro coarsely chopped
8 thinly sliced scallions including greens
1 teaspoon finely chopped saffron thread
2 tablespoons hot Hungarian paprika
2 teaspoon cayenne
2 tablespoon extra-virgin olive oil
1/2 cup fresh lemon juice
2 teaspoons cumin
1 teaspoon salt
1 cup water

Preparation
Mix all ingredients, except chicken, in a non-metallic bowl. Add chicken to the marinade; toss gently to coat pieces well. Cover and refrigerate for 1 to 2 days. Prepare a barbecue grill, so coals are white-hot. Spray the grill with a nonstick coating. Remove the chicken pieces from the marinade and place them on the grill. Cook by turning the chicken frequently, so it doesn't burn, until the juices run clear, and when large part of breast halves are pierced. The overall cooking time will vary between 12 and 20 minutes, depending on the heat of grill and the thickness of the breasts.

Serve 1 breast per person with tzatziki sauce, couscous, and grilled bell pepper strips. Recipe for Tzatziki sauce, a Greek sauce made with yogurt, cucumbers, and garlic is also in this cookbook.

Beef and Onion Stew (*Stifado*)

Preparation time: 15 minutes
Cook time: 105 minutes

Ingredients (4 servings)
1 (2 pound) boneless tip or round beef (cut into 1–inch cubes)
1 medium chopped onion
2 cloves garlic, minced
1 (8 ounce) can tomato sauce
3 tablespoons olive oil
1/2 cup dry red wine
2 tablespoons red wine vinegar
1/4 teaspoon coarsely ground pepper
Crumbled feta cheese
1 bay leaf
1 stick cinnamon
1 1/2 pound peeled pearl onions
1/2 teaspoon salt

Preparation
Cook and stir the chopped garlic and onion in oil in a Dutch oven over medium heat until the onion is tender. Remove with a slotted spoon. Cook the beef in the remaining oil about 25 minutes, stirring frequently, until all liquid is evaporated and the beef is brown on all sides. Next, drain fat. Return the onion and the garlic to the Dutch oven. Stir in all remaining ingredients except the cheese and the onions. Heat to boiling and reduce the heat. Cover and simmer 75 minutes. Add the white onions. Cover and simmer about 30 minutes until the beef and white onions are tender. Remove the bay leaf and add cinnamon. Garnish with cheese.

Zesty Chicken Oregano

Preparation time: 15 minutes
Cook time: 60 minutes

Ingredients (7 servings)
1 (3 pound) broiler– fryer chicken, cut up
2 teaspoons dried oregano leaves
1/2 cup olive oil or vegetable oil
1/4 cup lemon juice
1 clove garlic, chopped
Lemon slices
1 teaspoon salt
1/2 teaspoon pepper

Preparation
Place the chicken in an ungreased 13 x 9–inch baking pan. Mix the oregano, oil, garlic, salt, pepper, and lemon juice and pour over the chicken. Bake 25-30 minutes uncovered at 380 F, spooning the oil mixture over the chicken occasionally. Turn the chicken and cook until the thickest pieces are done, about 30 minutes longer. Garnish with lemon slices.

Braised Chicken in Aromatic Tomato Sauce (*Pastitsatha*)

Preparation time: 15 minutes
Cook time: 45 minutes

Ingredients (4 servings)
1 (3 pound) chicken, cut into 8 pieces
3 cups chopped red onions
12 ounces *perciatelli* pasta or spaghetti
1 (28 ounce) can whole Italian–style tomatoes (drained, juices reserved, tomatoes chopped)
6 whole allspice
1 teaspoon ground cumin
1/2 teaspoon ground nutmeg
1/2 teaspoon ground cloves
1 teaspoon paprika
Pinch cayenne pepper
2 tablespoon (or more) red wine vinegar
2 tablespoon tomato paste
1/4 cup olive oil
1 cinnamon stick
Pinch of granulated sugar
Freshly grated *Kefaltyri* cheese or *Parmesan* cheese
1 cup water

Preparation
Heat the oil in a heavy, large Dutch oven over medium–high heat. Add the chicken in batches and cook about 8 minutes until brown on all sides. Place the chicken on a platter. Add the onions to a Dutch oven and sauté until tender, 4-6 minutes. Add the spices and stir 1 minute until fragrant. Stir in tomatoes, their juices, and water.

Return the chicken to the Dutch oven. Cover and simmer about 35 minutes over medium–low heat until the chicken is very tender. Transfer the chicken to a platter. Make a tent with the foil. Add tomato paste, 2 tablespoons vinegar, and sugar to the Dutch oven. Simmer about 10 minutes until thickened to sauce consistency, stirring occasionally. Season with salt, pepper, and more vinegar, if desired. Remove from the heat. Cover to keep warm.

Cook pasta in large pot of boiling salted water until tender but still firm to bite. Drain. Transfer the pasta to a platter. Top with chicken, sauce, and cheese.

Stuffed Grape Leaves (*Dolmades*)

Preparation time: 20 minutes
Cook time: 60 minutes

Ingredients (8 servings)
1 (16 ounce) jar grapevine leaves
1 1/2 pounds ground round or turkey
1 finely chopped onion
1 cup undrained canned tomatoes
1/2 cup raw rice
1 tablespoon mint
1 tablespoon parsley
1 beaten egg
1/2 teaspoon dill
1/2 teaspoon oregano
3 bouillon cubes
1 tablespoon butter
Salt and pepper, to taste

Preparation
Combine ground round, onion, rice, salt, pepper, mint, parsley, egg, tomatoes, oregano, and dill by mixing well. Wash the grape leaves carefully and remove

the brine. Put any broken leaves into the bottom of a greased Dutch oven. Add a heaping teaspoon of the mixture in the center of each leaf (on the vein side). Fold edges over and roll tightly toward the point of the leaf.

Dissolve bouillon cubes in enough water to cover the rolls and then pour over the rolls. Dot tops with butter. Cover with a heavy plate to prevent the rolls from opening as the rice puffs. Cover the pan and steam over low heat for 50-60 minutes or until the leaves are tender.

Grilled Octopus With Oregano

Preparation time: 30 minutes (plus one day to marinate)
Cook time: 40 minutes

Ingredients (12 servings)
3 2-pound rinsed octopuses (thawed, if frozen)
1 lemon (cut into 1/4 slices)
2 teaspoon salt
1 teaspoon whole black peppercorns
1 1/2 cup extra-virgin olive oil
1/4 cup red-wine vinegar
2 1/2 tablespoon dried oregano

Preparation
Cut octopus pouches (heads) from tentacles, leaving enough pouch to keep tentacles attached in 1 piece (for small octopuses discard pouches.) In an 8 quart kettle, combine octopus pouches and tentacles, lemon, peppercorns, salt, and water to cover by 1 inch. Simmer gently, covered, until the octopus is knife-tender 25 to 30 minutes.

In a colander, drain octopus and cool until it can be handled. With hands, carefully rub off any purplish skin from the pouches and the tentacles (skin around suction cups may not come off completely). In a large bowl, whisk together the remaining ingredients and salt and pepper to taste. Finally, add the octopus, turning to coat. Marinate the octopus, covered and chilled, 1 day.

Prepare a grill. Transfer the octopus to paper towels to drain and reserve the marinade. Grill the octopus on an oiled rack set 5 to 6 inches over glowing coals, turning occasionally, until browned, 5-7 minutes. Cut the octopus into bite-size pieces (leave the small octopus whole) and toss with any reserved marinade. Octopus may be made 1 day ahead and chilled, covered. Serve the octopus at room temperature.

Greek Chicken with Olives

Preparation time: 10 minutes
Cook time: 15 minutes

Ingredients (5 servings)
1 (2 or 3-pound) cut up chicken
3 cups chopped tomatoes (fresh or canned)
5 chopped cloves garlic
3 chopped yellow onions
1 (6 ounce) jar green stuffed olives (or 3/4 cup salad olives)
3 tablespoons olive oil
1 tablespoon dried oregano (or 2 tablespoons chopped fresh)
1 cup dry red wine
Salt and Black pepper to taste

Preparation
Brown chicken in olive oil. Remove the chicken and sauté onions and garlic until tender. Add olives and tomatoes and sauté until tomatoes (if fresh) are soft. Add chicken, pepper, oregano, and wine. Cover and simmer about 30 minutes or until tender. Taste for salt preference, as the olives are inherently salty.

Tomato Pilaf

Preparation time: 10 minutes
Cook time: 15 minutes

Ingredients (8 servings)
2 medium coarsely chopped tomatoes
1 teaspoon instant beef bouillon
2 tablespoons chopped onion
2 tablespoons butter or margarine
1 cup uncooked regular rice
3/4 teaspoon salt
1/8 teaspoon pepper
2 cups water

Preparation
Cook and stir tomatoes and onions in butter in a 2–quart saucepan over medium heat for 2-3 minutes. Stir in remaining ingredients and heat to boiling. Stir once or twice and then reduce heat. Cover and simmer 13-15 minutes, without lifting the cover or stirring. Remove from heat and fluff rice lightly with fork. Cover and let steam 10 minutes. Serve with grated Parmesan cheese, if desired.

Greek Quesadilla

Preparation time: 10 minutes
Cook time: 15 minutes

Ingredients
1 flour tortilla
2 tablespoon feta cheese
¼ cup shredded mozzarella cheese
3 tablespoons diced Kalamata olives
1/8 cup finely diced onion
Pinch of finely diced oregano, basil, and rosemary to taste

Preparation
Sprinkle ingredients evenly over one side of a tortilla. Fold in half. Grill for about 1-2 minutes or bake at 350 F for 5 minutes. Slice in thirds and serve.

Chicken Casserole with Olives

Preparation time: 30 minutes
Cook time: 60 minutes

Ingredients (2 servings)

1 broiler–fryer chicken
1 stick of cinnamon
1 (14 ounce) can tomatoes
3 cloves
2 whole allspice
1 bay leaf
3 tablespoons olive oil
2/3 cup red wine
14 black or green olives
Salt and pepper, to taste

Preparation
Wash and dry chicken. Season with salt and pepper and fry in the olive oil. Pour wine into the pan, add tomatoes, spices, and the bay leaf. Cover and simmer for 60 minutes or until the meat is tender. Add olives the last 10 minutes, during which the sauce should be thick. Serve with rice or pasta.

Cinnamon Chicken (*Kota Kapama*)

Preparation time: 30 minutes
Cook time: 40 minutes

Ingredients (4 servings)
8 pieces chicken
1/2 cup chicken stock
4 tablespoons butter
1 teaspoon finely chopped or minced garlic
6 fresh garden tomatoes (alternative: 1 cup chopped, drained, canned plum tomatoes)
2 tablespoons tomato paste
1 (4–inch long) cinnamon stick
1/4 cup extra virgin olive oil
1 1/2 cups finely chopped onions
Freshly grated Parmesan cheese

Preparation

Grind some sea salt and black pepper over the chicken pieces. Heat the butter and olive oil over moderate heat in a sauté pan and brown the chicken pieces. Transfer them to a plate. Pour off all but a thin film of fat before adding the onions and garlic. Cook and stir for a few minutes until the onions are light brown.

Stir in chicken stock, tomatoes, tomato paste, cinnamon stick, 1/2 teaspoon of sea salt, and a few grindings of black pepper. Bring to a boil, and then return the chicken to the pan and baste it thoroughly with the sauce. Reduce the heat to low, cover and simmer 27-32 minutes, basting occasionally. Serve with white or brown rice or pasta. Spoon the tomato sauce over the chicken and rice or pasta. Sprinkle with Parmesan cheese, if desired.

Rice with Feta

Preparation time: 10 minutes
Cooking time: 45 minutes

Ingredients
1/2 teaspoon olive oil
1 medium chopped onion
3 garlic sliced cloves
1 cup brown rice
3 cups vegetable stock
Juice and grated zest of 1 lemon
2 tablespoons crumbled feta cheese
1 sliced scallion
1 tablespoon chopped fresh cilantro
Salt

Preparation

In a deep sauté pan or saucepan, keep the oil over medium heat and sauté garlic and onion for 3 minutes. Add the rice and continue cooking, stirring, for 2 minutes, until coated with oil. Add the stock, stirring and scraping the sides of the pan, until the rice is cooked. Season to taste with salt.

Cover and simmer for 27-30 minutes over low heat. Set aside, covered, to steam for five to 5-7 minutes. Uncover and test for doneness. If the liquid isn't absorbed and the rice isn't tender, return to the stove for a few minutes. Then add the scallions, feta, and cilantro. Stir gently just to mix. Serve immediately.

Shrimps with Feta Cheese (*Garides Me Feta*)

Preparation time: 10 minutes
Cook time: 20 minutes

Ingredients (4 servings)
1/2 cup minced onion
1 1/2 tablespoons butter
1 1/2 tablespoons vegetable oil
1/2 cup dry white wine
4 ripe medium peeled, seeded, and chopped tomatoes
1 small minced clove garlic
1 teaspoon salt
1/4 teaspoon freshly-ground black pepper
3/4 teaspoon oregano
4 ounces crumbled feta cheese
1 pound raw large shrimps (shelled and de-veined)
1/4 cup chopped fresh parsley

Preparation

In a heavy skillet, sauté the onion in butter and oil until soft. Add wine, tomatoes, salt, pepper, garlic, and oregano. Bring to a boil, lower heat to medium, and simmer until the sauce is slightly thickened. Stir in the cheese and simmer for 12 to 15 minutes. Adjust the seasonings. Just before serving, add the shrimps to hot sauce and cook for 5 minutes or until the shrimps are just tender. Don't overcook. Garnish with parsley and serve immediately in large bowls with crusty French bread. Pass the rice!

Meatballs (*Keftethes*)

Preparation time: 10 minutes
Cook time: 20 minutes

Ingredients (4 servings)
2 1/4 pound lean minced beef or lamb
2 cups unseasoned breadcrumbs, moistened in about 3/4 cup warm water
1 large finely minced onion
1 tablespoon vegetable oil
1 1/2 tablespoons finely chopped fresh parsley
2 beaten eggs
1 1/2 tablespoons finely chopped mint (if unavailable, use chopped, dried mint)
2 1/2 teaspoons salt
1 cup olive oil and corn oil mixed
Plain flour
Black pepper to taste
2 tablespoons Ouzo (optional)

Preparation

Fry onions with vegetable oil over low heat until golden. Remove to a large mixing bowl. Add meat and all other ingredients, except flour and olive/corn oil mix. Knead for about 10 minutes or until the mixture is a smooth paste. Heat the oil mix in a large frying pan to the point of a fragrance. Meanwhile, start to shape mixture into balls about the size of a large marble by rolling lightly between palms of hands (do them in batches of roughly 13-17), each batch should be enough to space evenly but separately in the frying pan. As each meatball is formed, place on a large plate which has been liberally covered with plain flour. When the batch is finished, lightly roll the meatball in the flour. Oil in the frying pan should be just ready. Put the batch of meatball into the pan.

Start on your second batch of meatballs, make them, and place them on the floured plate. At this point it's time to turn the meatballs over; and when you've completed this roll, add the second batch to the flour. Now it's time to remove the first batch from the frying pan using a slotted spoon or kitchen tongs and place on paper towels to drain. Put the second batch of meatballs into the pan to cook and continue with the process until you've finished the mixture. These meatballs are deliciously light and delicately flavored and you can serve them hot, warm or cold, or freeze for future use.

Athenian Stuffed Peppers

Preparation time: 15 minutes
Cook time: 75 minutes

Ingredients (4 servings)
1 pound ground beef
1 cup rice
2 onions, ground
1 clove garlic, minced
1/2 cup vegetable oil
1 (6 ounce) can tomato paste, divided
1 1/2 tablespoons salt, divided
3/4 teaspoon pepper, divided
1/2 teaspoon oregano
1 egg, well beaten
8 green bell peppers
6 cups water
5 medium potatoes, sliced

Preparation
Combine the meat, rice, garlic, onions, oregano, oil, 1 tablespoon tomato paste, egg, 1 tablespoon salt, and 1/2 teaspoon pepper. Wash the green peppers, cut, and remove seeds. Fill the peppers with meat mixture and place open side down in circle in roasting pan. Combine the remaining ingredients, except potatoes, and pour over peppers. Place potatoes in the center of the pan. Bake for 70-80 minutes at 400 degrees F.

Zucchini Pancakes (*Kolokythia Krokettes*)

Preparation time: 65 minutes
Cook time: 20 minutes

Ingredients (6 servings)
3 cups grated zucchini
1 cup grated feta cheese
3 eggs
1 1/2 teaspoons minced fresh mint leaves
3 tablespoons flour
1 teaspoon salt
Pepper
Butter

Preparation
Mix the zucchini with salt and let stand 1 hour. Squeeze out any moisture. Beat the eggs. Add the zucchini, flour, cheese, mint, and pepper to taste. Fry 1 tablespoon at a time in butter over medium heat. Brown on both sides.

Artichoke and Pea Stew

Preparation time: 10 minutes
Cooking time: 60 minutes

Ingredients
1 1/2 cups of fresh or frozen peas
6 fresh or frozen artichoke hearts (cut in half)
1 ¾ cup tinned salt reduced tomatoes
1/4 cup extra virgin olive oil
4 tablespoons chopped dill
3 chopped spring onions
1 cup of salt reduced vegetable stock
Juice of 1 lemon
Salt and pepper to taste

Preparation
Add oil to a medium sized pot on the stove on high heat. Add the spring onions and dill and stir fry for about 1 minute, until the spring onions begin to turn bright green. Add the tinned tomatoes. Lower the heat slightly, stir and cover and leave for about 10 minutes, occasionally stirring. Add the artichokes, peas, water, salt, and pepper. Bring to a boil. Then immediately cover the pot with a lid, turn the heat down. Let simmer for 30 minutes on the stove and stir occasionally. Turn off the heat and add the lemon juice. Don't stir, just gently shake the pan to distribute. Cover and let sit for about 12 minutes before serving.

Okra Stew

Preparation time: 10 minutes
Cooking time: 30 minutes

Ingredients

2 cups fresh or frozen okra (Optional Broad Beans, Diced Pumpkin)
1 large onion sliced finely
2 tablespoon tomato paste
1 can chopped tomatoes
2 garlic cloves diced finely
1 can of tomato soup
¼ cup red wine
Olive oil
Lemon juice
Salt and Pepper
Cinnamon and Cloves

Preparation

If using fresh okra, wash and remove stalks and just the top part of the bean, so that it doesn't open while cooking. Be careful not to cut the bean open as it'll make the cooking very slimy. Sprinkle with salt and a little vinegar or lemon juice. Rinse and drain prior to cooking.

Heat some olive oil in a frying pan and add okra, garlic and onions. Add additional vegetables at this stage, if required. Cook until they begin to brown. Add a little lemon juice, salt, and pepper while cooking. Add wine, reduce slightly, and then add tomato paste, diced tomatoes and tomato soup. Cook for 13-16 minutes or until vegetables soften and sauce reduces into a nice, thick consistency.

Green Peas with Veal

Preparation time: 5 minutes
Cooking time: 20 minutes

Ingredients
Lamb chops or Veal slices
1 large minced onion
Green peas
1 tablespoon dill weed
Olive oil
Salt and pepper to taste

Preparation
In a large saucepan, sauté the minced onion until brown. Add the lamb (or veal) and brown. Add the green peas, salt, pepper, and dill weed. Cook until tender.

Cabbage Dolmathes (*Lahanodolmathes*)

Preparation time: 15 minutes
Cooking time: 20 minutes

Ingredients
1 pound ground beef
1 whole cabbage
1 minced onion
1/2 cup rice
Salt
Dill weed
Egg lemon sauce (beat 1 egg and juice of 1 lemon with the recipe's juices in a blender until smooth)

Preparation
Boil cabbage and separate the leaves. Put the meat in a bowl and add the rice, onion, salt, and dill. Mix well. Put a bit of the mixture on each leaf and roll. Place in a cooking pot and simmer until done. Add the egg lemon sauce.

Soutzoukakia

Preparation time: 15 minutes
Cooking time: 60 minutes

Ingredients
1 pound ground beef
1 egg
1 can of whole tomatoes
1/3 of a cup sweet sherry
1 cup rice
2 slices of dry bread (or breadcrumbs)
1 minced clove garlic, minced
Pepper, salt and cinnamon
Flour

Preparation
Prepare 1 cup of rice with two cups of water in the usual manner. In a saucepan start heating the tomatoes and pour in the sweet sherry. Put the ground beef in a bowl. Add the egg, pepper, salt, grated dry bread, minced garlic, cinnamon, and salt. Mix all the ingredients well. Make "little barrels" from the mixture and dip them thoroughly in flour. Pour the olive oil in a frying pan and sauté the meat barrels until lightly brown. Add the barrels in the saucepan and simmer for about 1 hour.

Veal with Lemon

Preparation time: 10 minutes
Cooking time: 45 minutes

Ingredients
1 pound veal sliced
carrots sliced like wheels
1 minced onion
1 cup of rice
Olive oil
Juice of one lemon
Pepper and Salt

Preparation
Prepare the rice in the usual way. Boil the veal slices with a bit of water. Keep removing the foam from the veal by turning the meat until it absorbs the water. Next, add the olive oil and sauté. Add the juice of lemon, pepper, and salt to taste, as well as the carrots and onion. Next, simmer for about 35 minutes. Serve it over the rice or with fries.

Fish Plaki

Preparation time: 20 minutes
Cooking time: 45 minutes

Ingredients
1 pound cod or sole fish, boned and skinned
1 can whole tomatoes
1 large onion cut in rings
Fresh minced parsley
1 clove minced garlic
Juice of 1 lemon or lime
1 lemon or lime sliced in rings with the skin
Dill weed
Salt

Preparation
Sauté the garlic and onion rings with olive oil in a frying pan. Add some olive oil at the bottom of the baking pan and lay the cod filets. Pour lemon juice over the cod, add salt, and dill weed. Place the sautéed onions and garlic on the fish. On top of this, add the sliced tomatoes to cover the whole fish. Sprinkle the parsley and add the onion rings on top. Bake for 35 – 46 minutes in a preheated 350 F oven.

Grilled Salmon & Zucchini with Red Capsicum Sauce

Preparation time: 10 minutes
Cooking time: 15 minutes

Ingredients (4 servings)
⅓ cup sliced almonds, toasted
¼ cup chopped roasted red capsicums
¼ cup halved cherry tomatoes
1 small clove garlic
1 tablespoon olive oil
1 tablespoon sherry vinegar or red-wine vinegar
1 teaspoon paprika
½ teaspoon salt, divided
½ teaspoon divided freshly ground pepper
1 1/3 pound salmon fillet, skinned, and cut crosswise into 4 portions
2 medium zucchinis, halved lengthwise
2 tablespoon additional olive oil
1 tablespoon chopped fresh parsley

Preparation
Preheat the grill to medium. Process the tomatoes, garlic, almonds, and peppers; first, measure the olive oil, vinegar, paprika, ¼ teaspoon of salt and ¼ teaspoon of pepper in a food processor or blender until smooth.

Coat the salmon and zucchini on both sides with olive oil, and then sprinkle with the remaining ¼ teaspoon of salt and ¼ teaspoon of pepper. Grill, turning once, until the salmon is just cooked through and the zucchini is soft and browned, 3-4 minutes per side.

Transfer the zucchini to a clean cutting board. When cool enough to handle, slice into ½ inch pieces. Toss in a bowl with half of the reserved sauce. Divide among 4 plates along with a piece of salmon. Top with some of the remaining sauce. Garnish with parsley.

Herbed Fish Fillets

Preparation time: 15 minutes
Cooking time: 20 minutes

Ingredients (2 servings)
1 tablespoon olive oil
2 large or 4 small fillets of salmon, gurnard, terakihi, or snapper
1 tablespoon fresh parsley
1 tablespoon thyme
1 tablespoon tarragon
1 tablespoon minced garlic

Preparation
Spread a little olive oil onto a foil lined baking sheet or dish. Arrange the fish fillets on it. In a small bowl, blend the parsley, thyme, tarragon, garlic, and olive oil. Spread thinly over the fillets. Bake at 390 F for 20 minutes or until the fish flakes easily in the center. Serve with garden beans, fresh asparagus, or on a bed of fresh spinach.

Shrimps with Spinach and Zucchini

Preparation time: 10 minutes
Cooking time: 10 minutes

Ingredients (2 servings)
½ pound frozen shrimps
1 finely chopped medium onion
3 finely chopped cloves of garlic
½ inch piece of peeled and finely chopped fresh ginger (or grated)
2/3 pound of fresh spinach leaves
1 - 2 sliced in flat rounds medium zucchini
2 tablespoon soy sauce
1 tablespoon hoisin sauce
2 - 3 tablespoon olive oil for stir-frying

Preparation
Heat the olive oil in a wok or a large fry-pan. Add the ginger, garlic, and onions. Cook for about 2 minutes before adding the frozen shrimps and then covering. After 3 minutes, add soy sauce and hoisin sauce. Add the zucchini, stir well and cook an additional 3 minutes. Next, add the spinach and cover. Once that spinach has wilted, stir and serve with basmati rice.

Tuna Patties

Preparation time: 10 minutes
Cooking time: 10 minutes

Ingredients (2 servings)
1 can tuna canned in water, drained
2 tablespoon chopped onion or spring onion
1 egg white
1 tablespoon vinaigrette dressing
2 teaspoon finely chopped mixed garden herbs
¼ cup dry breadcrumbs
2 teaspoon olive oil
1 tablespoon pickle relish (optional)

Preparation
In medium bowl, combine relish, vinaigrette dressing, tuna, onion, egg white, and breadcrumbs. Shape into four patties. Begin heating a non-stick skillet over medium heat. Coat the surface with oil. Add the patties and fry on both sides until lightly browned. Serve with a mixed salad.

Hearty Turkey Stew

Preparation time: 15 minutes
Cooking time: 35 minutes

Ingredients (4 servings)
1 pound chopped cooked turkey (or chicken)
4 cups rinsed and drained cooked or canned kidney beans
2 cups chopped zucchini
1 tablespoon olive oil
1 cup chopped onion
2 cups chopped celery
1 cup chopped capsicum
2 teaspoon chopped fresh garlic
1 teaspoon cumin seed
2 cups diced canned tomatoes
2 cups vegetable broth
1 teaspoon brown sugar
Chili powder to taste (optional)

Preparation
Preheat the oven to 430 F. Coat a glass baking dish with cooking spray or a little olive oil. Arrange the zucchini in a single layer within the baking dish. Roast for 8 to 10 minutes until slightly tender and lightly browned. While the zucchini is roasting, add the olive oil and chopped onions to a Dutch oven or soup pot. Sauté over low heat until the onions are browned. Add the celery and peppers and continue to sauté. Add the garlic, cooked turkey, cumin seed, and chili powder to taste. Cover and simmer for about 6 minutes. Stir in brown sugar, the tomatoes, kidney beans, vegetable broth, and the roasted zucchini. Cover and simmer for 15 minutes. Ladle into warmed individual bowls and serve immediately.

Lamb and Apricot Hot Pot

Preparation time: 10 minutes
Cooking time: 120 minutes

Ingredients (4 servings)
1 2/3 pound lean diced lamb
2/3 cup dried apricots
2 finely chopped onions
1 tablespoon flour
1 teaspoon each cinnamon, coriander, and cumin
Salt and pepper
1 tablespoon olive oil
2 teaspoon corn flour
¼ cup flaked almonds
1 cup boiling water
Fresh coriander leaves

Preparation
Soak the apricots in boiling water for 30 minutes. Preheat the oven to 360 F. Combine salt, flour, spices, and pepper in a bowl. Add the lamb and toss until evenly coated. Transfer to a casserole dish. Add the apricots and boiling water. Stir well. Cover and bake for 60 minutes. Mix the corn flour with 1 tablespoon water to make a paste. Add to the casserole and mix in well. Cook for an added 14-16 minutes. Garnish with almonds and fresh coriander. Finally, serve with a generous portion of broccoli and seasonal vegetables. If desired, add a small portion of baby potatoes (baked in their skins), or brown rice.

Baked Potato

Preparation time: 10 minutes
Cooking time: 60 minutes

Ingredients
1 can tuna in brine water, drained
1 chopped spring onion
Chopped handful cherry tomatoes, halved ½ small bunch coriander or parsley
1 medium-sized potato, baked in its skin
½ cup low-fat cottage cheese
½ red chili, chopped (optional)

Preparation
Preheat the oven to 360 F. Prick the potato several times with a fork and put it straight onto a rack in the hottest part of the oven. Bake for approximately 60 minutes, or until it's soft inside. Mix tuna with chili (if added), spring onion, coriander, and cherry tomatoes. Cut the top off the potato and scoop out about half of the potato inside. Fill with the tuna mix and cottage cheese

Artichoke Cod with Tomatoes

Preparation time: 10 minutes
Cooking time: 25 minutes

Ingredients (6 servings)
6 cod fillets
1 can quartered water-packed artichoke hearts, drained
1/2 cup julienned soft sun-dried tomatoes (not packed in oil)
2 chopped green onions,
3 tablespoons olive oil
1 minced garlic clove
1 teaspoon salt
1/2 teaspoon pepper
Salad greens and lemon wedges

Preparation
Preheat oven to 400 F. In a small bowl, combine the first artichoke, tomatoes, onions, olive oil, and garlic. Toss to combine. Sprinkle both sides of cod with salt and pepper and place in a 13x9-inch baking dish coated with cooking spray. Top with the artichoke mixture. Bake uncovered for 17-22 minutes or until the fish just begins to flake easily with a fork. If desired, serve over greens with lemon wedges.

Pork Souvlaki with Tzatziki

Preparation time: 25 minutes
Cooking time: 20 minutes

Ingredients (4 servings)
1 1/4 pounds trimmed pork shoulder, cut into 3-by- 1/2-inch strips
1 large onion, cut through the root end into 1/2-inch wedges
1 cup Greek-style whole-milk yogurt
1/2 seeded and diced European cucumber
1/4 cup plus 2 tablespoons extra-virgin olive oil
3 tablespoons fresh lemon juice
2 tablespoons chopped fresh oregano
2 mashed garlic cloves
Salt and Pepper
2 tablespoons chopped fresh mint
Warm pita
lemon wedges

Preparation

In a medium bowl, toss the pork strips and onion wedges with half of the garlic paste, olive oil, lemon juice, and chopped oregano. Season with 1 1/2 teaspoons of salt and 1/2 teaspoon of pepper. Next, let stand for 20 minutes.

Meanwhile, in a bowl, mix the mint, the remaining garlic paste, the yogurt and the cucumber. Season the tzatziki with salt and pepper. Heat a large cast-iron griddle or grill pan until very hot. Add the pork and onion wedges, along with any marinade, and cook over high heat 9-11 minutes, turning once or twice, until the pork and onion are tender. Transfer the pork and onion to plates and serve with the tzatziki, lemon wedges, and pita.

Recipe for tzatziki is also part of this cookbook.

Feta-Brined Chicken Breast with Rosemary

Preparation time: 40 minutes (plus overnight)
Cooking time: 40 minutes

Ingredients (4 servings)
4 medium skinless and boneless chicken breasts
4 cups water
4 ounces feta cheese (about 1 cup crumbled)
2 teaspoons salt
2 teaspoons freshly ground black pepper
1 head garlic
6 sprigs fresh rosemary, broken into small pieces
1 tablespoon olive oil
½ large lemon
Crostini

Preparation
Combine feta, salt, pepper, and the water in a blender and blend until smooth. Place the chicken breasts in a resealable plastic bag or container large enough

to submerge the meat. Pour the brine over the chicken, cover, and refrigerate at least 8 hours or overnight.

Arrange a rack in the middle of the oven and heat to 400 F. Meanwhile, remove the chicken breasts from the brine, pat dry with paper towels, and place in a single layer in a baking dish or on an aluminum foil-lined rimmed baking sheet. Let sit for about 30 minutes at room temperature. Break off a few cloves of garlic from the head, peel, smash, and scatter around the chicken. Cut the top off the remaining garlic head to expose the cloves, cut in half horizontally, and then place the 2 pieces in the pan. Sprinkle the rosemary sprigs over the chicken, and then drizzle with the oil. Roast until an instant-read thermometer inserted in the thickest part of the breasts reads 165°F, about 40 minutes. Remove the chicken breasts from the oven, squeeze the juice from the lemon half over the chicken, and let rest for 5 minutes before serving. Squeeze the roasted garlic cloves from their peels onto crostini.

Lamb En Papilotte (*Arnaki Klephtiko*)

Preparation time: 20 minutes
Cooking time: 70 minutes

Ingredients (6 servings)
2 pounds boneless lamb, cut into cubes
1/4 cup extra virgin olive oil
2 large peeled and coarsely chopped onions
4-6 trimmed scallions, cut into thin rounds
2-3 peeled and minced garlic cloves
1 1/2 cups fresh peas (or frozen and thawed)
1/2 pound yellow cheese, cubed
2 cored and sliced medium tomatoes
2 teaspoons oregano
Salt and Pepper

Preparation

Season the lamb with salt and pepper. Heat 2 tablespoons olive oil in a large skillet and brown the meat on all sides over high heat. Add the remaining olive oil and sauté the onions, scallions and garlic until wilted. Add the peas and cook for 4-6 minutes.

Preheat the oven to 350 F. Cut 6 large sheets of aluminum foil or parchment paper. Distribute the lamb, vegetables, and cheese cubes evenly among them. Season with salt and pepper. Top each with 2 slices of tomatoes, and a little oregano. Seal each "parcel" either by folding it at the top to close thoroughly, or by tying it with a cotton butcher's cord. Place the parcels in a roasting pan and bake at 350 F for about 60 minutes. Serve immediately.

Beef and Quince Stew (*Moschari me Kydonia*)

Preparation time: 15 minutes
Cooking time: 80 minutes

Ingredients (6 servings)
2 1/2 pounds lean boneless beef, cubed large
4-6 tablespoons extra virgin olive oil
2 large peeled, halved and sliced red onions
2 large peeled and cored quinces, submerged in a bowl of lemon water until ready to use
1/4 cup fresh chopped mint
1 cup peeled chopped plum tomatoes
1 small cinnamon stick
1 bay leaf
1/2 teaspoon ground allspice
3/4 cups water
Salt and pepper to taste
Flour for dredging

Preparation

Combine the salt, paper, and flour in a large plate and dredge the beef lightly, shaking off any excess. Heat 4 tablespoons of the olive oil in a large Dutch oven or casserole and sauté the onions over medium heat until lightly golden, about 9-10 minutes. Add the quince and sauté lightly, to color and soften a little. Remove both with a slotted spoon.

Add the remaining olive oil to the pot and brown the meat, over a high flame and turning to color on all sides. Toss the onions back into the pan, add salt, paper, allspice, tomatoes, cinnamon, bay leaf, and 3/4 cup of water. Cover, reduce heat, and simmer for 28-31 minutes. Add the quinces to the pot and continue cooking, covered, another 20-25 minutes, until the beef is tender and the pot juices thicken. Five minutes before removing from heat, toss in the mint and adjust the seasoning with salt and pepper.

Corfiot Veal with Vinegar Sauce (*Sofrito*)

Preparation time: 10 minutes
Cooking time: 20 minutes

Ingredients (4 servings)
1 pound veal, preferably top round, cut into 1 1/4-inch slices
3 tablespoons extra virgin olive oil
1 1/2 cups canned unsalted beef broth
1/2 cup chopped flat-leaf parsley
4 minced garlic cloves
1/4 cup red wine vinegar
1/3 cup all-purpose flour
Pinch of cayenne pepper
Salt to taste

Preparation

Combine the flour and cayenne and lightly dredge the veal. Heat olive oil in a large non-stick skillet over medium heat and brown the veal for about 1 minute on each side. Transfer to a platter. Add the garlic to the skillet and sauté for 1 minute. Return the veal to a skillet and pour in the vinegar. As soon as the vinegar steams, pour in the beef broth. Boil until the sauce is reduced by half and the veal is tender, about 9-10 minutes. Transfer the veal to a platter, add chopped parsley to the skillet, and cook another 6 minutes, until the sauce is thick. Season to taste with salt and pour sauce over the veal before serving.

Octopus with Ouzo and Olives
(*Htapothi me Elies kai Ouzo*)

Preparation time: 10 minutes
Cooking time: 110 minutes

Ingredients (5 servings)
1 large octopus (3-4 pounds)
2 peeled and minced garlic cloves
1 small can (1 1/2 cups) plum tomatoes
1/3 cup extra virgin olive oil
2 medium peeled, halved, and sliced thin onions,
1/2 teaspoon whole black peppercorns
1/2 cup rinsed and drained pitted Kalamata olives
1/4 cup ouzo
1 bay leaf
Salt to taste
Water

Preparation

Remove the head from the octopus and discard. Squeeze out its beak-like mouth and rinse. Place the octopus in a large pot with no liquid. Cover the pot and let the octopus cook in its own juices over very low heat for 50 minutes. Remove, leaving all the pot juices inside. Cut the octopus into eight pieces, by separating each tentacle.

Heat the olive oil in the pot and sauté the onions until wilted. Add the garlic and stir for 1 minute. Place the octopus back in the pot, cover with tomatoes and their juices, and add the peppercorns, bay leaf, and water just to cover the octopus. Cover and simmer for another 50 minutes over low heat.

Ten minutes before removing the octopus from the heat, add the olives and ouzo. Taste and adjust seasoning with salt. Serve immediately.

Red Mullet Baked in Grape Leaves (*Barbounia Psita sta Klimatofylla*)

Preparation time: 20 minutes
Cooking time: 30 minutes

Ingredients (5 servings)
2 pounds red mullet, cleaned, and gutted but whole
Grape leaves in brine (as many as there are fish, plus about 6 for spreading on the bottom of the pan)
3/4 cup extra virgin olive oil
Strained fresh juice of 2 lemons
1 tablespoon oregano
Ground black pepper to taste
Water

Preparation

Whisk together the olive oil, lemon juice, oregano, and pepper. Bring a large pot of water to a rolling boil and blanch the grape leaves, steeping them for about 5 minutes, until soft. Remove with a slotted spoon and rinse immediately under cold water. Trim off the stems. Preheat the oven to 350 F. Brush 1 tablespoon olive oil on the bottom of an ovenproof glass baking dish large enough to hold all the fish. Spread 6 grape leaves on the bottom. Wrap each fish in a grape leaf. Place in the pan and seam side down. Pour the sauce over the fish, and bake, covered, until the fish and grape leaves are tender, about 25-30 minutes. Remove and serve.

Pork Braised with Celery and Leeks
(*Hirino me Selina kai Prasa*)

Preparation time: 15 minutes
Cooking time: 100 minutes

Ingredients (5 servings)
2 pounds boneless pork, cut into stewing pieces
2 large leeks, trimmed, tough upper greens removed
1 small peeled and diced celeriac
3-4 trimmed and coarsely chopped large celery stalks
1/2 cup extra virgin olive oil
2 eggs
2 cups dry white wine
Water
Salt and white pepper to taste
Strained juice of 1 lemon

Preparation

In a large casserole or Dutch oven, heat the olive oil and sauté the leeks, celeriac, and celery until wilted. Remove with a slotted spoon. Add the pork to the pot and brown. Place the leeks and celery back in, pour in the wine and add enough water to cover and bring to a boil.

Reduce heat, season with salt and white pepper, and simmer for about 90 minutes or until the pork is very tender. Add more water during cooking, if needed. Beat the eggs until frothy and add the lemon and beat to combine. Take a ladleful of the pan liquids from the pork and gradually stream them into the egg-lemon mixture, beating all the while.

Pour the egg-lemon mixture back into the pot, stir to combine, and remove immediately from the heat. Serve hot.

Egg Noodles with Warm Tahini-Yogurt Sauce

Preparation time: 15 minutes
Cooking time: 15 minutes

Ingredients (4 servings)
3 tablespoons tahini
1 juiced lemon
2 peeled and minced cloves garlic
1 cup plain yogurt
1/2 teaspoon cayenne
1 pound egg noodles or fettucine
2-3 tablespoons extra virgin olive oil
1/4 cup finely chopped fresh flat-leaf parsley
1 cup water
Salt

Preparation
Beat together the water, tahini, and lemon juice until smooth and creamy. Place the mixture in the food processor, add the garlic, yogurt, and cayenne and pulse until creamy and frothy. Meanwhile, boil the noodles in ample salted water until tender. Drain and reserve 1/3 cup of the liquid. Toss the

noodles with olive oil. Add the pasta liquid to the tahini-yogurt mixture, place in a small saucepan, and heat for 3-4 minutes, in order to warm through. Pour over the pasta and combine, together with chopped parsley, and serve immediately.

Green Peppers Stuffed with Feta
(*Piperies Gemistes me Feta*)

Preparation time: 15 minutes
Cooking time: 20 minutes

Ingredients (6 servings)
8 green Italian peppers
1/2 teaspoon cayenne peppers
2 tablespoons extra virgin olive oil
1/2 pound feta
1 teaspoon oregano

Preparation
Wash and pat dry the peppers. Cut them at the stems carefully and keep the stems on the side. Using a dull knife, scrape out the seeds. In a mixing bowl and using a fork, mash together the feta, oregano, cayenne, and olive oil until smooth. Take a butter knife or other dull knife, and stuff the peppers, so that they're each 2/3 full with the cheese mixture. Preheat the oven to 400 F. Close the peppers with their stem ends, place side by side in a lightly oiled shallow baking dish and bake for about 18 minutes, until the peppers are soft and the cheese melted. Serve hot.

Chicken Gyros with Tzatziki

Preparation time: 20 minutes (plus 3-4 for marinade)
Cooking time: 10 minutes

Ingredients (5 servings)
Tzatziki (*see separate recipe in this cookbook*)
2 lbs boneless, skinless chicken thigh fillets
5 - 6 pita breads or flat breads

Salad
3 de-seeded and diced tomatoes
3 diced cucumbers
½ peeled and finely chopped red Spanish onion
¼ cup fresh parsley leaves
Salt and pepper

Marinade
3 minced large garlic cloves
1 tablespoon white wine vinegar
3 tablespoon lemon juice
1 tablespoon extra-virgin olive oil
3 tablespoon Greek yogurt
1 ½ tablespoon dried oregano
1 teaspoon salt
Black pepper

Preparation
Salad
Combine salad ingredients in a bowl.

Marinade
Place the marinade ingredients in a Ziploc bag and massage to mix. Add the chicken into the Ziploc bag and massage to cover all the chicken in the marinade. Marinate between 3 and 12 hours.

Chicken

Brush the outdoor grill with oil and then preheat on medium high. Or heat 1 tablespoon of oil in a fry pan over medium high heat. Remove the chicken from the marinade. Cook the chicken for 3 minutes on each side, until golden brown and cooked through: Adjust the cooking time to the size of chicken. Remove the chicken from the grill onto a plate. Cover loosely with foil and allow to rest for 6-7 minutes before serving.

Gyros

Get warmed pita bread or flatbread and place it onto a piece of parchment foil or (baking) paper. Place some salad down the middle of the bread, then top with chicken and tzatziki. Roll the wrap up, enclosing it with the parchment paper. Twist the end with the excess parchment paper to secure it and cut, if desired.

Greek Lamb Patties with Tabbouleh

Preparation time: 15 minutes
Cooking time: 20 minutes

Ingredients (4 servings)
Tabbouleh
1/4 cup bulgur
3 seeded and diced roma tomatoes
1 chopped finely red onion
2 cup coarsely chopped parsley
1 cup coarsely chopped mint
1/3 cup olive oil
1/3 cup lemon juice

Patties
1 1/3 pound lamb mince
1 tablespoon finely grated lemon rind
2 teaspoon dried oregano
3 crushed clove garlic
1/4 cup dry breadcrumbs
1 lightly beaten egg
2 tablespoon olive oil

Preparation

Patties

In a large bowl, combine mince, breadcrumbs, egg, rind, oregano, and garlic. Season to taste. Roll the mixture into 7-8 even-sized patties. Chill for 20 minutes. Heat the oil in a large frying pan on medium. Cook the patties in batches, for about 5 minutes each side, until browned and cooked through. Drain on a paper towel.

Tabbouleh

Place bulgur in a large bowl. Cover with cold water. Set aside for 15 minutes until most of the water has been absorbed. Drain off excess water and fluff with a fork. Toss through onion, herbs, and tomato. Add the oil and juice and mix well. Chill until required. Serve lamb patties with tabbouleh.

Salads

Warm Chickpea and Silver Beet Salad with Sumac

Preparation time: 20 minutes (plus overnight)
Cooking time: 120 minutes

Ingredients
1 ½ cup dried chickpeas
1 onion, cut into wedges 2 tomatoes
½ cup olive oil
1 teaspoon sugar
¼ teaspoon ground cinnamon
2 chopped cloves garlic
3 1/3 pound silver beet
3 tablespoons chopped fresh mint
2-3 tablespoons lemon juice
1½ tablespoons ground sumac

Preparation
Place chickpeas in a large bowl, cover with water, and leave to soak overnight. Drain and place in a large saucepan. Cover with water and bring to boil, simmer for 2 hours, or until tender. Drain. If choosing canned chickpeas, rinse well with cold water and drain. Wash the silver beet and dry with paper towel. Trim the stems and shred the leaves. Stand in a colander until ready to add to the pan.

Heat the oil in a frying pan, add the onion, and cook over low heat for 3-4 minutes, or until soft and just starting to brown. Cut the tomatoes in half, remove the seeds, and dice the flesh. Add the tomatoes to the pan with the sugar, cinnamon, and garlic, and cook for 3 minutes, or until soft. Add well drained, shredded, silver beet to the tomato mixture in the frying pan. Add the chickpeas and cook for 4 minutes, or until the silver beet wilts. Add the mint, lemon juice, and sumac. Lastly, season and cook for another minute. Serve immediately.

Boiled Leafy Greens (*Horta Vrasta*)

Horta vrasta or boiled greens are a staple in any Greek household. They're super easy to prepare; and when dressed with a bit of lemon and olive oil, you'll really enjoy the clean, pure taste. Like spinach, boiled greens wilt and reduce when cooked to a fraction of their original quantity. It may seem like quite a lot, but for four ample servings, You'll need approximately three pounds of greens.

Preparation time: 15 minutes
Cook time: 20 minutes

Ingredients (4 servings)
3 pounds curly endive (or any leafy green of your choice, like chicory or Swiss chard)
1 cup white vinegar for adding to soaking water)
2 tablespoons extra-virgin olive oil
1 juiced lemon
1 tablespoon salt
Salt and pepper to taste

Preparation

Wash the greens well before cooking and trim any coarse stems. Discard any brown leaves. Soak the greens in a clean sink with plenty of water and about a cup of white vinegar. Any sand or residue will fall to the bottom of the sink while the greens will float on top. Remove the greens to a colander before draining the water.

Bring a large pot of water to a boil and then add about a tablespoon of salt to the water. Carefully submerge the greens in the pot and boil for about 20 minutes or until the thickest parts of the stems are tender. Be careful not to over boil. Drain in a colander and place in a bowl. Dress with extra virgin olive oil, lemon juice, and a bit of salt and pepper to taste. Serve the greens warm or at room temperature.

Greek Salad

Preparation time: 15 minutes

Ingredients (12 servings)
6 medium tomatoes, cored and cut into wedges
6 cucumbers, peeled and sliced 1/2 inch thick
1/2 pound feta cheese, crumbled (about 1 1/2 cups)
1 cup black olives, pitted (6 ounces)
1/2 cup extra-virgin olive oil
2 tablespoons chopped oregano
Salt and freshly ground pepper
4 romaine lettuce, torn
3 tablespoons red wine vinegar
3 tablespoons lemon juice

Preparation
In a small bowl, whisk together the lemon juice, olive oil, vinegar, and oregano. Season with salt and pepper. In a large bowl, combine the cucumbers, cheese, romaine, tomatoes, and olives. Toss the salad with the dressing and serve at once.

Cypriot Cracked Wheat Salad

Preparation time: 45 minutes

Ingredients
1 cup cracked bulgur wheat
1 finely chopped bunch coriander
1 finely chopped bunch parsley
3 finely diced tomatoes
2 diced Lebanese cucumber
1 finely diced medium red onion
1 cup boiling water

Dressing
½ cup olive oil
1 juiced lemon
Salt and pepper to season

Preparation
Soak the bulgur wheat in boiling water for 30 minutes and set aside to cool. Place the coriander, parsley, tomatoes, cucumber in a large bowl and mix until all ingredients are combined. Add the bulgur wheat to the salad. Dress with lemon juice and olive oil.

Twirls Salad

Preparation time: 15 minutes

Ingredients (4 servings)
1 (12 ounce) package uncooked rainbow twirled macaroni
1 cup crumbled feta, Roquefort or blue cheese
1/2 cup chopped black olives
3/4 cup sliced radishes
1/4 cup sliced scallion
1 cup marinated artichoke hearts
1/2 cup olive or vegetable oil
2 tablespoons lemon juice
2 tablespoons chopped fresh parsley
1 clove garlic, minced
1 teaspoon oregano

Preparation
Cook macaroni according to the package directions and drain. In a large bowl, toss the hot cooked twirls with olives, radishes, cheese, scallions, and artichoke hearts until well blended. In a small bowl, combine remaining ingredients. Toss with the twirl mixture until evenly coated. Salt and pepper to taste and chill.

Greek Hot Potato Salad

Preparation time: 15 minutes

Ingredients (4 servings)
5 large potatoes
1 sliced large onion
1/2 cup diced celery
1/2 cup olive oil
Chopped Parsley
Juice of 2 lemons
Salt and pepper

Preparation
Boil the potatoes until tender and keep hot. Slice the onion into a large bowl. Sprinkle with salt and cold water and allow to stand about 5 minutes, then drain. Slice the hot potatoes and add to the onions. Add celery, lemon juice, and olive oil. Mix well to absorb the dressing. Season to taste, and garnish with chopped parsley. Serve warm.

Greek Avocado Salad

Preparation time: 15 minutes

Ingredients (4 servings)
Dressing
¼ cup olive oil
2 tablespoons red wine vinegar
1 teaspoon minced garlic
2 teaspoons dried oregano
¼ teaspoon salt

Salad
1 halved lengthways and sliced large cucumber
1 deseeded and sliced green pepper (capsicum)
½ sliced thinly red onion
4 vine ripened tomatoes, cut into wedges
7 oz cubed good quality creamy feta cheese
½ cup pitted Kalamata olives
1 diced large avocado

Preparation
Whisk together dressing the ingredients in jug or jar and mix together all of the salad ingredients in a large bowl. Toss with the dressing. Season with extra salt, if needed. To serve, sprinkle over extra oregano to taste. Serve with any meat (or without)!

Goddess Salad

Preparation time: 15 minutes

Ingredients (4 servings)
1 head romaine or green-leaf lettuce, rinsed and torn into bite-size pieces
2 medium tomatoes, cut into 8 wedges each
1 medium green bell pepper, thinly sliced (about 1 cup)
1/4 cup crumbled feta cheese
1/4 cup pitted, sliced olives, Kalamata or other oil-cured variety (optional)

Dressing
1 teaspoon chopped fresh oregano or 1/4 teaspoon dried oregano
2 1/2 tablespoons fresh lemon juice
1/4 teaspoon black pepper
2 teaspoons olive oil

Preparation
In a small bowl, combine the oregano, lemon juice, oil, and pepper. Mix well and set aside. Dry the lettuce thoroughly in a salad spinner or with a double layer of paper towels. Place in a large salad bowl. Add the bell pepper, olives, feta, and tomatoes. Pour the dressing over the salad. Toss gently to coat. Divide the salad among serving plates and serve immediately.

Athenian Salad

Preparation time: 15 minutes

Ingredients (8 servings)
1 medium sliced cucumber
6 scallions (with tops), cut into 1/2–inch pieces
1 medium head lettuce
1 bunch romaine
10 sliced radishes
1/4 cup crumbled feta cheese
1/2 cup olive or vegetable oil
1/3 cup wine vinegar
1 teaspoon salt
1 teaspoon dried oregano leaves
24 Greek or ripe green olives
1 (2 ounce) can rolled anchovies with capers, drained

Preparation
Tear the lettuce and romaine into bite–size pieces. Place the cucumber, lettuce, romaine, radishes, and scallions in a large plastic bag. Close the bag tightly and refrigerate. Shake the oil, salt, vinegar and oregano in a tightly covered jar and then refrigerate. Just before serving, shake the dressing. Add the dressing and olives to vegetables in a bag. Close the bag tightly and shake until all ingredients are well coated. Pour salad into large bowl. Top with cheese and anchovies.

Greek Country Salad (*Horiatiki*)

Preparation time: 15 minutes

Ingredients
1 thinly sliced onion
1 small thinly sliced green pepper (pith and seeds removed)
1 pound diced tomatoes
1/2 peeled and sliced cucumber
5 ounces feta cheese
12 black olives
Pinch of oregano
4 tablespoons olive oil
Salt and pepper, to taste

Preparation
Place onion, tomatoes, cucumber, and pepper in a bowl. Dress with olive oil, salt, and pepper. Arrange the olives and feta cheese on the top and sprinkle with the oregano.

Carrots Sauté

Preparation time: 5 minutes
Cooking time: 15 minutes

Ingredients
Carrots sliced thin (1/2 inch) like wheels
1 minced clove garlic
1 minced large onion
Oregano
Lemon juice
Olive oil
Salt, pepper

Preparation
Parboil (or microwave) the carrots for 5 minutes. Sauté the garlic and onion in olive oil. Add salt, pepper, lemon juice, and oregano. Put a lid on the frying pan and let it braise for 7 – 11 minutes.

Salmon and Pumpkin Salad

Preparation time: 15 minutes
Cooking time: 40 minutes

Ingredients (4 servings)
2 x ½ pound cans salmon, drained and flaked
2 sliced scallions
Vegetables 6 cups cubed peeled pumpkin
1 tablespoon olive oil
½ teaspoon freshly ground pepper
¼ teaspoon divided salt

Salad
8 cups mixed salad greens
1 avocado, chopped in chunks
2 tablespoon olive oil
¼ teaspoon freshly ground pepper
¼ teaspoon divided salt
2 tablespoon sherry vinegar or red-wine vinegar
1 tablespoon minced garlic
1 teaspoon whole-grain mustard
1 teaspoon minced anchovy fillet or paste

Preparation
Preheat oven to 450 F.

Vegetables
Toss root vegetables in a large bowl with ¼ teaspoon salt, 1 tablespoon oil, and ½ teaspoon pepper. Spread in a single layer on a large rimmed baking sheet. Roast for 15 minutes. Stir and continue roasting until soft and golden brown in spots, about 14-16 minutes more.

Salad
Whisk 2 tablespoon oil, mustard, vinegar, garlic, anchovy, and the remaining ¼ teaspoon each pepper and salt in a large bowl. Reserve 2 tablespoons of the dressing in a small bowl. Add the salad greens to the large bowl and toss to combine; divide among 4 dinner plates.

Assembly
When the vegetables are done, transfer them to the large bowl and gently combine with the avocado, reserved dressing, salmon, and scallions. Serve over the salad greens.

Mediterranean Grain Salad

Preparation time: 40 minutes

Ingredients (2 servings)
½ cup crumbled feta cheese
½ cup bulgur wheat
2 cups cherry tomatoes, halved
¾ cup chopped fresh parsley
2 very finely chopped spring onion
1 tablespoon balsamic vinegar
2 tablespoon olive oil
Salt and ground pepper
Finely chopped Sprig garden mint (optional)

Preparation
In a heatproof bowl, mix the bulgur with 1½ cups boiling water and ¼ teaspoon salt. Cover, and let stand until tender but slightly chewy, about 30 minutes. Drain the bulgur in a fine-mesh sieve, pressing to remove any liquid and return to the bowl. Add the spring onion, tomatoes, parsley, vinegar, and oil. Season with salt and pepper. Toss to combine. Top with cheese and sprinkle with chopped mint.

Pomegranate Orange and Baby Spinach Salad

Preparation time: 10 minutes

Ingredients (4 servings)
2 handfuls baby spinach
½ seeded pomegranate
2 teaspoon pomegranate juice
1 orange in separated segments
Juice of 1 orange
½ teaspoon caster sugar

Preparation
Place the washed baby spinach on a plate. Mix the juice of half the orange with sugar and the pomegranate juice for dressing. Place the orange segments and pomegranate seeds on the spinach. Pour the dressing over the salad.

Orange and Olive Salad
(*Salata me Portokalia kai Elies*)

Preparation time: 15 minutes

Ingredients (4 servings)
4 navel oranges, peeled, pith removed, sliced into 1/4-inch rounds
1 small red onion, peeled and cut into very thin rings
2 tablespoons fresh strained orange juice
2 teaspoons red wine vinegar
1/4 cup extra virgin olive oil
1 cup rinsed and halved kalamata olives
1 garlic clove
1/2 teaspoon dried thyme
1/2 teaspoon black peppercorns
4 arugula leaves, washed, patted dry, and shredded

Preparation
Arrange the oranges, onions, and olives on a platter. Using a mortar and pestle, crush together the garlic, thyme, and peppercorns. Combine the orange juice, vinegar, olive oil and crushed spices in a jar and shake very well. Sprinkle the shredded arugula leaves over the oranges and onion slices, and drizzle with the dressing. Serve immediately.

Roasted Red Pepper Salad With Feta and Herbs (*Piperies Florinis*)

Preparation time: 80 minutes

Ingredients (6 servings)
1 16-ounce jar roasted red peppers
3 tablespoons extra virgin olive oil
2 tablespoons red wine vinegar
1-2 peeled and minced garlic cloves
1 teaspoon oregano
3 tablespoons crumbled feta cheese

Preparation
Drain and rinse the peppers very well under cold water. Let them stand in a colander for a few minutes to drain off any excess water. Cut the peppers in half lengthwise and place them neatly on a platter. In a small bowl, whisk together the olive oil and vinegar and pour the dressing over the peppers. Sprinkle oregano and the garlic over the peppers and let them marinate, covered and at room temperature, for 1 hour. Just before serving, sprinkle feta on top and serve.

Watermelon Feta Salad

Preparation time: 15 minutes

Ingredients
35 oz seedless and cut into chunks watermelon
9 oz feta cheese, cut into cubes or crumbled
Chopped bunch of mint
1 finely sliced small red onion
4 oz pitted Kalamata olives
1 peeled and diced small cucumber

Dressing
1/4 of a cup extra virgin olive oil
2 tablespoon lemon juice
1 teaspoon brown sugar
Salt and Pepper to taste

Preparation
Remove the rind and seeds from the watermelon and cut into triangular chunks. Cut the feta cheese into small cubes, or bigger if you prefer, and place both into a large bowl. Slice the onions into paper-thin slices and add into the bowl with the rest of the ingredients. Add the chopped mint leaves, cucumber, and the Kalamata olives and set aside. In a small bowl add the olive oil, lemon juice and brown sugar and season. Whisk the ingredients to combine, taste, and adjust the seasoning. Pour the dressing over the watermelon feta salad and toss to coat. Serve immediately.

Soups

Easter Soup with Avgolemeno Sauce

Preparation time: 15 minutes
Cook time: 20 minutes

Ingredients (4 servings)
1/2 cut up chicken
1/2 cup (1 stick) butter
1/2 cup fresh dill
1/2 cup rice
1/2 cup parsley, finely chopped
4 finely chopped scallions
5 cups water or chicken consommé
3 cups water
Salt and pepper

Egg–Lemon Sauce (Avgolemeno Sauce)
7 eggs (at room temperature)
2 tablespoons water
Juice of 3 lemons

Preparation

Boil the chicken in the 3 cups water for 50 minutes. Remove from heat and strain broth and set aside. Chop the chicken into pieces. Cook dill, onion, and parsley in butter with 1 teaspoon salt and a dash of pepper until soft and transparent, being careful not to brown. Add the chopped chicken and cook over moderate heat for about 5 minutes and stirring frequently. Add the chicken broth and enough water to make 2 quarts liquid and bring to boil before adding rice. Reduce heat and cook until the rice is done. Remove from heat and blend in the Avgolemeno Sauce.

Avgolemeno Sauce

Beat egg whites with water until stiff. Blend in egg yolks, then add lemon juice, beating until thick. With a ladle, add a small amount of hot broth to the egg mixture, blending quickly. Pour sauce into the soup and serve immediately.

Greek Lentil Soup (*Faki Soupa*)

Preparation time: 15 minutes
Cook time: 20 minutes

Ingredients (4 servings)
3/4 cup brown lentils
1 large sliced onion
2 crushed cloves garlic
1 (3 ounce) can tomato purée
8 ounces fresh peeled and seeded tomatoes
Pinch of oregano
2 tablespoons olive oil
3 3/4 cups water
Salt and Pepper to taste

Preparation
Cover lentils with cold water and bring to boil. Drain lentils and return to the pan with garlic, onion, 1 1/2 pints water, tomato purée, fresh tomatoes, olive oil, and oregano. Bring to a boil and simmer until the lentils are soft. Remove from the heat and blend but stop blending before the mixture gets too smooth. Season to taste.

Bean Soup

Preparation time: 10 minutes
Cooking time: 120 minutes

Ingredients
1 pound dry white beans
1 can whole tomatoes (or tomato paste)
1 minced onion
1 beef bouillon
2 chopped carrots
Chopped celery
Pepper, salt and mint to taste
Olive oil

Preparation
In a large boiling pot boil 10 cup water and add the beans and bouillon. Add the tomatoes sliced, carrots, celery. Add the spices and a bit of olive oil. Bring to a boil and simmer for 2 hours or until are ready.

Meat Ball Soup (*Youvarlakia*)

Preparation time: 15 minutes
Cooking time: 60 minutes

Ingredients
1 pound ground beef
1 can of whole tomatoes
1 cup rice
1 beef bouillon
1 egg
Pepper and Salt
Flour

Preparation
In a large boiling pot, boil a half gallon of water, add the beef bouillon, and the tomatoes sliced. Put the ground beef in a bowl. Add the pepper, salt, egg and rice. Mix all the ingredients well. Make "little barrels" from the mixture, dip them thoroughly in flour, and put them in the boiling pot. Bring to a boil and simmer for an hour.

Chickpea and Pomegranate Dip

Preparation time: 10 minutes
Cooking time: 20 minutes

Ingredients (24 servings)
½ cup olive oil, plus extra for the crisps
3 x 1 pound tins drained chickpeas
2 tablespoon pomegranate molasses
6 - 8 pieces whole meal pita bread
2 seeded and chopped red chilies
1 finely chopped garlic clove
Juice of one lemon
2 teaspoon cumin seeds, toasted in a dry frying pan
1 finely chopped small red onion
A small bunch of finely chopped mint or parsley

Preparation
Put the lemon juice, chickpeas, olive oil, chili, and garlic in a food processor, season, and then pulse until just crushed. Remove and mix in the cumin seeds, red onion, and mint or parsley. Season. Mix the pomegranate molasses with a little water to thin down. Drizzle the pomegranate syrup over the chickpea dip. Serve with warm pita crisps.

Pita Crisps
Heat the oven to 390 F. Cut 6 - 8 pita breads into triangles and separate the layers. Brush with olive oil, season, and bake for 8 minutes until crisp and golden.

Greek White Bean Soup with Garlic and Lemon

Preparation time: 15 minutes
Cooking Time: 120 minutes

Ingredients (2 servings)
8.8 oz cannellini beans or small white beans soaked in water overnight
6 tablespoons extra virgin olive oil
½ minced onion
3 chopped garlic cloves
1 carrot cut into very thin slices
1 chopped stick of celery finely
1 lemon zest and juice
Salt and freshly ground pepper

Preparation

Beans
Drain the beans from the water they've soaked in overnight. Half fill a cooking pot with water and add the beans. Bring to a boil over high heat. Cook for 4 minutes and then drain beans in a strainer.

Soup
In a medium-sized cooking pot, add the olive oil and heat over medium-high heat. Add the onion and garlic and cook until softened and golden in color. Add the beans, along with 6 cups of water (part of it could be vegetable stock), and bring to a boil. Then reduce the heat to medium-low; and with the lid on partly open on the side, simmer for about 120 minutes or until beans are completely soft and tender. Cooking time depends specifically on the variety and quality of the beans.

Add the celery and carrot and season with salt and pepper. Continue simmering, stirring occasionally until the soup gets nice and thick. Then add the lemon juice and zest and cook for 3 minutes more. Remove from the heat and serve with freshly ground pepper on top and an extra squeeze of fresh lemon to taste.

Greek Fish Soup (*Psarosoupa*)

Preparation time: 15 minutes
Cooking Time: 45 minutes

Ingredients (4 servings)
1 fresh grey mullet or sea bass
2 small potatoes cut into ½ inch squares
1/2 cup celery root cut into ½ inch squares
1 small carrot cut into 1/2 inch squares
1 finely chopped small onion
A handful of chopped fresh celery leaves
1 large tomato grated
1/2 cup extra virgin olive oil
1 lemon zest and juice

Preparation
Clean and prepare the fish. Remove its scales with a fork, open the belly with a knife, and remove its innards and the gills. Cut the fish into 5-6 pieces and place in a pan. Next, season with salt and freshly ground pepper on both sides.

In a cooking pot, add the olive oil and the onion, along with 5 cups of water. Bring to a boil over high heat and then reduce heat to medium and with the lid on slightly open on the side, simmer for 16 minutes. Add the celery root, grated tomato, and the carrot and simmer for another 15 minutes. Add the celery leaves, the potatoes, and season the soup with a bit of salt and pepper. Simmer for another 5 minutes and then add the fish. Place the fish in the pot and bring the heat to medium-high. Cook for 10 minutes more, adding the lemon juice and zest 2 minutes before removing the pot from heat.

Greek Goat Soup

Preparation time: 15 minutes
Cook Time: 150 minutes

Ingredients (8 servings)
4 ½ pound male goat meat with bone cut in large pieces (alternatively lamb or beef meat)
2 medium-sized tomatoes
1/3 pound spaghetti or pasta
1 dried bay leaf
Crumbled feta cheese

Preparation
Add the meat in a large cooking pot and cover with 17 cups of water. Bring to a boil over high heat. Once it starts boiling, reduce the heat to medium-high. Skim off any foam that forms on the surface. Simmer for about 2.5 hours or until the meat feels soft when you prick it with a knife. Remove the meat from the pot and transfer to a large pan, setting it aside to cool. Pass the stock through a sieve to remove any small bones. Add the stock back to the pot.

Soup

The remaining stock should be about 3 liters; if not, add more water to it. Season with salt, pepper, a bay leaf, and bring back to a boil. Using a blender, blend the tomatoes until smooth and add to the pot. Simmer over medium-high heat for about 16 minutes more.

If using the spaghetti, cut it in smaller parts with your hands, to 5 pieces of each. Add spaghetti or pasta to the pot and simmer until pasta is cooked as well. Remove the bones from the meat, shred the meat into small pieces, and add to the pot. Serve with crumbled feta cheese on top.

Classic Vegetable Soup (Lahanosoupa)

Preparation time: 10 minutes
Cooking time: 60 minutes

Ingredients (7 servings)
1/2 cup dry and slightly salty cheese
3 peeled and chopped large onions
3 peeled and cut into large carrots
1/2 pound spinach, washed, trimmed, and shredded
1/4-inch slices
2 trimmed and cut into celery ribs
2 peeled and diced large potatoes
4 peeled and chopped large ripe tomatoes
1 finely chopped bunch parsley
8 cups water
1 cup olive oil
Salt
Freshly ground black pepper
Juice of 1/2-1 lemon

Preparation

In a large soup pot, heat half the olive oil and add onions. Cook while stirring over medium heat until wilted 6-8 minutes. Add the celery and carrots and toss to coat with oil. Sauté in the pot for 5 minutes, stirring. Add the potatoes and stir to coat. Add the parsley and the tomatoes. Pour in the water, season with salt, and bring the soup to a boil.

Reduce the heat and simmer for 30 minutes. Add the spinach and simmer another 20 minutes. Adjust the seasoning with salt, pepper, and lemon juice. Pour in the remaining raw olive oil just before serving. Ladle into individual bowls and sprinkle a few teaspoons of the grated cheese on top.

Dips, Pastries and More

Tzatziki

Preparation time: 75 minutes

Ingredients
4 cucumbers
3 cloves peeled and minced garlic
1 tablespoon olive oil
Salt and pepper, to taste
2 cups yogurt or sour cream mixed with yogurt

Preparation
Peel and seed the cucumbers and put through a fine grater (not a blender). Allow to drain in a colander until the juices have stopped running. In a small bowl, mash the garlic with salt, pepper, and the olive oil. Stir in the cucumbers and yogurt. Chill, covered, for at least 70 minutes. Serve as a dip with crackers or raw vegetables.

Skordalia

This one is my favorite Greek dip! It's a creamy, garlicky dip I love to serve on many different occasions. It's made from potatoes and walnuts that's smooth and creamy and always a hit. Serve it with toasted pita.

Preparation time: 10 minutes
Cook time: 15 minutes

Ingredients (2 servings)
8 oz. russet potatoes, peeled and cut into 2" pieces
1/2 cups walnuts (and more for serving)
2 peeled cloves garlic
3 tablespoon lemon juice
2 tablespoon white wine vinegar
1/2 cups extra-virgin olive oil (and more for serving)
2 tablespoon freshly chopped parsley for serving
Pita bread and cucumber spears for serving
Salt

Preparation
In a large pot, cover the potatoes with water and season generously with salt. Bring to a boil and cook until totally soft, 12 to 14 minutes. Drain and let cool. Meanwhile, add the walnuts to a food processor. Grate the garlic over the walnuts and process, while drizzling in the lemon juice and vinegar, until the nuts are thoroughly ground.

Add the cooled potato and olive oil and process until a thick but creamy spread form, also adding a few splashes of water to thin, if needed. Season well with salt. Top with olive oil, chopped walnuts, and parsley. Serve with bread and cucumbers.

Greek Olive Spread (*Alifi apo Elies*)

Preparation time: 15 minutes

Ingredients (7 servings)
1 cup rinsed and drained pitted Kalamata olives
1 anchovy fillet, soaked for 10 minutes in water and drained
2 peeled and minced garlic cloves
1/4 cup rinsed and drained capers
1 tablespoon grated orange zest
1-2 tablespoons ouzo
1 teaspoon dried oregano

Preparation
Place the capers, olives, ouzo, anchovy fillet, garlic, and orange zest in the bowl of a food processor and pulse on and off for a few seconds to combine. Add the herbs and pulse for a few more seconds. Remove to a bowl and serve at room temperature or chilled, either as a dip with raw vegetables or with toasted bread or pita wedges.

Greek Fried Cheese (*Saganaki*)

Preparation time: 10 minutes
Cook time: 20 minutes

Ingredients (7 servings)
1/2 pound kasseri cheese (sliced 1/2 inch thick)
2 tablespoons brandy
4 tablespoons butter
1 well beaten egg
1 teaspoon flour
Juice of 1/2 lemon

Preparation
Heat the butter in a large heavy skillet over moderate heat. Beat the egg and flour together and dip the cheese slices into the mixture. Fry until well browned on both sides. Remove from the heat and add the brandy.

Carefully ignite the brandy with a match and shake the skillet until the flame is extinguished. Squeeze the lemon juice over the cheese and serve directly from the skillet with crusty bread.

Spinach–Cheese Pie (*Spankopita*)

Preparation time: 10 minutes
Cook time: 20 minutes

Ingredients (8 servings)
2 pounds fresh spinach
1 finely chopped onion
4 tablespoons butter
1 cup cream sauce
6 beaten eggs
1 cup finely crumbled feta cheese
Salt and pepper
Dash of nutmeg
1/2 pound phyllo pastry sheets
Melted Butter

Preparation

Wash the spinach and discard stems. Dry thoroughly on absorbent paper and cut into pieces. Sauté the onion in butter until soft. Add the spinach and sauté a few minutes longer. Cool and add cheese, cream sauce, eggs, and seasonings. Mix well.

Place 7 layers of phyllo pastry sheets in an 11 x 14 x 2–inch pan, brushing each sheet well with melted butter. Add the spinach mixture, then place 8 phyllo pastry sheets on filling, again buttering each sheet. Bake at 355 degrees F for 28-32 minutes, or until the crust is golden brown. Cut into small squares before serving.

Easy Tiropita in Pan

Preparation time: 20 minutes
Cook time: 90 minutes

Ingredients
1 pound grated feta cheese
3/4 g crumbed ricotta
4 eggs whisked
Filo pastry
1 cup fresh cream
1/2 cup Parmesan cheese
1/4 cinnamon
1/2 teaspoon sugar
1 cup soda water

Preparation
Preheat the oven to 360 F. Butter a baking dish. Layer a few sheets of pastry and butter them enough to just drape over the sides of the tray. Mix the cheeses and nutmeg. Take one sheet at a time and sprinkle with cheese mixture.

Scrunch up the pastry using both hands—one on each end, pick up and place it in the pan. Keep going until the pan is filled and all the cheese mixture is used up. It should be firmly packed. Beat the eggs, add cream and soda, and then pour over filling. Tuck in the sides of pastry, around the pan. Bake in the oven until golden brown.

Greek Trinity Loaf

This recipe honors the traditional Greek Easter bread that's cut when the entire family is seated at the Easter table. Each person receives one thin slice from each of the three loaves.

Preparation time: 15 minutes
Cook time: 100 minutes

Ingredients
2 packages fast-acting yeast
3 1/2 cups all-purpose flour (divided)
1/4 cup granulated sugar
1 teaspoon anise seed
1 teaspoon salt
1/2 cup water (75 F)
1/3 cup butter or margarine
2 whole eggs
1 divided egg
1 cup golden raisins

Preparation
In large bowl, combine the sugar, 1 cup flour, undissolved yeast, anise seed, and salt. Heat the water and butter until very warm (130 F). Stir into the dry ingredients. Stir in 1 egg yolk, 2 eggs, and enough remaining flour to make soft

dough. Knead on a lightly floured surface until smooth and elastic, about 6 minutes. Cover and let rest 11 minutes.

Remove 1/2 cup dough and reserve. Knead the raisins into the remaining dough and divide into 3 equal pieces. Form each into smooth ball and arrange on a greased baking sheet in the shape of a 3-leaf clover. Divide the reserved dough into 4 equal pieces and roll each into a 10-inch rope.

Place 2 ropes side by side and twist together, pinching ends to seal. Repeat with the remaining ropes. Arrange the twisted ropes on 3-leaf clover in the form of a cross, tucking the ends under carefully. Cover and let rise in warm, draft-free place until doubled in size, about 45 to 60 minutes.

Lightly beat the reserved egg white; brush on the dough. Meanwhile, heat the oven to 375 degrees F. Bake the bread for 35 minutes or until done, covering with foil after 10 minutes to prevent any excess browning. Remove from the pan and cool on a wire rack.

Saint Basil's Bread (Vasilopeta)

Preparation time: 20 minutes
Cook time: 50 minutes

Ingredients
6 eggs
2 cups granulated sugar
3 cups all-purpose flour
2 teaspoons double-acting baking powder
1 cup lukewarm milk
1/2 teaspoon baking soda
1 1/2 tablespoons fresh lemon juice
1/2 cup chopped walnuts or almonds
1/4 cup granulated sugar

Preparation
Preheat oven to 350 F. Combine the butter and sugar together until light. Add the flour and stir until the mixture resembles coarse meal. Add the eggs, one at a time, beating well after each addition. Stir the baking powder into the milk and add into the egg mixture. Mix the lemon juice and baking soda and stir in. Mix well.

Pour into a greased round layer cake pan 10 inches in diameter and 2 inches deep. Randomly throw in a clean coin. Bake for 18-22 minutes. Sprinkle with nuts and sugar and bake about 25 minutes longer or until cake tests as done. Cool 15 minutes in pan and invert onto a serving plate. Serve right side up.

Galaktoboureko

Preparation time: 20 minutes
Cook time: 50 minutes

Ingredients
Syrup
3/4 cup water
1 cup granulated sugar
Juice of 1 lemon
1 edge of orange rind
1 cinnamon stick

Pastry
2 quarts milk
1 cup farina
6 eggs
3/4 pound unsalted sweet butter
2 teaspoons vanilla extract
20 phyllo sheets

Preparation

Boil all syrup ingredients for 10 minutes. Cool and prepare this before making the pastry.

Heat the milk to scalding. Beat the eggs until thick, add farina, and mix. Add the mixture to milk with 1/4-pound butter. Heat, stirring, until thickened. Remove from heat. Add the vanilla extract. Melt the remaining butter and butter the bottom and sides of a 10 x 14 x 2–inch pan.

Place 10 buttered phyllo leaves in the pan. Pour the farina mixture in and cover with the remaining phyllo, buttering each leaf as it's laid. Butter the top sheet very well and sculpt into diamond–shaped pieces. Bake at 350 degrees F for 50-60 minutes. Pour the cooled syrup over the hot pastry.

Haloumi Cheese Pastries

Preparation time: 15 minutes
Cooking time: 80 minutes

Ingredients
Filling
2 ¼ pound Ricotta Cheese
2 ¼ pound grated haloumi
4 eggs
1/2 cup semolina
1 teaspoon dried mint
1 cup fresh mint, finely chopped

Pastry
2 ¼ pound self-rising flour
2 cup Greek style yogurt
4 eggs
1 cup canola oil
4 egg yolks for brushing
2 tablespoon milk for brushing

Preparation
Filling
Add haloumi, ricotta, semolina, and mint into a bowl. In a separate bowl, beat the eggs with a fork and then add to the cheese mixture.

Pastry
Preheat a fan-forced oven to 360 F. Sift the flour into an electric mixer or food processor and add eggs, yogurt, and oil. Mix at a slow speed until mixture comes together and forms a ball. Remove the mixture from the bowl and knead into a ball. Place the pastry into a plastic bag and allow it to rest for 35 minutes. Divide the pastry into 10 even balls. Using a rolling pin, roll out each ball into a rectangular sheet, ensuring it's as thin as possible.

Assembly

Add 5 tablespoons of filling consistently along the bottom half of the long edge of the pastry. Starting on the long edge of the pastry, roll up to form a long log. Cut the log into 1 ½ inch pieces and place onto tray with the filling facing up. Repeat this process with the remaining sheets of pastry. In a separate bowl, whisk the egg yolk and milk; next, brush over each pastry. Bake at 360 F for 33-37 minutes or until golden brown.

Baked Feta Parcels with Thyme-Infused Honey

Preparation time: 20 minutes
Cooking time: 20 minutes

Ingredients
3 sheets filo pastry
½ cup melted butter
1/3 pound feta, cut into 3 thick slices

For serving
5–6 tablespoon thyme-infused honey
1 tablespoon sesame seeds
1 tablespoon nigella seeds

Preparation
Preheat the oven to 380 F. In a non-stick frypan, gently toast the sesame seeds and nigella seeds. Allow to cool. Lay the filo sheet flat and lightly brush with butter. Fold in half and lightly brush again. Place the feta on top and fold the pastry, enclosing the feta completely, like an envelope.

Generously brush again and repeat this process with the other two pieces of feta. Place on a baking tray lined with baking paper. Bake for 17-20 minutes, until golden. Remove from the oven, drizzle with the honey, and sprinkle with the seeds. Serve warm with ouzo, if available.

Homemade Phyllo

Preparation time: 20 minutes

Ingredients
1 pound all-purpose flour
Salt
Olive oil
Warm water
Lemon or vinegar

Preparation
Place the flour in a bowl and add salt and olive oil. Keep mixing the flour with one hand, while slowly adding water with the other. Continue mixing until dough is made. Place the dough on a counter and make phyllo. Adding lemon (or vinegar) will make the phyllo crispy.

Homemade Greek Yogurt

Preparation time: 20 hours

Ingredients
1 quart cow's, whole goat's or sheep's milk
2 tablespoons plain full-fat yogurt with live active cultures

Preparation
Spoon 2 tablespoons of milk into a bowl and stir in the yogurt. In a saucepan, bring the remaining milk to a boil. Let stand off the heat without stirring, until it registers 190 F on an instant-read thermometer. It'll take about 15 minutes and a skin will form on the surface. Using a table knife, make a small opening in the skin and pour the yogurt mixture into the milk in the saucepan. Cover the pot with a kitchen towel and transfer to an oven. Turn the light on and close the oven door. Let stand for 15-17 hours.

Using a skimmer or slotted spoon, lift off the skin and discard it. Carefully ladle the yogurt into a sieve lined with a double layer of cheesecloth and refrigerate until much of the whey is drained and the yogurt is thick, at least 5 hours. Transfer the yogurt to a bowl.

Desserts

Baklava With Walnuts and Almonds

Baklava is the dish most people think of when they envision a Greek dessert. Baklava is a perennial favorite, a classic Greek pastry made with flaky phyllo dough that's layered with a cinnamon-spiced nut filling and bathed in sweet syrup. It's crunchy and sweet and very decadent, but isn't Greek only. Many other Balkan nations have their own versions of baklava.

Preparation time: 40 minutes
Cook time: 45 minutes

Ingredients (24 servings)
For the Filling and Phyllo
1 pound walnuts (coarsely ground)
18 (9x12-inch) sheets phyllo pastry sheets
1/2 pound almonds (coarsely ground)
1 tablespoon cinnamon
½ pound butter (unsalted, melted)
1/2 cup sugar

For the Syrup
10 cloves (whole)
1 1/2 cups sugar
2 cups water
Juice of 1/2 lemon

Preparation
Prepare the Filling and Phyllo
Mix the walnuts, almonds, sugar, and cinnamon in a bowl. Set aside. Preheat the oven to 325 F. Carefully remove the phyllo roll from the plastic sleeve. If needed, using scissors or sharp knife to cut the sheets to make ones that measure 9 x 12 inches. To prevent drying, cover one stack with wax paper and a damp paper towel while working with the other.

Using a pastry brush, brush the bottom and sides of a 9 x 12 inch rectangular pan with melted butter. Begin by layering 6 sheets of phyllo, ensuring to brush each with melted butter. Add half of the nut mixture in an even layer. Pat it down with a spatula to flatten. Continue layering another 6 sheets of phyllo, brushing each with melted butter. Add the remaining nut mixture in an even layer. Top with the remaining phyllo sheets. Before baking, score the top layer of phyllo (making sure not to go past the top filling layer) to enable easier cutting later. You can place the pan in the freezer for 10 minutes or so to harden the top layers and then use a serrated knife to score. Bake in a preheated oven for about 45 minutes or until the phyllo turns a rich golden color.

Make the Syrup

In a medium saucepan, combine the water and the sugar and mix well. Add the cloves and simmer over medium-high heat for about 20 minutes. You want the syrup to be slightly thickened. Remove from the heat and discard the cloves. Stir in the lemon juice. Allow the syrup to cool slightly. When the baklava is out of the oven and still warm, ladle the syrup carefully over the entire dish. Baklava can be refrigerated or stored at room temperature.

Almond Shortbread (*Kourambiethes*)

Preparation time: 10 minutes
Cook time: 45 minutes

Ingredients (4 servings)
1/2 cups blanched almonds
1 pound unsalted softened butter
1 pound confectioners' sugar
2 egg yolks
3 tablespoons of Cognac
1 teaspoon vanilla extract
3 cups cake flour
1/2 teaspoon baking powder

Preparation
Heat oven to 350 F. Spread the almonds in a single layer on a baking sheet. Bake, stirring occasionally, until lightly toasted, about 10 minutes. Remove from the oven, cool and chop coarsely. Beat the butter in large bowl of electric mixer on medium-high speed until very light and fluffy, 4-5 minutes. Add 3 tablespoons of the confectioners' sugar; continue beating 3 minutes. Add egg yolks, Cognac, and vanilla and beat until smooth. Beat in the almonds, flour, and baking powder until mixed well. If the dough is too soft to handle, add the additional flour. Shape the scant tablespoons full of dough between your palms into round balls or crescents.

Bake on ungreased baking sheets until set and very pale golden in color; 15 minutes. Remove the cookies to a cooling rack. Place the remaining confectioners' sugar into a sifter. While cookies are still hot, sift confectioners' sugar over the tops. Repeat twice at 20-minutes intervals.

Greek Diples

Preparation time: 10 minutes
Cook time: 40 minutes

Ingredients
5 egg yolks
1 egg
1/4 cup melted and cooled butter
1 teaspoon finely shredded peeled orange
1/4 cup orange juice
2 tablespoon brand
1 tablespoon lemon juice
2 1/2 cup flour
1 teaspoon baking powder
cooking oil for deep fat -frying
1 cup honey
2 tablespoon water
Ground cinnamon
3/4 cup ground walnuts

Preparation

In a small bowl beat the egg yolks and egg at a high speed about 4 minutes. Stir in the butter, orange peel, orange juice, brandy, and lemon juice. Stir together 2 cups of the flour and the baking powder and add to the egg mixture. Stir in as much of the remaining flour as you can mix using a spoon.

On a lightly floured surface, knead in remaining flour to make moderately stiff dough. Continue kneading until the dough is smooth and elastic (6-8 mm.). Divide dough into quarters and cover. Let it rest 10 minutes.

Roll each quarter too 16-inch square. If dough is difficult to roll, cover, and let rest a few minutes more. Cut the dough into 4-inch squares. Drop one square into deep hot oil (360 degrees). Slip the dough between the tines of a long-tined fork and quickly twist dough into a roll, using a second fork to guide the dough.

Continue cooking until the roll is browned, turning once. Transfer to a paper towel and remove with fork. Repeat with the remaining dough squares. Store in a covered container. Just before serving, combine the honey and water in a saucepan. Heat until warm. Dip the desired number of rolls, one at a time, in the syrup. Sprinkle with cinnamon and walnuts.

Kourabiedes

Preparation time: 10 minutes
Cook time: 60 minutes

Ingredients
1/2 cup coarsely grated or finely chopped almonds
3 1/2 cups flour
1 1/2 cups butter
2 tablespoons confectioners' sugar
1 egg yolk
2 pounds confectioners' sugar

Preparation
Preheat the oven to 280 F. Cream the butter until light and fluffy. Mix in the egg yolk, the 2 tablespoons confectioners' sugar, and cream well. Beat in the almonds. Stir the flour and measure while gradually adding just enough flour to make a soft dough that you can shape with your hands.

Pinch off pieces of dough the size of a walnut and roll between your hands. Shape into half-moons or stylized S shapes. Place on an ungreased baking sheet and bake for 40-50 minutes or until lightly browned. Remove from the oven and let cool in pan until lukewarm.

Sift confectioners' sugar onto wax paper. Carefully transfer the cookies from the baking sheet to the sugared paper. Sift more sugar over the top, coating them with at least 1/4 inch of sugar. Let stand until cool and then store in a cookie jar or crock.

Greek Coffee Cake

Preparation time: 10 minutes
Cook time: 60 minutes

Ingredients
1 cup butter
1/2 cup margarine
1 2/3 cups granulated sugar
6 eggs
2 cups flour
1 tablespoon vanilla extract
1 tablespoon orange or lemon juice

Preparation
Mix cream butter, margarine, and sugar. Add the eggs and mix well. Add the remaining ingredients and mix well. Bake in a greased and floured Bundt pan at 325 F for about 60 minutes. Cool for 10 minutes, remove from the pan, and sprinkle with confectioners' sugar.

Cheese and Honey Pie (*Melopita*)

Preparation time: 30 minutes
Cook time: 40 minutes

Ingredients (8 servings)
For the filling
1 pound Myzithra cheese (soft, or ricotta cheese)
3 eggs (lightly beaten)
1/2 cup honey
1 lemon (the zest, grated)
3 teaspoon flour
1/4 cup sugar
Garnish: cinnamon (ground)
Garnish: honey

For the crust
1 1/4 cup flour
1/3 cup sugar
1/4 teaspoon salt
1 yolk from egg
1 teaspoon vanilla extract
1 tablespoon brandy or cognac
2 tablespoons of iced water
8 tablespoon (1 stick) unsalted butter, cut into 1/4-inch pieces

Preparation
Preheat the oven to 350 F.

Crust in Food Processor
Add the sugar, flour, and salt to the bowl. Pulse a few times to mix. Add chilled butter pieces and process until crumbly, like wet sand. Add the vanilla, egg yolk, brandy, and 1 tablespoon of ice water. Process until the dough pulls together and forms a ball away from the sides. Add an additional tablespoon of water if it seems too dry. Turn out onto a lightly floured surface and flatten dough into a round disk. Chill dough while you prepare the filling.

Crust by Hand
In a large mixing bowl, add flour, salt and sugar. Mix to combine. Add the butter pieces; and using two forks or a pastry blender, cut the butter into the flour. You can also use your hands for this. The mixture should resemble coarse sand when the butter is incorporated fully. Add brandy, water, egg yolk, and vanilla. Next, mix to incorporate, kneading the dough into a smooth ball. Flatten into a round disk and chill while mixing the filling.

Making the Filling

In a medium-sized bowl, add Myzithra or ricotta cheese, eggs, lemon zest, honey, flour, and sugar. Mix well until all ingredients are combined. Using a rolling pin, roll out your dough to the approximate size of your baking pan. If possible, use a 10-inch tart circle with a removable bottom. You can substitute a spring form pan, a round cake pan, or even a pie dish.

Lightly grease the pan's bottom and sides. Dough should be large enough to push up the sides of your pan. The easiest way to transfer the dough from the counter to the pan is to roll it back onto your rolling pin and then unroll it over the pan. Press the dough into the sides and bottom of the pan.

Add the filling and bake in a preheated 350 F oven until the filling sets (no jiggle in the center) and it begins to turn a golden-brown color. Baking times will vary according to the size you choose to make. For a 10-inch tart, it should take 38-42 minutes. A deeper, 9-inch pie plate could take up to 45-55 minutes. Be sure to monitor your pie after 35 minutes of baking time. Serve on a plate drizzled with honey and sprinkle with ground cinnamon.

Greek Butter Biscuits (*Koulourakia Voutirou*)

Preparation time: 10 minutes
Cook time: 15 minutes

Ingredients (40 servings)
3/4 cup butter
3/4 cup granulated sugar
1 egg
2 egg yolks
3 1/2 cups flour
1 beaten egg
2 teaspoons baking powder
Cream butter and sugar

Preparation
Add the egg and egg yolks and beat until light and fluffy. Add flour, sifted with baking powder. Knead to make a soft dough, chill for an hour and form into small rings. Arrange on greased baking sheets, brush with beaten egg, and bake in a moderate oven for about 12 minutes.

Greek Chocolate Balls

Preparation time: 15 minutes

Ingredients
1/2 pound walnut meats
1/2 pound sweet cooking chocolate
9 pieces zwieback
1 1/2 tablespoons granulated sugar
1/2 teaspoon cinnamon
2 tablespoons rose water
Confectioners' sugar

Preparation
Put walnut pieces, cooking chocolate and zwieback through the fine blade of a food chopper. Add rose water, sugar, and cinnamon. Form into 36 small balls. Roll in confectioners' sugar. Store the balls airtight.

Greek Rice Pudding

Preparation time: 15 minutes
Cook time: 20 minutes

Ingredients (7 servings)
1/2 cup short grain rice
1 cinnamon stick
6 cups milk
1 1/2 tablespoons cornstarch mixed with 2 tablespoons milk
1 teaspoon vanilla extract
1/2 cup sugar
Zest of 1 lemon
A grating of fresh nutmeg
2 cups water
Ground cinnamon (for garnish)

Preparation
Combine rice, cinnamon stick, and water in a saucepan and bring to a boil. Lower the heat and simmer covered for 15 minutes. Add the milk, cornstarch mixture, and sugar to the pan. Increase the heat to moderate and stir constantly 16 minutes, until the mixture thickens. Add lemon zest, vanilla extract, and nutmeg and stir to combine. Spoon into individual serving bowls or glasses and refrigerate for at least 2 hours. Dust with a little cinnamon before serving.

Melomacarona

Preparation time: 15 minutes
Cook time: 20 minutes

Ingredients
1 cup (2 sticks) margarine
5 cups flour
1/4 cup granulated sugar
1 1/2 teaspoons baking powder
1/2 cup orange juice
1 1/4 cups vegetable oil
1 teaspoon baking soda

Preparation
Beat the oil, sugar, and margarine. Add the baking powder and beat well. Add the baking soda to orange juice and stir until foamy. Add to the first mixture and beat well. Add the flour and form cookies. Knead by hand and form cookies in an oblong shape.

Bake at 375 F on an ungreased cookie sheet. When slightly brown on the bottom, remove from the oven to let cool. When cooled, dip the cookies in 1/2 water and 1/2 honey which has been brought to a boil. Do this one at a time. Sprinkle with chopped walnuts and hint of cinnamon.

Yogurt Cake

Preparation time: 15 minutes
Cook time: 20 minutes

Ingredients

Syrup
2 cups water
2 cups granulated sugar
1 slice lemon
1 slice orange

Batter
1 cup flour, sifted
1 teaspoon baking powder
4 eggs, thickly beaten
1 cup granulated sugar
2 cups plain yogurt
1 1/2 teaspoons grated orange rind

Preparation

Combine lemon, water, sugar, and orange slices in a small saucepan. Cook at a slow boil until clear and syrupy. Set aside. Mix and sift the flour and baking powder. Add sugar to the eggs gradually, beating constantly, until smooth and thick. Stir in the yogurt and add the orange rind and flour–baking powder mixture while mixing smooth.

Pour into an 8–inch square baking pan. Bake at 375 F for 33-36 minutes and then remove. Cake will have a delicate brown color. Pour the cool syrup slowly over hot cake until absorbed and then cool. Cut cake diagonally into diamond shapes. Serve plain or garnished with diced orange sections, whipped cream, toasted almonds, or chopped pistachios.

Greek Almond Macaroons (*Amigdalota*)

Preparation time: 15 minutes
Cook time: 20 minutes

Ingredients
1 pound ground almonds
3/4 cup granulated sugar
2 tablespoons toasted bread crumbs
4 egg whites
1 teaspoon vanilla extract
1/2 teaspoon lemon juice
Pinch of salt
Rose water
Confectioners' sugar

Preparation
Beat the egg whites with salt until stiff, and then add lemon juice. Add crumbs, almonds, and sugar to the egg whites, folding them in gradually. Add the vanilla extract. Cut a brown paper bag to fit a cookie sheet and grease the paper. Drop teaspoon–size macaroons onto the paper and bake at 275 F about 20 minutes, checking after 14 minutes, so that Amigdalota don't burn.

Brush the cookies with rose water when they come out of the oven. Loosen them from paper by moistening the paper slightly and lifting off macaroons. Sift confectioners' sugar over them and let cool.

Greek Christmas Cookies

Preparation time: 15 minutes
Cook time: 40 minutes

Ingredients
1 1/2 cups semolina
1 grated lemon rind
1 grated orange rind
4 cups flour
1 1/4 cups light olive oil
1/3 cup granulated sugar
1 cup orange juice
2 1/2 teaspoons baking powder
1 teaspoon cloves
1/2 teaspoon cinnamon

Syrup
1 cup honey
1 cup granulated sugar

Topping
2 teaspoons ground cloves
1 cup walnuts, coarsely ground

Preparation
Beat olive oil with sugar and add the orange juice. Mix 2 cups of flour with baking powder and add to oil and orange mixture. Beat in semolina, orange, brandy, lemon peel, cloves, and cinnamon. Knead dough on a floured surface, adding more flour as needed for strong elastic dough. Let stand covered for 20 minutes.

Preheat the oven to 350 F. Shape the dough into oval cookies about 2 1/2 inches long. Bake on an oiled cookie sheet for 23-26 minutes and let cool. In a saucepan bring sugar, honey, and water to a boil. Simmer 9-11 minutes and remove from the heat. Mix the walnuts with cloves and sprinkle over the cookies. Cool before serving.

Zwieback (*Paximadia*)

Preparation time: 15 minutes
Cook time: 30 minutes

Ingredients
1/8 teaspoon nutmeg
1/2 cup chopped walnuts
1/4 cup toasted sesame seeds
1 cup vegetable oil
1 cup granulated sugar
3 large eggs
4 cups divided flour
1 tablespoon baking powder
1 1/2 teaspoons cinnamon

Preparation (5 servings)

Preheat the oven to 350 F. Lightly grease two baking sheets and beat the oil and sugar. Add eggs one at a time. In a bowl, measure and mix together the baking powder, cinnamon, 2 cups flour, nutmeg, sesame seeds, and nuts. Add the flour mixture to the egg mixture and add remaining flour, as necessary, to make a soft dough.

Divide the dough into four equal balls. Roll each to 12 inches long x 3 inches wide and 1/4–inch thick. Bake for 14-17 minutes on a prepared baking sheet. Remove the loaves from the oven. While warm, slice 3/4–inch thick diagonally or straight across. Place each slice cut side down back on a baking sheet. Return to the oven and lightly brown 4-6 minutes per side to make a light toast.

Pistachio and rose semolina cakes

Preparation time: 15 minutes
Cooking time: 50 minutes

Ingredients (20 servings)
1 cup semolina
¾ cup roughly chopped pistachios
2 cups self-rising flour
1 teaspoon baking powder
1 tablespoon lemon zest
¾ cup freshly squeezed orange juice
6 eggs
½ pound softened butter
½ cup white sugar

Syrup
3 ½ cups water
1 wedge lemon
3 cups white sugar

Icing
1 cup icing sifted sugar
1 tablespoon boiling water
2 tablespoon rose water
Rose petals
Roughly chopped pistachios

Preparation

Preheat the oven to 325 F. Grease and line two muffin trays or petite cake trays. Prepare the syrup by bringing the water, sugar, and lemon to a boil. Lower the temperature and simmer for 10-15 minutes before removing from the heat and allowing to cool at room temperature.

Using an electric mixer, beat the butter and sugar at a high speed until pale and creamy. Add the eggs one at a time, beating after each addition. Reduce the mixer's speed and add the lemon rind and orange juice. Add the flour, semolina, and baking powder and mix until well combined. Stir the chopped pistachio nuts and transfer to a baking dish. Bake for about 30 minutes or until golden and cooked through. Remove from the oven and pour the cooled syrup over the hot cakes. Cover and allow to the syrup to absorb before removing from the baking dishes.

To make the icing, whisk the icing sugar, boiled water, and rose water in a bowl. Add more water, as necessary, since the icing should be thick and glossy. Top the cakes with a dollop of icing and sprinkle with rose petals and pistachios to garnish.

Orange Cake in Syrup (*Pontica*)

Preparation time: 15 minutes
Cook time: 40 minutes

Ingredients
Cake
1/4 cup (1/2 stick) melted butter
1 teaspoon orange rind
1 teaspoon vanilla extract
1 cup all-purpose flour
6 separated eggs
1 cup granulated sugar
1 tablespoon baking powder

Syrup
1 cup granulated sugar
1 cup orange juice
1 cup water

Preparation
Preheat the oven to 355 F. Butter an 8 x 12-inch pan with 1/4 cup melted butter. Make a syrup by combining orange juice, water, and sugar in a saucepan. Bring to a boil, reduce heat, and simmer 18-21 minutes. Remove from the heat and allow to cool. Beat the egg whites until stiff. In another bowl, beat the egg yolks until light yellow and add sugar, orange rind, and vanilla extract. Blend well into a cream.

Mix the flour and baking powder together and set aside. With the egg yolk mixture, add the egg whites, alternating with 2 tablespoons of flour, ending with egg whites. Pour the batter into a prepared pan. Bake for 35 minutes or until a wooden pick inserted in center of the cake comes out clean. Remove the cake from the oven and cut into diamond shapes. Pour cold syrup over the hot cake. Cool completely before serving.

Kataifi with cheese and syrup (*Kunefe*)

Preparation time: 15 minutes
Cooking time: 100 minutes

Ingredients

Filling
4 cups ricotta cheese
½ cup heavy cream
½ cup milk

Syrup
2 tablespoons lemon juice
3 cups cold water
3 cups sugar
1 piece of lemon rind (optional)
1 stick cinnamon (optional)

Kunefe
1 packet Kataifi (shredded filo dough)
1 cup roasted and finely ground pistachio
¾ cup unsalted clarified butter
4 tablespoons rose water

Preparation

Preheat the oven to 375 F. To make the syrup, combine water, sugar, and cinnamon in a saucepan and boil for 5-6 minutes; next, then lower the heat and simmer, uncovered, for about 14-16 minutes. The syrup is ready when light yellow and when a small amount dropped onto a wooden surface is sticky or tacky when cool. Stir the lemon rind into the syrup and cool.

To make the filling, mix the cheese, milk, and heavy cream together well.

To assemble kunefe, brush the inside of a 10x15x2 inch baking dish all over with a little of the clarified butter. Separate the shredded dough in half by holding up and pulling it apart. Spread half the dough evenly in the pan. Dip a wide pastry brush into butter and drizzle half the butter over the dough. Spread the filling over the pastry evenly. Place the other half of the shredded dough over the kunefe and gently press down all over. Drizzle any remaining butter over the dough.

Bake the kunefe in the center of the preheated oven for 33-37 minutes, until golden. Remove from the oven and immediately pour over the rosewater, followed by the cooled syrup. Cover the kunefe and allow the pastry to absorb the syrup. Sprinkle with roasted, ground pistachio nuts. Serve warm or cool to room temperature.

Nutella Baklava

Preparation time: 10 minutes
Cooking time: 45 minutes

Ingredients (8 servings)
1 pound packet of filo pastry
½ pound jar of Nutella
3 tablespoon almonds coarsely ground
½ teaspoon of ground cinnamon
1 cup unsalted butter melted for brushing

Syrup
1 cups of caster sugar
4 cloves whole
1 tablespoons of lemon
2 tablespoons of honey
½ cup of water
2 cinnamon sticks

Preparation
Syrup
In a medium saucepan, combine the sugar with water. Bring to a boil over medium heat, stirring until all sugar has dissolved. Add the lemon juice, cinnamon sticks, and whole cloves to a saucepan. Reduce the heat to a simmer for 9-10 minutes. Remove from the heat and stir in the honey. Set aside to cool completely.

Nutella Baklava Fingers
Using 5 sheets of filo pastry at a time, brush each layer with melted butter and place on-top of each other. Brush the top of the first sheet with butter, place the next sheet on-top, and brush with butter. Be sure to continue until all five sheets have been buttered. Keep any remaining filo covered with a damp towel always and don't dry it out.

Sprinkle 1 tablespoon of almonds on the top layer of the filo pastry. Pipe a small line of Nutella (approximately 1/3 cup) along the long side of the pastry closest to you and fold left and right: ensure that the short ends are slightly in (approximately ¾ inch on either side) and then fold slightly on the long side over Nutella (approximately ¾ inch). Gently roll away from you to create a long roll. After rolling into a long roll, lightly grip both ends of the roll and gently push roll into the center until there's a slightly gathered look. Place on a lined backing tray / sheet and cut into 4 equal pieces. Bake at 320 F for approximately 25 minutes and then the increase temperature up-to 360 F until golden brown. Pour the cold syrup over the hot baklava fingers and allow to cool. Drizzle with Nutella and serve.

Almond Halva Cake

Preparation time: 15 minutes
Cooking time: 20 minutes

Ingredients
1 ¾ cup water
3 ½ cup glucose
2 ½ pound sugar
¼ cup soapwort
5 ¾ pound Tahini
1 tablespoon vanilla
½ pound almonds
½ pound chocolate
½ pound almonds (for the base)

Preparation
Add water, glucose, and sugar to a pot and boil to 310 F. Whip the soapwort to stiff peaks. Add the heated caramel to the soapwort by pouring slowly and using a medium mixer speed. When fully incorporated, add the whipped caramel to the tahini and then add the vanilla. Start to mix with a silicone glove until you see a grainy texture. Next, then begin to knead it like a bread dough. Add the almonds and continue to knead. Add the chocolate and continue to knead until almost set. Then fold the mix a few times. Line a 11-pound steel bowl with oil and add the final amount of almonds to the base and pour in the not quite set caramel-tahini mixture. Let it set overnight, then invert, and unmold onto a wooden serving board.

Greek Amaretti Cookies

Preparation time: 15 minutes
Cooking time: 30 minutes

Ingredients (15 servings)
1 cup almond flour (or 3 cups finely ground almonds)
3 egg whites
½ teaspoon vanilla extract
1 teaspoon almond extract
1 cup fine sugar

Preparation
Preheat the oven to 300 F. In a food processor mix together the almond flour and sugar. Add the vanilla and almond extract and pulse for a few seconds. Add the egg whites, one at a time, and continue to process until the dough is smooth. Place the dough in teaspoonful amounts on baking paper on oven trays. Dust lightly with sugar. Bake for 25 - 30 minutes, depending on whether you prefer them slightly chewy or crispy. Store in a cool, dry container.

Baked Quince with Yogurt
(*Kythoni Psito me Yiaourti*)

Preparation time: 15 minutes
Cooking time: 40 minutes

Ingredients (8 servings)
4 large quinces
1/3 cup honey
3-4 tablespoons fresh strained lemon juice
2 cups strained Greek yogurt or sour cream
1/3 cup currants
1/3 cup chopped lightly toasted pine nuts
Fresh mint for garnish
Water

Preparation
Preheat the oven to 350 F. Peel the quinces and halve lengthwise. Using a sharp paring knife or spoon, scoop out the core and seeds. Place the quince cut side

down on a shallow baking sheet. Pour a little water into the pan to keep the quinces from burning.

Combine the honey and lemon juice and pour evenly over the quince. Bake about 40 minutes uncovered, until tender, then remove and cool.

Place each quince half on a small serving dish. Fill with a dollop of yogurt or sour cream. Sprinkle with currants and nuts, drizzle with additional honey if desired, and serve, garnished with fresh mint leaves.

Figs Poached in Mavrodaphne with Manouri Cheese

Preparation time: 70 minutes
Cooking time: 40 minutes

Ingredients (6 servings)
12 ounces dried figs
2/3 cup black wine (Mavrodaphne wine, if possible)
1 cinnamon stick
3-4 whole cloves
1-2 pounds yellow cheese
Fresh mint for garnish

Preparation
Place the figs in a wide saucepan and cover with hot water. Steep them for 60 minutes. Pour in the Mavrodaphne and the spices. Bring to a boil, reduce heat, and simmer for about 30 minutes, until the figs are very plump and tender.

Remove the fruit with a slotted spoon, and strain the poaching liquid, discarding the spices and any seeds that may have leaked out from the figs. Return the poaching liquid to the pot, add sugar, and boil until reduced and thick and the consistency of syrup. Slice the manouri cheese into 1/2-inch rounds or crescents, carefully to keep the pieces intact. Place the cheese slices in one overlapping row on a large platter. Place the poached figs evenly over them and pour over the syrup. Garnish with mint and serve immediately.

Honey Soaked Walnut Cake (*Karydopita*)

Preparation time: 15 minutes
Cooking time: 60 minutes

Ingredients (12 servings)
Syrup
1/2 cup honey
1/2 cup orange liqueur
1/2 cup water

Cake
1/2 pound melted unsalted butter
3 large eggs
1 cup sugar
1 1/4 cups ground walnuts
1 cup plain yogurt
2 cups all-purpose flour
2 teaspoons grated orange rind
2 teaspoons baking powder

Preparation

Syrup

In a small saucepan, combine the honey and water, and heat over medium heat until the honey dissolves. Bring to a boil, reduce the heat, and simmer for 9-11 minutes. Remove from the heat and stir in the liqueur. Brush a 9-inch tube pan with melted butter and dust with flour. Set aside.

Cake

Beat the eggs until light and fluffy. Add the sugar and the remaining melted butter, orange rind and mix until creamy. Combine the walnuts, flour, and baking powder in a large bowl. Add the egg and sugar mixture to the bowl and beat thoroughly. Fold in the yogurt.

Pour the batter into the prepared pan and bake in a preheated oven at 350 F for 50 minutes or until a cake taster comes out clean. Remove the cake from oven and cool on a rack for 5 minutes. Spoon the cooled syrup over the cake and let it stand for at least 3 hours before serving.

Tahini cake (*Keik apo Tahini*)

Preparation time: 15 minutes
Cooking time: 45 minutes

Ingredients (9 servings)
1/2 cup tahini
1 3/4 cups all-purpose flour
2 teaspoons baking powder
1/2 teaspoon baking soda
1 tablespoon ground cinnamon
1 teaspoon ground cloves
1 cup strained fresh orange juice
1/4 cup honey
1 teaspoon vanilla extract
Grated rind of orange
Pinch of salt
1/2 cup water
Confectioner's sugar (optional)

Preparation
Preheat the oven to 350ºF and lightly grease and flour a 10-inch round cake pan. Sift together the soda, salt, flour, baking powder, cinnamon, and cloves. In a separate bowl, whip together the tahini with the orange juice, honey, and water. Add the vanilla and grated orange rind as you continue beating for 5 minutes.

Add the flour to the tahini mixture, beating all the while, until a thick batter forms. Pour into a prepared baking pan and bake for 45 minutes, until a cake tester inserted in the center of the cake comes out clean. Remove and cool for 30 minutes in the pan. To serve, sprinkle with confectioner's sugar.

If you liked Greek food, discover to how cook DELICIOUS recipes from other Balkan countries!

Savor *Sarma*, *moussaka* from other Balkan countries, and original *kajmak* recipes inside!

Within these pages, you'll learn 35 authentic recipes from a Balkan cook. These aren't ordinary recipes you'd find on the Internet, but recipes that were closely guarded by our Balkan mothers and passed down from generation to generation.

Main Dishes, Appetizers, and Desserts included!

If you want to learn how to make homemade *moussaka*, *sarma* (stuffed cabbage rolls), Croatian green peas stew, and 32 other authentic Balkan recipes, then start with our book! Also, I reveal the best homemade versions of *kajmak* west of Serbia! *Kajmak* is a delicious butter cheese cream spread that's a staple at Balkan tables.

Order HERE now for only $2,99

If you like Greek food, but you're a Mediterranean dieter who wants to know the secrets of the Mediterranean diet, dieting, and cooking, then you're about to discover how to master cooking meals on a Mediterranean diet right now!

In fact, if you want to know how to make Mediterranean food, then this new e-book - "The 30-minute Mediterranean diet" - gives you the answers to many important questions and challenges every Mediterranean dieter faces, including:
How can I succeed with a Mediterranean diet?
What kind of recipes can I make?
What are the key principles to this type of diet?
What are the suggested weekly menus for this diet?
Are there any cheat items I can make?
... and more!

If you're serious about cooking meals on a Mediterranean diet and you really want to know how to make Mediterranean food, then you need to grab a copy of "The 30-minute Mediterranean diet" right now.

Prepare **111 recipes with several ingredients in less than 30 minutes!**

Order HERE now for only $2,99!

ONE LAST THING

If you enjoyed this book or found it useful, I'd be very grateful if you'd post a short review on Amazon. Your support really does make a difference and I read all the reviews personally, so I can apply your feedback and make this book even better.

Thanks again for your support!

Please send me your feedback at
www.facebook.com/balkanfoodonly
www.balkanfood.org

BLINDSPOTTING

Harry~

Marty Dubin

MARTIN DUBIN

BLINDSPOTTING

HOW TO SEE WHAT'S HOLDING YOU BACK AS A LEADER

HARVARD BUSINESS REVIEW PRESS · BOSTON, MASSACHUSETTS

HBR Press Quantity Sales Discounts

Harvard Business Review Press titles are available at significant quantity discounts when purchased in bulk for client gifts, sales promotions, and premiums. Special editions, including books with corporate logos, customized covers, and letters from the company or CEO printed in the front matter, as well as excerpts of existing books, can also be created in large quantities for special needs.

For details and discount information for both print and ebook formats, contact booksales@harvardbusiness.org, tel. 800-988-0886, or www.hbr.org/bulksales.

Copyright 2025 Martin Dubin

All rights reserved

Printed in the United Kingdom

10 9 8 7 6 5 4 3 2

No part of this publication may be reproduced, stored in or introduced into a retrieval system, or transmitted, in any form, or by any means (electronic, mechanical, photocopying, recording, or otherwise), without the prior permission of the publisher. Requests for permission should be directed to permissions@harvardbusiness.org, or mailed to Permissions, Harvard Business School Publishing, 60 Harvard Way, Boston, Massachusetts 02163.

The web addresses referenced in this book were live and correct at the time of the book's publication but may be subject to change.

Library of Congress Cataloging-in-Publication Data

Names: Dubin, Martin, author.
Title: Blindspotting : how to see what's holding you back as a leader / Martin Dubin.
Description: Boston, Massachusetts : Harvard Business Review Press, 2025. | Includes index.
Identifiers: LCCN 2025000200 (print) | LCCN 2025000201 (ebook) | ISBN 9798892790536 (hardcover) | ISBN 9798892790543 (epub)
Subjects: LCSH: Executives—Psychology. | Leadership. | Problem solving.
Classification: LCC HD38.2 .D83 2025 (print) | LCC HD38.2 (ebook) | DDC 658.4/092—dc23/eng/20250326
LC record available at https://lccn.loc.gov/2025000200
LC ebook record available at https://lccn.loc.gov/2025000201

ISBN: 979-8-89279-053-6
eISBN: 979-8-89279-054-3

For the Loves in My Life

My Eternal Love
Barbara

My Parents
Charlotte and Frank

My Children
Emily and Jon

My Grandchildren
Josie, Naomi, Remy, and Levi

"O wad some Power the giftie gie us /
To see oursels as ithers see us!"

—Robert Burns

"'Tis wealsome Pow'r the gift to gie us,
To see oursel' as ithers see us."

—Robert Burns

CONTENTS

INTRODUCTION
THE BLINDSPOTTER
1

CHAPTER 1
IDENTITY
Who Do You Think You Are?

21

CHAPTER 2
MOTIVE
Are You Blind to the Core Forces
Driving Who You Are?

49

CHAPTER 3
TRAITS
Are Your Superstrengths Enabling
Unseen Weaknesses?

81

CHAPTER 4
EMOTION
Are Your Feelings Managing You or
Are You Managing Your Feelings?

107

CHAPTER 5
INTELLECT
Are You Smart Enough to Realize That Being Smart Is Never Enough?

137

CHAPTER 6
BEHAVIOR
Are You Mastering Three Key Areas of Behavior the Way a Leader Should?

163

CONCLUSION
ADDRESSING YOUR OWN BLINDSPOTS

193

Appendix: Blindspot Checklist

213

Notes

219

Index

221

Acknowledgments

227

About the Author

229

BLINDSPOTTING

INTRODUCTION

THE BLINDSPOTTER

A few years ago, I received a panicked call from Dara, an investor in Aesthetics, a tech startup specializing in augmented reality (AR) devices.* I knew of the company from the significant media coverage it had garnered, and I had recently read a fawning profile of its founder, Marcus, whose brilliance, it was said, had thus far led Aesthetics to tremendous success. From the outside, this was a business on fire, with technology that was well ahead of its competitors', creating entirely new product categories and swimming in preorders for its latest innovation, an indestructible AR camera. The company had raised hundreds of millions of dollars in capital and was valued at well above a billion dollars—a "unicorn," in startup parlance. Marcus was a visionary making his own—and his employees'—wildest dreams come true.

Yet Dara was desperate for help. Though no one knew it yet, she told me there were signs that Aesthetics' new product was coming out of the factory malfunctioning—it wasn't quite as indestructible as the company had advertised—and it was set to disappoint millions of users. Marcus, the founder, had ignored the warning signs that could

---

* The clients and companies discussed throughout this book are anonymized but are versions of real stories, or combinations of stories.

have prevented this. Dara bemoaned that at a time when Marcus should have been consumed with fixing the manufacturing issue, or even just empowering someone else to do it, he was instead off trying to raise more money and keep the good press and hype around the company rolling in.

While this seemed like a disaster on its own, Dara further revealed that one by one, her fellow investors had started dropping out of Aesthetics' latest funding round, to Marcus's bewilderment. The panicked call I got was her last-ditch attempt to help Marcus see what he'd been missing, change his behavior, and set a new course before the ship met the iceberg.

As Dara explained, Marcus had been an incredible leader when things were going well, a charismatic and articulate presence for employees, investors, and the press, and a remarkable generator of ideas and potential, but this current challenge had exposed deep flaws in his leadership that he and they hadn't known were there. While the specifics were new to me, the general outline of the story wasn't. Things go well until they don't. We succeed until the moment a problem emerges that we think we can handle—but we actually can't. We use all of the tools that have gotten us this far, but somehow they stop working. We don't understand; what are we missing? What we don't see is what we *can't* see: there's a blindspot in our self-awareness, and until we uncover it, we are unable to get past the crisis.

This was Marcus's problem, but it's everyone's problem at one point or another. We all have biases, errors in judgment, and gaps in our thinking. But we're not very good at identifying them, and we're even worse at dealing with them.

There actually is no professionally accepted personality model for what it takes to be a successful leader—no model for identifying and changing elements of our personality that are standing in our way. As a clinical psychologist turned business coach (with my own relevant experience in the business world in between, as a CEO and successful entrepreneur; more on that in a bit), I spent years honing my intuition to recognize when previously successful executives were getting in their own way and to come up with tailored solutions to help them. What I didn't have was a blueprint that could help me validate that intuition, to tell me what needed adjustment and to give me a toolbox of techniques to fix the problem.

It didn't exist, so I decided to create it. The result is this book, and my assertion that if only we could see our blindspots, we could address what's holding us back and thrive in the moments when we currently fall short.

Defining Blindspots

Most of us understand the idea of blindspots in a general sense—areas we can't see, to take the term most literally, or places we have gaps we may not even realize, to be a little more abstract. But in the context of this book, I'm defining blindspots quite specifically: they are what we don't know about ourselves that hold us back as leaders and prevent us from achieving our highest success. They are the particulars of who we are—our behaviors, our emotions, our intellect, our inborn traits, our core motives, and the identities we embody—that we are unable to see, and thus unable to take action to address.

The good news is you can compensate for your blindspots. The bad news is first you have to know what they are. That's the challenge this book is here to address. If you were working one-on-one with a leadership coach like me, I'd start by giving you some tests aimed at discovering how you see yourself and how you see the world. I would talk to you and observe you, notice how you respond to challenges, listen to your stories, and try to unlock your true potential. I would ask the people around you for honest feedback, and I would listen closely—for what they say, and what they don't say. I'd put all the information I gathered into a report, all about you—your gifts and your gaps, and everything in between.

Report in hand, we'd meet, and, quite often, to your surprise and mine, you'd reach for the Kleenex. Executives who have to keep their emotions together 24/7 and who can't afford to show their vulnerability—who know that literally any inkling of weakness can cause a stock price to plummet, employee morale to soften, or investors to start questioning their decisions—tend to be bottled tight. But, brought in with a promise of confidentiality, a coach is one of the few people (along with perhaps spouses or partners) with whom it's safe for them to let their guard down.

I've had people tell me that even with their peers, all they can talk about without considering the repercussions is how well their company is doing. But when they do feel comfortable enough to speak freely and unburden themselves, incredible things emerge. CEOs have said to me that on the first day they walked into the office—with floor to ceiling windows—all they could think was, *Don't jump out.*

It's not that our strengths and struggles necessarily come as a surprise. Most of us know, in a general sense, what we're good at and where we need help. "I'm not a detail guy," for instance. But what we don't recognize is how those struggles impact the people around us, or that the things we see as superstrengths ("I can outwork anyone!") can actually turn into supernovas when relied upon too heavily, exploding any positive impact those characteristics might have ("My boss sends emails and texts at all hours of the day and night—I'm afraid if I don't respond immediately, he'll think I'm sleeping on the job!").

What reports like mine reveal—through true feedback from others and a trained observer listening and watching closely—is that we are not as self-aware as we believe. We all tend to feel as if most of our traits, instincts, and feelings are like everyone else's, except for the qualities where we think we're exceptional—where we perceive ourselves as being gifted in ways that can only serve as a positive. As an example, suppose your partner complains that you are too organized and rigid about where things belong. It's easy to think you're no more fixated on this than the average person—or that in fact it's a strength to be celebrated rather than criticized—but we don't necessarily realize when we are truly an outlier, or when a positive quality has tipped over into something that is hurting us (or at least hurting our relationships).

I call this the Perception Gap. Psychologists accept that nearly all human characteristics are arranged along a normal distribution, a bell curve, typically with two-thirds of people in the middle and one-sixth at each extreme. We often think we're at least in the middle, even when it comes to characteristics where we are firmly in the bottom sixth—think about how no one is inclined to believe they're a bad driver. Likewise, on characteristics we see as strengths, we may think we're in the top sixth when we're in the middle of the curve. The tendency to overestimate our own skills is known as the Dunning-Kruger effect: in David Dunning and Justin Kruger's studies, they found that the lowest performers on tests of logical reasoning, English grammar, and appreciation of humor had scores placing them in the 12th percentile, but ranked themselves a full fifty points higher, in the 62nd percentile, well above average.[1]

Anecdotally, I think about an executive who told me how much he loved speaking at all-staff meetings, and how he was "killing it" whenever he talked. When I mentioned this to his HR leader, she rolled her eyes and said, "Yes, I know he thinks that, but he is terrible—there is an almost-audible groan whenever he steps up to the microphone."

Turns out we're not always great judges of ourselves, even when we think we are. We believe we are behaving normally even in areas where others see tremendous deficits, and even in situations that, from an outsider's perspective, are clearly leading to problems.

Being self-aware—eliminating the Perception Gap—is about knowing your gifts and your gaps and how each can lead to blindspots that put your success at risk.

Presenting: The Blindspotter

Once you accept that you may have blindspots, the challenge becomes figuring out where to find them. As you'll see in the stories throughout the book, there are six blindspots that line up with the areas I have seen hundreds of high-performing executives struggle with throughout my career. Together, they form an awareness model that can help us each to understand our personality and provide a pathway for using that understanding to create change. To the extent the model relies on any theoretical underpinning, it is phenomenological—that is, it relies on our conscious awareness and an understanding of how we think about ourselves and each other.

Leadership literature typically focuses on how leaders influence organizations, in part because the writers of those books are often trained in business or organizational psychology—the study of human behavior in the workplace. This book and this model approach things differently. I am a *clinical* psychologist by training, and my lens is naturally turned more inward. We often ignore how the inner makeup of leaders influences their behavior; we must understand who we are before we can modulate our behavior in the context of our work. And to understand who we are, we must *see* what we have until now been missing. Hence, the focus on our blindspots.

Each of the six blindspots is a common term and is distinct from the others, but we are complex creatures and there is inevitably some blurring of the lines. You may at times ask yourself, "Is this a motive or an emotion?" or "Is this a trait or an identity?" These questions are natural and expected, because the six areas interact with and influence each other. In the end, we are made up of the synthesis of the six elements, and attacking a particular issue from multiple angles—working with the tools found in each relevant chapter—will enable the greatest amount of change.

The outer layer of awareness represents those blindspots closest to the surface: *identity* and *behavior*. (See the self-awareness model in figure I-1.) These are the elements we are most aware of and that are most under our conscious control, representing perhaps our largest opportunities for recognizing blindspots and making meaningful change. If your identity, for instance, is to be a peacemaker, you can become aware of when it makes more sense to be a fighter, or at the very least surround yourself with fighters who can take the reins when necessary.

FIGURE I-1

The self-awareness model

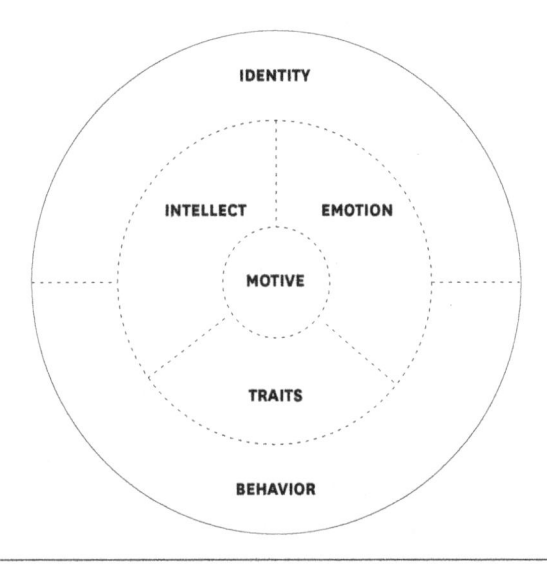

```
            IDENTITY

    INTELLECT  |  EMOTION
           MOTIVE

            TRAITS

           BEHAVIOR
```

If your blindspot is behavioral—say, you talk too much in meetings or express yourself too bluntly—you can direct your attention to talking less, or to taking a breath and reflecting on what you're about to say before you say it. These are the most solvable types of blindspots once they're identified; the trick, of course (and we'll master it in the chapters ahead), is to see them in the first place.

Identity and behavior are in fact the outward expressions of the other four blindspots, which is why those four appear within the inner circles. By identifying those other blindspots, even if they are so hardwired that you can't fully change them, you can become aware of how they show up in your identity and in your behavior, and make the necessary adjustments in those two areas.

Next, we have a layer containing your *traits*, your *emotions*, and your *intellect*. We can become aware of blindspots here and sometimes make changes within this layer, with great effort, but even when we can't, we can certainly adjust their expressions in the outer ring to compensate for issues that may arise. You might have a short fuse in meetings, for instance, but you can ask a colleague to give you a signal when you look like you're losing it, to remind you to take a deep breath or leave the room.

At the core are our *motives*, most hidden from our awareness and most difficult to change. If mismatched motives are a strong element in your life, there are tools to address this—but it also may be the case that if this is the blindspot area that keeps coming up, you might get to the end of this book thinking more broadly about your goals and whether you're in the right role in which to achieve them.

We will use the model throughout the book, peeling back the layers to show how these blindspots play out in our lives and intersect with each other, and we will shine a light on how we can embark on successful change. But the best way to begin to understand how our blindspots show up in the world is to return to the story of Marcus, the founder of Aesthetics, who was suddenly struggling after years of remarkable success.

Blindspotting in Action

Marcus had done so many things right on his journey to the top. Most notably, he had been able to pivot his company, Aesthetics, from one remarkable invention to the next—category-creating innovations in the tech space—staying ahead of the market even as copycats of his initial products began to emerge and growth flatlined. Unlike many leaders, he knew when to move on—and, after his first success, he had launched a second brand-new product line and was on his way to a third, his indestructible AR camera.

The product sounded great and looked great, and the vision seemed to be unfolding exactly as Marcus had planned. But Marcus needed more than vision once the manufacturing flaws became apparent. The investor who called me in a panic wanted me to meet with Marcus and answer some simple questions: Why had this amazing company, led by this supremely talented individual with a spotless track record up to this point, suddenly turned into a mess? Why hadn't Marcus acted yet to fix the problem, and what was he going to do—now hemorrhaging investors and about to have a public unveiling of his product's flaws—to turn things around?

If the investor hadn't briefed me in advance, I'm not sure I would have known there were any issues as I walked into my initial meeting with Marcus. Nothing in the Aesthetics offices hinted at any kind of problem. I had done this walk so many times before, but still I was a bit awed by Aesthetics. I couldn't escape the sharp design sense that came through everywhere I looked. It was evident that everything from the color of the walls to the contour of the chairs had been selected with careful intention. The attention to detail, from the paintings, to the positioning of furniture, to the signage pointing the way to the carefully named conference rooms, was unusual for a young startup. Most of them convey a scrappiness, or at least the intentional projection of scrappiness—with mismatched furniture, exposed brick and concrete, a kind of temporariness that matches most of these startups' prospects, a sense that the office could vanish just as quickly as it appeared. There was absolutely none of that here.

Marcus's administrative assistant told me Marcus was running a few minutes late for our meeting. Not every leader at a company this size would have had an administrative layer between me and the CEO; most CEOs preferred to communicate with me directly. After nearly half an hour, Marcus strode into the office and nodded in my direction. No small talk. He handed his designer backpack to his assistant to deal with. She didn't seem fazed; she understood that her role in this company was to serve.

As a coach, you learn a lot by listening to where someone begins. Marcus betrayed a great deal as soon as he started talking. I felt an immediate attraction to him; his calm confidence was charismatic and drew me in. But the words he was saying gave me pause. He was almost instantly name-dropping, steering the conversation to the influential thinkers and leaders he knew and socialized with. He talked about his travels, both for work and for pleasure. He eagerly boasted about the substantial fundraising he had engaged in already and his plans for Aesthetics to get much, much bigger. His company had experienced a lot of success, no doubt, and his anecdotes were compelling—but I began to get a sense of his priorities.

I couldn't help but notice that Marcus wasn't anxious, even though his investors clearly were. This meeting was a result of their panic. The quickest way to get to the heart of any issue is to find the emotion and then drill deeper. I kept trying to press him on the manufacturing issues and investor desertion, how he felt and what he planned to do, but he kept moving the conversation elsewhere. He was polite and friendly, but to me it began to feel like a fencing match. No matter where I poked, he maneuvered away.

Marcus was focused on vision, not execution. He kept trying to convince me—as if I were one of his investors—of the business's amazing potential but seemed either unwilling or unable to take responsibility for the mistakes that had been made. It became clear that either he did not have a concrete plan to turn things in a new direction or, if he did, he had no interest in sharing it. His avoidant behavior was telling me he needed my help—but it was also showing me he would resist it, strongly.

It became clear to me that the problem with Aesthetics was sitting right in front of me. Until he wasn't. After forty-five minutes, and one last story about an incredible meal he'd shared with the president of an island nation with a GDP that barely exceeded Aesthetics' market cap, Marcus told me he needed to bring our meeting to a close.

As he urged me out the door, he told me a few of his leaders might be able to use my help, since he wasn't able to give them all the time they needed. I did end up working with three of his senior leaders, but through that work it became even more apparent the problem was at the top. As I got Marcus's team to work more effectively together, I noticed that Marcus was in fact the bottleneck slowing down any plans they made. He had insisted on signing off on every important decision, but he was usually unavailable to engage, due to jetting around the world for investor meetings. His failure to empower them made my efforts ultimately ineffective. They couldn't make final decisions, and he wouldn't acknowledge what was really wrong. I tried to meet with him again to tell him what I'd discovered. He wasn't interested in meeting and said he'd read my report and get back to me if he had any questions. I never heard from him again, and the next thing I knew, he and Aesthetics were in the news: the business had been shut down, and despite Marcus's tremendous talents, he lost nearly everything.

Was the failure preventable? We can never know for sure, but I do have confidence that an understanding and acceptance of his blindspots would have at least made a different outcome more possible.

Marcus Was a Victim of His Blindspots

Marcus had experienced so much success, and while success is of course a good thing, it has the perverse effect of growing any blindspots because we don't receive signals we need to change our behavior. We think, of course, that our success is due to how exceptional we are, which is only partially true. Success is due to a match between our qualities and the demands of the situation. Those same exceptionalities with a different set of circumstances become hindrances that can accelerate failure if we don't recognize what's going on. Merely having blindspots isn't the problem. We can think of them metaphorically like allergies: we may be allergic to a particular flower, but until we encounter it, we're fine. And then we find ourselves in a new garden, and we can't stop sneezing. That's when the allergy—the blindspot—needs to be addressed.

Along similar lines, successful entrepreneurs are often asked if luck has played a role in their success. The more self-aware of them acknowledge that in addition to their hard work and personal abilities, luck did play a role. Good luck, I would make the case, is when life presents you with challenges and opportunities that match your personal gifts. Bad luck is when those same strengths make difficult situations worse, and you don't have the self-awareness to pivot effectively at times of crisis.

Marcus's story is an unusually fortunate one for our learning purposes, because Marcus can be used to shine a light on all six of our blindspots. Like so many of us, he was a "Swiss cheese leader"—filled with holes—and the holes just happen to line up with the most common missteps I repeatedly see from leaders.

First, it was clear from the moment Marcus started talking to me that he saw himself as an innovator. This was his *identity*. And yet, Aesthetics at that point needed someone who could execute. They needed a business builder and a leader, and Marcus didn't see himself that way—so he didn't focus on those aspects of the job, to his extreme detriment. Marcus had one more obvious identity—the hero, who solves all of a company's problems. While he didn't get involved enough in the details of his supply chain and manufacturing, he also didn't fully empower others to fix what was broken. He always had to be at the table . . . yet he was often away meeting new investors. In chapter 1, we'll dive deep into identity and help you figure out if the way you see yourself is holding you back from embracing certain parts of your job that are critical for success.

Next, as soon as Marcus started name-dropping the famous people he knew and telling me about his lavish trips and the massive amounts of money and attention he was earning, I suspected he had a *motive* blindspot as well. He wanted to be famous, to live the good life, and to be respected and esteemed by the world. There's nothing wrong with that motive, except when it becomes such a priority that it excludes other motives that would lead to what's necessary for success in the moment. He needed to be in the office, puzzling out the execution issues, and not on the road, trying to gin up as many glowing media profiles as he could. That drive for fame overwhelmed his ability to recognize what he ought to have been focusing on. Interestingly, he wasn't all that motivated by money, at least not the investors' money, or money as a scorecard to demonstrate his company's success. He just wanted enough money to fuel his lifestyle—and once he had that, his motives drove him away from the substance of the job. In chapter 2, we'll look at the most common motives, how to discover the core motives that are unique to you, and how you can harness the forces deepest inside of you to shape your behavior in the right way.

Third, Marcus was clearly gifted with so many incredible *traits*. Like a lot of successful entrepreneurs, he had perseverance and confidence, passion, responsibility, a comfort with risk, and a bias to action. He was a brilliant creative, an exceptional visionary. But often we lean on our strengths too much. Marcus's blindspot here was that he didn't understand that vision and creativity could get him only so far. He didn't see that his extreme self-confidence had tricked him into thinking only he could solve the execution problems. He thought leadership was about being responsible, and being the one to make the tough decisions, but he failed to see that leaders also empower others. Sometimes your company is best served when you lead from the rear, but Marcus's trait of responsibility wouldn't allow him to relinquish authority to his talented team. In chapter 3, we'll explore how our innate personality traits can drive us to victory but also blind us to the reality that success requires something other than what we are good at, and that investing too much in our superstrengths can lead to our downfall.

Fourth, Marcus had a blindspot in his *emotions*. He couldn't read the room and acknowledge that the struggles of his team were largely about their struggle with him, and his unwillingness to give up his position of authority or acknowledge that he couldn't be the hero. He did not empathize with the customers who had received imperfect goods or the investors who were risking their money on his success. He only wanted to live in the excitement of the adventure, and that was a big part of his struggle. In chapter 4, we'll discuss emotional awareness, self-regulation, and how the best leaders strategically deploy their emotions, bringing out what's needed in order to meet the moment, even if those emotions make them feel uncomfortable inside.

Fifth, Marcus truly believed his outsize *intellect* was going to be enough to save the day. He was the smartest person in the room, and he knew it. Because he thought he understood everything, he assumed the things he didn't understand weren't important, and he also assumed he was done learning. He leaned too much into his intellectual gifts. He thought he needed to be present to solve all the difficult problems, and that they wouldn't get correctly fixed without him, which created a bottleneck. Marcus underinvested in the areas that were boring to him, like the actual manufacturing of his products, and failed to recognize that even if he wasn't passionate about certain aspects of the business, that didn't mean he didn't need to learn about them. In chapter 5, we'll discuss intellect and how intellectual horsepower, while a great strength, is never enough, and how you can't simply power through problems without drawing on other types of thinking.

Finally, sixth, Marcus's *behaviors* were a huge blindspot for him. He was great at selling—but that meant he was *always* selling, and often he needed to act not like a salesman but like a problem solver or a team leader. He needed to do what was important for his role as CEO, yet he couldn't. He needed to deploy the right kinds of influence for every situation, yet he behaved exactly the same way whether he was on stage in front of an audience, one-on-one with a concerned investor, or in a conference room with a psychologist coach who was genuinely trying to help him. He needed to prioritize what was needed to fix the company's problems, and he didn't. In chapter 6, we'll work through influence along with two other key behaviors leaders need to understand so that the way they act doesn't bring down their career or their company.

How to Use This Book

The reality is that leaders are not born; leadership is a set of choices and is formed by experience. No matter who you are, you can become a greater leader—but you need to deeply understand your strengths, your limitations, your default responses, your motivations, and more, and you need to put the structures in place around you to take advantage of what you do well and compensate for where you struggle. When you aren't moving forward—in your career, or in your company—it is time to look inward and see if your blindspots may actually be the problem.

In fact, I wish I'd had a book like this long before I ever became a coach, because before I was a coach, I was in the business world just like my clients, and I could have used the help to avoid succumbing to my own blindspots. Being a coach is actually the third phase of my career. I started out with a doctorate in clinical psychology, with a busy psychotherapy practice for a dozen years. And then, just as I was getting comfortable, the health-care business began to shift. I found myself drawn into the industry's business challenges and cofounded a company to manage mental health benefits for large insurers, figuring (accurately, as it turned out) that my partners and I knew more about mental health care than the insurance companies did. We grew the business to a $50 million concern, with 250 employees. And then, like Marcus at Aesthetics, I ran into a roadblock. All of a sudden, after fifteen years of growth, we were failing.

My innate curiosity had carried with it the risk of getting bored. This meant I eventually delegated and took my eye off the ball. We bid for a new contract with an insurer that would become our largest customer, but it turned out we were basing our contract on inaccurate data we had received from the insurer. I should have reviewed the data more closely and realized it was inaccurate. I didn't notice until too late that we were losing money on this new contract, month after month. It put our entire company at risk of failure. There was a period where I couldn't sleep or eat as I tried to figure out what we could do to save ourselves. I told myself in those moments of panic that I was not cut out for this. I was trained to treat patients; what did I know about running a business? My strengths had helped us grow and establish ourselves, but now I was flailing.

I later realized that my blindspots were part of the reason for our failure. The biggest one concerned my *identity*. I wasn't fully embracing the fact that I was supposed to be building a sustainable business for the long term. My identity was as a psychologist with a business, not as a businessperson who just happened to have psychological knowledge. In practice, this meant I felt like I had an escape hatch—returning to my private psychotherapy practice—and the stakes of failure didn't feel especially high. This caused me to miss details a fully focused businessperson would have recognized.

Beyond that, I had a *traits* blindspot. I was leaning too far into the superstrengths that had served me well as an entrepreneur—my intellectual curiosity and my agreeableness, most notably—but these created gaps that ended up hurting me. My curiosity kept me from remaining laser-focused on what my job required, and my agreeableness kept me from acting strategically with the bad actor that had supplied us with the flawed data. To wit, I admitted to our customer we had bid on the contract using "incomplete" data it had provided, with the hope we could collaboratively agree on a higher fee. In my attempt to minimize the conflict and be agreeable, I gave away too much information. This put us in a weaker bargaining position.

I was also struggling with my *emotions*. I was overwhelmed but didn't want to admit it to myself until it was almost too late. I let my anxiety cloud my decision-making process.

In the end, my partner saved us, or at least he pushed us in the right direction. He insisted we had to sue the customer that had given us the bad data. And while the last thing I wanted to do was sue someone—especially a company we were in a contract with—he was right. We ended up working it out, but it was a major blow to the company, and when we eventually sold the business, it was not at the top of our value.

The experience left me wondering about what separates a successful leader from one who fails or has mediocre results. Digging deeper into that question, I spent the next part of my career as an undercover psychologist, in a way. I became a vice president at the *Fortune* 50 public company that had acquired our business and paid close attention to the leaders around me. I began to notice firsthand how some executives are completely unaware of the blindspots holding them back. I couldn't help but find myself drawn to thinking about the minds of the people around me—and so, after a few years, I shifted again, to the intersection of business and psychology as a leadership coach, first at the Center for Creative Leadership, then at the industry-leading RHR International, and now in my own private practice. After almost two decades of this work, I have seen again and again that understanding blindspots really is the key to unlocking performance in the talented executives I have been fortunate to work with.

In his *New York Times* bestseller, *The Hard Thing About Hard Things*, venture investor Ben Horowitz writes, "By far the most difficult skill I learned as CEO was the ability to manage my own psychology.... I've never read anything on the topic."[2]

This book is my answer to Ben's concern—a pathway to understanding how we all struggle, plus guidance on how to prepare yourself to succeed, make better business decisions, and achieve more-favorable outcomes. The book is story-driven by design—that's the way I think people learn best. And I want you, as a reader, to imagine yourself in the shoes of the leaders whose stories I share throughout.

You can approach your reading in multiple ways: you can jump right in and, as you read, notice what stories resonate for you, highlighting them. Then, once you get to the appendix, look at those potential blindspots you noted, and go back to the exercises at the ends of those particular chapters. Or you can stop along the way, reflect on what is speaking to you, and pause to dive into the exercises. For me, especially since the six blindspots are so interconnected, I would find it most natural to read the whole thing first and give myself a complete picture before doing the work of self-reflection. But you may find it useful to be a more active reader throughout.

No matter how you approach it, understand that there will be some work involved if you truly want to change. Easy-to-apply, one-size-fits-all leadership advice—as offered in typical self-help books—too often falls short because while it is undoubtedly true that there are specific leadership skills that can separate good executives from great ones, the most critical skill comes from realizing all leadership is expressed through one's unique personality. The way I can lead effectively is different from the way you can lead effectively, because we are different people, with our own individual identities, motivations, traits, emotions, intellectual gifts, and default behaviors.

This means that in most books, the help is present, but the self is absent. So if you are looking for a traditional "how to" book, some of what follows might feel disappointing, and this book may ask you to do a fair bit more reflection than you might have been expecting. That is actually the point. Other books provide advice, assuming the reader can easily apply it to their personality and their situation. As a psychologist, I know this is unlikely, if not impossible. People are endlessly unique. Only by helping you understand what about you is holding you back can books offering leadership advice be of much use.

My goal in writing this book was to create and convey a system of discovery, to help you find the particular blindspots interfering with your effectiveness. You will find "how to" in this book, but only after you have found *you*. And, as it happens, once you find your blindspots, and address them using the techniques offered here, you will be able to make much better use of the advice in other leadership books that speak to you.

I'm sometimes asked if the right changes depend on what business you're in, but the truth is that they don't. As a leader, your awareness of yourself is your primary leadership tool, no matter your industry, your role, or your responsibilities. I'm also asked if some types of blindspots are worse than others and cause bigger problems. The answer is that it is entirely situational. Emotional blindspots can result in interpersonal problems, cultural missteps, and a lack of empathy with clients, customers, and suppliers. Intellectual blindspots can result in bad judgment, coupled with traits of arrogance or perseverance that can cause one to miss the need to pivot. An identity blindspot can stop career momentum in its tracks. In other words, any blindspot can have serious consequences depending on the context.

Finally, I'm asked about whether there is one perfect set of attributes we should all aim for, to avoid blindspots. The answer is that we can't avoid blindspots; we can only become aware of them, and then adjust. And to be clear, there is not one type of leader, or one set of attributes required to effectively lead.

There are many combinations of identities, motivations, traits, intellectual abilities, emotional sensitivities, and behavioral characteristics that can result in success or failure. The lesson of this book isn't about becoming someone other than who you are; it's about becoming the best, most self-aware, most flexible and adaptable leader you can be, without hampering the magic that led you to be able to get where you've gotten in the first place.

It's really all about being conscious and strategic with what is within your power to adjust. And you can adjust, make no mistake. People can change. While basic personality characteristics are relatively stable, we can certainly alter how we show up in any given situation, and in changing how we show up, we change our impact. If you love to socialize, and decide it is taking away from time you would rather be working, you can track your social time and potentially reduce it; if you realize you make decisions too quickly, you can remind yourself to wait and take in more information. Executives often don't even have to change all that much to make a meaningful difference in how their coworkers perceive them and how effective they are as leaders. The problem is figuring out the meaningful changes, which is where this book comes in.

But first you must become aware of your gifts and your gaps and how they each can become blindspots—others see them, but you probably don't. In the end, I want you to close this book with the realization that you don't have to constantly be at the mercy of your default responses. There are so many things you deal with in business and in your careers that are completely out of your hands; the things you do have power over are how you behave, how you make choices, and how you lead. *Blindspotting* can help with all three.

So let's dive in.

CHAPTER 1

IDENTITY

WHO DO YOU THINK YOU ARE?

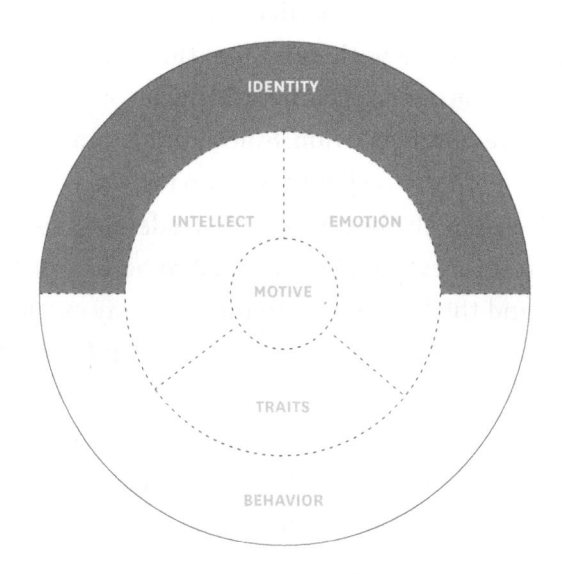

We begin with identity, which we can think of as the nametag you wear as you make your way in the world. The outer layer of the self-awareness model holds the blindspots that are easiest to bring to our consciousness, and where we have the most opportunity to effect change. Once we recognize an identity blindspot, it is relatively easy to adjust and improve. While later chapters will highlight blindspots that may be more difficult to see and then address, identity is the right place to start—in

part because it is often where we can achieve our greatest "aha" moments and then use our newfound self-awareness to take dramatic steps forward in our careers.

Elizabeth came to me after I completed an assignment for Admiral Products, helping the company hire a new president for its US consumer goods division. These kinds of engagements are relatively common in my field. A company has a handful of final-round candidates, and it brings in someone like me to interview the finalists and the people they work with, put them through some psychological exercises, evaluate them against the needs of the role, and produce a selection recommendation. Since all the final candidates are typically qualified to do the job they're up for, the request is generally to identify who is the best fit for the leadership demands of the role, with the interpersonal skills needed to be successful with the existing team and the best match to the company culture. I was already onto a new project when I received a call from Elizabeth, a senior executive at Admiral I'd spoken to in the course of gathering information about the various candidates. To my surprise, she wanted to hire a coach on her own, driven by one big question she wanted help answering: Why wasn't she even *considered* for the role as president?

As we sat down to talk—in her spotless, nicely decorated office—I found Elizabeth to be thorough and organized in her thinking, and undeniably intelligent. She told me how she had risen up the ranks at a variety of consumer packaged goods companies through unfailing execution. As a technical expert on the operations side, she didn't have a particularly high profile in the industry or even within the companies she'd worked for—but she had the respect of the people who mattered and saw herself as a secret weapon who contributed massively to her companies' successes.

And yet, she worried she was doing something wrong that was leading to her being ignored when her bosses looked for executives to promote to the next level. She worried her career had stagnated; she loved being a number two, but she felt ready for more and knew she had the knowledge and capability to do her boss's job. She was frustrated that she couldn't identify what was standing in her way. She wondered if it was time to switch industries, and if the experiences she'd collected perhaps weren't the ones that companies respected when it was time to hire a leader, or if she was missing skills she didn't realize she needed.

Missing skills or experiences weren't bad hypotheses; people in a hiring position often have an archetype in mind when they set out to fill a position, and it can be an enormous challenge to overcome the image someone has in their head for a particular role. But after our first meeting, I felt with a great deal of confidence that the problem wasn't Elizabeth's experience, or Elizabeth's competence. The problem here was an *identity* blindspot, and it was standing in the way of Elizabeth ever ascending that final step to the senior leadership ranks.

The Power of Identity

Before I dive deeper into Elizabeth's story, let me explain what I mean by identity, because it's a concept most of us don't spend a lot of time reflecting on. Our identities are how we define ourselves. They are the roles we see ourselves playing in our own lives and careers, and sometimes the roles others assign us, consciously or not. As humans, we are innately programmed to search for patterns, some of which we recognize will lead to pleasure and others that may pose danger. Identities are a shorthand for defining the roles that help us to sort through people and situations we encounter, in order to figure out who they are—and who we are in relation to them.

We are deeply, almost inherently aware of some of our identities—spouse, parent, daughter, sibling, computer scientist, reader, runner, foodie, hockey fan, Buddhist—but others may be hidden, and at risk of becoming blindspots.

For instance, as a child we're often told things about ourselves: "you're shy," "you're funny," "you're great at sports," "you're too little," "girls don't do those things." Some of these identities we gladly accept and some we brush off, deciding they don't fit—but some of them stay with us even when we don't realize it, and direct how we present ourselves to the world. If you're told as a child, for instance, "It's tough to argue with you; you'll make a good lawyer like your father," or "Your brother's the jokester; I'm glad you're so serious," those impressions may have a real impact on how you see yourself, and the behaviors you adopt.

We like to believe we are our own scriptwriters, authoring our own identities—"I'm a finance whiz," "I stand up to authority," "I am the hero behind the scenes"—but whether the identities originate in our own minds or are inspired by what we hear others say about us, they can get sticky, defining us even if they no longer truly fit, or affecting our performance in situations that may call for entirely different approaches. Thinking of yourself as "the funny one" works if you're a stand-up comic, but perhaps not if you're a criminal-defense lawyer trying to show your client how seriously you're taking his case.

People with differing identities can approach the same job in completely opposite ways. In a leadership role, the person who sees herself as a consensus builder and a team player is likely to approach decision-making differently from someone who sees himself as a person responsible for having all the answers. The math whiz is going to gravitate toward the numbers, while the marketing genius is likely to overindex on that aspect of any role.

Think about the first thing you say when a stranger asks you about your job. Do you lead with the company name, your title, the industry, or some quick description of what you do or how you do it? How you see your job matters. Even when I was running a business full-time, I was still quick to tell people I was a psychologist. It was how I saw myself, but I realized only after the fact that it was not the identity best suited for my role at the time.

One thing you learn in clinical psychology training is to pay close attention to the very first (and, for that matter, the very last) things that a client tells you. For my executive coaching clients, as they introduce themselves, they instantly reveal what they want me to know about their identities, and I know right away how they see themselves and how they present themselves to others. Recall how Marcus from the introduction told me about all the famous people he socialized with. In the next chapter, we'll meet someone who found a way to tell me he got a perfect score on the SAT. It made an impact on how he was seen—though it wasn't the impact he intended, I'm sure.

When Elizabeth introduced herself, she didn't lead with her title or the scope of her role. She said: "I'm the *invisible glue*. I anticipate where problems might occur, and try to fix things before anyone knows they're broken." That's a great quality, and of tremendous benefit for the business—but no wonder she wasn't top of mind for a promotion; she herself was literally telling me that she was trying to be invisible!

At its most fundamental level, your identity is how you complete the sentence, "I am _____." If someone tells you, "I'm a musician, but I'm working in marketing," you'd better believe that marketing job is the first thing they're leaving behind when they get a record deal. If someone tells you, "I'm in finance, but I'm sure you don't want to hear about it—it's boring," they are telling you their identity lies elsewhere.

This is not a superficial point. For any of us, in most any role, it's hard to do everything. A successful person—or a struggling one—lives in a world of too much to do, too much to learn, too much to pay attention to, and too many people and projects competing for time. We are constantly choosing what to focus on and where to engage. Even when our job gives us very specific tasks—but especially when it doesn't—our moment-to-moment actions are at the discretion and direction of our inner voices. And sometimes our inner voices are more in line with how we see ourselves—our identities—than they are with what the role demands of us.

Our identities, therefore, to a large and unseen extent, determine how we define our jobs and how people define us. Identity becomes a filter selecting what we see, and it orients us as to where we invest our energy. The purpose of an identity is to reduce the confusion that an endless task list might lead to. But this works well only if there is alignment between your identity and the role, and you end up paying attention to the right things.

A Misalignment Is Your Identity Blindspot

Think about Marcus from the introduction. His calendar turned out to be a perfect embodiment of his identity blindspot. He saw himself as an inspirational visionary—one of his identities—so he spent much of his time flying around the world, raising money and wowing people with his company's incredible story. That worked when things were going well, but not when he needed to be in the office, figuring out how to fix product quality problems, or deep in meetings with his leadership team.

He also saw himself as his company's hero—a different identity—and believed that good decisions couldn't be made without him. He insisted on being in the middle of every crisis, even though his availability was spotty at best. This meant meetings were constantly being rescheduled around him, pushing important decisions further and further into the future. If his identity was more grounded in building a successful company, growing his leaders, and satisfying his investors and customers, his behavior would have been different—and a different outcome for his company may well have followed.

As it was, the number of meetings Marcus planned to attend was well beyond what it should have been for the CEO of a company the size of Aesthetics, extending deep into the weeds—design meetings at the lowest levels, taking every media call himself. People sometimes run into a problem where they only engage in the areas they're interested in—we'll see this later in the discussion of prioritization in the behavior chapter—but this actually wasn't Marcus's issue. He wanted to be involved in everything he deemed important whether he was interested or not, where he might be able to step up and be seen as the hero. But no one can do it all, and he wasn't empowering his leaders to take control.

This was his identity blindspot at play. What Marcus needed at this stage of his company was to think of himself primarily not as a visionary or a hero, but as a leader. That was what his role required. Similarly, Elizabeth wanted to be seen as a person capable of leading an entire enterprise, but she had an identity blindspot as well. She thought of herself not as a leader but as an incredible executor, the person behind the scenes who got things done. They were focused on what they did well, but they failed to ensure that how they saw themselves matched what was needed to fill their roles, or, in the case of Elizabeth, her desired role.

Why had it taken so long in Elizabeth's career for this to become a problem? It was only when she wanted to be a senior leader that her identity as an executor no longer made sense and caused a career-limiting blindspot.

The Identities That Often Become Blindspots

Marcus's identity blindspot was not unique to him. In fact, there is a set of identities that just about every entrepreneur must shift between as their company grows, as well as a set of more general business identities for established companies, and on top of that a number of common personal identities many of us hold.

For entrepreneurial companies—startups—the misalignment between identity and role comes as the company grows and shifts. At the beginning, these companies need innovators as they try to develop a product and prove its feasibility in the marketplace. Then, as the enterprise moves to a new stage, the requirements change, and the company needs a business builder to establish market success. Finally, to go from successful business to an enduring company, a true leader is needed—another shift in role:

Entrepreneurial companies

ROLE	IDENTITY
Founder	Innovator
Founder/CEO	Business builder
CEO	Leader

For established companies, it is not that the business is necessarily changing, but as an executive follows a career path, the needs shift as the role matures, from individual contributor to operational leader and then to being the leader of the entire enterprise. Identity must shift as those responsibilities and demands change, in order to remain in alignment:

Established companies

ROLE	IDENTITY
Individual contributor	Subject-matter expert
Individual contributor	Tactical operator
Manager	Leader of individual contributors
Operational leader	Leader of managers
Enterprise leader	Leader of leaders

Alongside these identities related to role and business live our personal identities, which can also cause blindspots as they rub against the requirements of any particular job:

Common personal identities

- Impostor
- Independent thinker
- Rule follower
- Unworthy
- Entitled
- Rebel
- Peacemaker

Despite the entrepreneurial journey being reasonably predictable, it is a rare entrepreneur who understands when identity shifts must occur, and many entrepreneurs wind up with identity blindspots as their role matures but their identity does not. Founders almost always start out naturally as innovators who want to change the world. Their identity is fused with their product and expressed through passion and perseverance. Founders who have remained in control of the great tech companies—think Jeff Bezos at Amazon, Steve Jobs at Apple, Bill Gates at Microsoft, and Mark Zuckerberg at Facebook (Meta), to name a few—have been able to shift their identities from innovator to business builder and then to leader.

As the company grows, innovating becomes less important. Founders must instead build sustainable businesses and then lead teams of people to execute. Magic happens when a founder is able to shift identity effectively without succumbing to a blindspot that keeps them from realizing they need to change. Identity transitions can be emotionally heavy. Moving beyond innovator, in particular, involves real loss. Many founders love the intimacy that the early stage of business building inevitably engenders. Marcus loved being the innovator, the visionary, and the hero. He didn't *want* to be the guy working on the details of the manufacturing process or empowering one of his key leaders to solve problems that he still wanted a hand in. He wanted to be flying around impressing people and making every decision himself. It wouldn't have been as personally gratifying to take on the internal-facing, power-sharing leader identity that the business required. So he remained perhaps willfully blind to the need for change, to some extent. But whether willful or not, failing to shift meant that he took the risk of losing his company.

Ultimately, innovators who are blind to the business builder and leader identities are confusing and frustrating to their teams. Employees expect a leader and don't understand why the CEO is failing to lead. The company ends up with high turnover on the executive team as team members realize they aren't being allowed to do their jobs; the innovator CEO doesn't empower them to make the big decisions, and decisions in functional areas outside the innovator CEO's sphere of interest end up being delayed or simply wrong.

As one cofounder once told me, "My partner and I agreed that one of us will only adopt the CEO role when the investors force us to." The two partners were desperate to avoid the role shift—blind to the need for it. And the fact they didn't understand it would be a natural result of the company growth, hoping instead that the investors would never "force" the issue, became a true identity blindspot.

Beyond startups, in almost any career, there are shifts. People start out as individual contributors—subject-matter experts and tactical operators—and over time need to transition their identity to become managers, or leaders of workers. From leaders of workers, people become leaders of managers and then leaders of leaders. The roles are different, but many people don't recognize the need for change, and they succumb to an identity blindspot. They're still judging their own effectiveness based on selecting the right font for the brochure—getting deep in the weeds of individual-contributor-type decisions—when they're managing a team of one hundred marketing professionals.

I worked with Helen, a top-notch graphic designer who had just been promoted to design lead, supervising a team of twelve designers. She came to me because she was frustrated. She loved designing, and she hated managing people. She still saw herself as a designer—her identity—and would redo the designs of her team members when she didn't think they were up to snuff. This made them resent her and dislike having her as a boss. She disliked their resentment and didn't like being their boss, either. The supervisor's job paid almost double what she had been making as a designer. And further opportunities for promotion were only going to come from remaining on the leadership path.

Helen had an identity blindspot. She was a designer forced into the role of manager and never shifted. She didn't think the shift was necessary; she didn't think managing people was important, at least not compared with actually creating great designs, so she was blind to the need to change her actions. Once I framed her conflict in terms of identity, Helen saw what she had been missing. She realized that in order to be effective as a manager, she needed to see herself as a manager and actually manage. *Framed in that way, her next step was easy.* Helen may well have had the skills to succeed as a leader, but that wasn't the role—or the identity—that she wanted. Seeing her blindspot could have led her to change her behavior; instead, she decided to change her role. She left the company and opened up her own independent design consultancy, where she is making even more money than she was as a design lead, and is far, far happier. She loved her identity as a designer and did not want to give it up—a reasonable choice, but far better to make an active choice than to fail at a new role and wonder why. That's the power of seeing your blindspots: full awareness gives you the ability to make the right choices for yourself.

The seven personal identities described earlier are a good place to start when thinking about what other identities might be lurking where you can't see them. Do you feel like an impostor, a rebel, a peacemaker? Do you think you are unworthy of your role or entitled to more? Is being a rule follower keeping you from taking appropriate risks? Is being an independent thinker keeping you from serving as a productive team player? There are many other idiosyncratic identities, of course, and some of the listed ones may not speak to your specific issues, but this is how to begin the search.

Finding Your Identity at Work

Even if the chart gets you thinking about a few possible identities that could be blindspots for you, it is sometimes hard to be certain. We don't always know what our identity is, at least not consciously. Sometimes it takes some digging. To get at the answer, a coach will often ask executives: What brand are you developing? We all understand the importance of product brands and the signals that even small packaging or design decisions can send (the difference between a luxury bar of soap and one for the masses might just be a fancier box and a more delicate scent), but we don't think about our own brand in the workplace despite the fact that it's a far bigger deal in our careers than we realize. This gets right at the heart of the identity blindspot. I usually get blank stares when I ask someone to tell me about their brand, or they start talking about their subject-matter expertise—but identity is about more than expertise.

"I probably do have a brand," they eventually say, "but I guess I don't know what it is." Indeed, whether we realize it or not, we all have a brand. We are all perceived in various ways by the people around us, but without deeper investigation, we don't always know what they're thinking.

The more I learned about Elizabeth, the more convinced I was that this "brand identity" was the reason why she wasn't being seen as a leader, and her blindspot was her failure to understand the identity she was presenting to her colleagues. She had all the tools she needed to lead, but it was how she saw herself, and thus how her identity showed up in her behavior, that was her main roadblock. With Elizabeth's permission, I interviewed her managers and coworkers, and the responses I got were absurdly consistent. Nine out of nine people raved about Elizabeth's expertise, her ability to build trust among her team and create mentoring relationships, her skill at organizing and communicating, and her ability to self-reflect, take responsibility, and learn from failures.

"She acts with integrity, and you can rely on her," one person said. "She has built relationships with key stakeholders; they really trust her decision-making; she can deliver tough messages, and because of those strong relationships, she can make people understand what they need to do and what to expect."

And she had the expertise to match the soft skills. "She is very intelligent and understands the technical side extremely well. She has a tremendous amount of experience in a variety of arenas. She is open to going into innovative, new areas; some people never get out of their lanes; she likes variety."

Elizabeth's career path had been a testament to her ability to build lasting relationships—and execute masterfully. She had followed several bosses as they took on new roles and new companies: they brought her with them as a trusted lieutenant. As we talked, she told me she prided herself on making things easy for her boss, using her people skills to solve problems so her boss wouldn't need to deal with them. "I like that my job is so complex," she said. "I like dealing with hard problems for the people in charge and taking away headaches for senior leadership, even when they don't realize what I've done."

As soon as she said that, I interrupted her—something a good coach will try not to do, but I wanted her to repeat what she had just said: *even when they don't realize what I've done*. It was back to the same point she opened with, about being invisible. If people don't realize what you've done, how can you expect them to reward you for it? But even more, she talked about the people in charge, doing things for *senior leadership*, as if that was some other group of people she was not a part of. Elizabeth *was* a senior leader, with dozens of direct reports. But she didn't talk about herself that way. Aha! Her identity blindspot was that she neither talked nor acted like a member of the executive leadership team. She did not fully see "senior leader" as her identity.

When we reviewed Elizabeth's peer and manager feedback, what struck me were the things no one was saying about her. Missing from the comments were statements like, "She has a great runway ahead of her," or, "She could do her boss's job," or, "She's such an incredible thought partner." As we walked through the report, I could tell that Elizabeth was upset no one saw her as an executive leader, but of course it was hard to find fault with them when she didn't even see it herself.

Elizabeth wanted to be a number one, but instead—through her actions, and thus in the eyes of everyone around her—she was a loyal, dedicated, supremely effective number two. She couldn't see it until it was called out to her in big, bold letters: *You want to be x, but your expressed identity is y. You have an identity blindspot.*

When I pointed all of this out, Elizabeth gasped. She admitted that she really did see herself as a number two, and she always had. "In high school, I loved theater," she told me. "I excelled as the stage manager . . . but even though part of me wanted to, I never took the risk to become a performer."

Elizabeth was a middle child, always looking up to her older brother, always trying to impress her parents, her teachers, anyone in a position of authority. She worried what they thought of her, which drove her to seek to be better, even perfect. She never wanted to disappoint, so she agonized over every decision, fell on her sword when things went wrong, and worked hard to repair relationships, reestablish trust, and stay in people's good graces. She believed she hid her anxiety well, did what she could to make herself liked and respected by everyone, and never took credit for triumphs. At work, Elizabeth told her team they were all in it together, which built strong relationships. She led from the side when possible, only exerting authority when it was absolutely necessary. She was masterful at all of it, but what it got her was a loyal team of people who saw Elizabeth as their friend and champion, not necessarily their boss.

Elizabeth believed she did everything a good leader ought to do—and she was right, which is why she had every reason to feel frustrated and flummoxed at never getting chosen. Now that we were both aware of her identity blindspot, we realized we could address the problem by changing Elizabeth's brand. Despite how hard she had worked on becoming a loyal number two, and how well that brand fit her, it was the wrong brand for the kinds of roles she wanted in the next phase of her career. She needed to see herself as the leader she was, and then find ways to communicate that new identity to the stakeholders at work. Otherwise, they would remain confused about who she was and what she wanted. "I don't know what Elizabeth wants to do with her career," one of her colleagues had said to me, and I had put that statement in her report. "I don't think Elizabeth knows either."

Elizabeth read that comment and smiled. "That's wrong," she said, with a confidence I hadn't yet seen from her. "Because I do know what I want. I can do my boss's job. I'm ready to do my boss's job. I just need to know how to make everyone else see it."

Deciding You Want to Change

So you see the mismatch. You want to be a leader, like Elizabeth, but everyone sees you as a team player. What do you do? Look at your behaviors and see how strongly they might be reflecting the wrong identity.

The higher you rise in a company, the greater freedom you have in determining what you do each day. If your attention is being directed by the inner voices of your identity, rather than your actual (or desired) role, you may not be consciously choosing the activities that best align with how you hope to be seen. This is especially a problem if your role has recently changed or if, like Elizabeth, you want your role to change. Your identity might lag behind reality, and thus you find yourself paying attention to what was important in the previous role, and blind to what is important in the current or future one. I frequently ask clients to go back through their calendars for the past three months and categorize how they have spent their time. Then we look at the responsibilities and priorities of their role and see how well (or, too often, how poorly) they match. This is how we shine a light on the identity blindspot we've been talking about.

To that end, a story emerges from a board I was advising on whom to promote to CEO. The company's chief marketing officer seemed like an ideal fit—but multiple board members pushed back on my recommendation and said it wasn't clear to them that he even wanted the role. "He never asked for it," they said. "And while he's wonderful in situations where he's a leader, he never seems to want to take on that responsibility." Indeed, on his calendar there were almost no circumstances where he was doing things that might get him noticed as an entire enterprise leader.

In talking to me, the CMO took pride in the idea that he *wasn't* a self-promoter and *didn't* take on tasks that would make him stand out. He felt that if he got the job, it would be because the board recognized how good he was, not because he lobbied for it—and that would make the promotion feel even sweeter.

He, too, had an identity blindspot. He thought of himself as the unsung hero, the modest leader plucked from obscurity despite his own reluctance to serve—but didn't see how that identity was getting in his way as he sought a bigger role. Maybe he had grown up being told to never trumpet his own accomplishments, never brag, always be humble. Humility is great, and I would never advise anyone to be obnoxious about their ambition. After all, boastfulness can be as much of a blindspot (see chapter 3 on trait blindspots), or even more of one, than failing to advocate for yourself. But the business world is generally not a place where silence is rewarded, in part because quiet leadership is not the model in our society. Leaders need to step up and lead, especially if they want to advance to the scarce roles available at the top of organizations.

Of course, as with Helen the graphic designer, not everyone has to be a leader.

The confidence I saw from Elizabeth when she insisted that she really did want to change her identity was striking—but she didn't have to feel that way. Elizabeth could have remained content as a number two. She was, after all, very strong in so many ways—and she knew it. She was a terrific team player, someone who had great relationships, knew how to execute, and could get the job done. She was prized at the company for her knowledge, her care, and her honesty. Changing is a choice, and it's not the only choice when you discover you have an identity blindspot.

I can return to my own story as an example. After my behavioral health-care company was bought by the *Fortune* 50 enterprise, I became a vice president, and I was not a great employee—thanks to my own identity blindspot. I had been my own boss for nearly my entire career. When I worked as a clinician, in my own private practice, I controlled my schedule and my patient relationships. And then, at my company, I was the CEO, with no one to answer to. So being inside a corporate hierarchy was new to me. I remember a meeting shortly after I started, when I introduced myself as the person "in charge" of our particular product.

"What do you mean you're in charge?" they asked. "What's your title?"

I was caught off guard. Titles had never meant much to me. The company had acquired my business, and my identity was still as the person in charge of it—but that wasn't the role. I had a boss, and my boss had a boss, and it didn't particularly matter what I thought we should do if my boss and my boss's boss didn't agree.

My initial instinct was much like Elizabeth's—confusion that others saw me differently from how I saw myself. But then I realized two things:

1. This was an identity blindspot. There was a mismatch where I still saw myself as a leader, when my role was to instead be a supporting player, take direction, and keep my ego in check.

2. Changing my identity to become that supporting player was a choice, not a necessity.

Elizabeth wanted to change her identity and needed tools to do that. But I raise my own situation to show that's not always the direction you'll go. Before you jump to changing your identity, it's important to ask yourself whether that's something you actually want. I liked my identity. I liked the freedom of being on my own. I liked being accountable for the decisions I made. I liked "owning" my professional endeavors. Sometimes your identity isn't wrong. *The role is wrong.*

Fernando, another client I worked with, was scrappy and self-made, and had chased a gap in the marketplace—high-end hair care products for men. He developed his own formulas, launched a website, and was gaining traction. He was so successful that a leading mass-market competitor in the space made him an acquisition offer that was impossible to refuse. Fernando's brand was folded into the larger business, and, at first, he couldn't have been more excited. He had reached the limits of what he could do on his own and was ready to learn from the best and figure out how to scale.

I was called in shortly after the acquisition to help Fernando. The acquirer really wanted Fernando to stay and instill some of his entrepreneurial ambition in others. But they also needed him to rein it in a bit. Fernando's instincts were to act first and ask permission later—which can work when you're a solo entrepreneur (and there's no permission required), but not when you're part of a larger business. He would approve ideas or spend finances without checking with corporate or his peers, and they ended up frustrated beyond their limits. His marketing materials didn't match the corporate style; his ad spending was wildly out of control; his organizational chart was a mess in a company where hierarchy was clear.

With help, he began to understand his identity blindspot. We determined that he had no interest in corporate processes slowing him down. He did not want to spend the necessary time and energy pushing his ideas through proper channels, even if that was going to be the only way to play. Before our engagement was even finished, he was fired for operating outside corporate protocols one too many times.

That might seem like a failure.

And, sure, getting fired was probably not the best outcome. But Fernando's identity wasn't "corporate executive," and as much as he wanted to learn from the executives around him, he didn't want to become one. The relationship was going to end in separation sooner or later. He should have made the active decision to leave—but the second-best option was probably what happened. Fernando didn't want to change his identity. And *you* don't have to change *your* identity. But if there's a mismatch between role and identity, one of them absolutely does need to change.

In my case, I stayed at the big company until I completed my buyout obligations—*and then it was off to coaching*, a much better fit with how I saw myself, and who I wanted to be. Elizabeth made a different choice. She saw the conflict—blindspot uncovered—and realized she needed to act.

Evolve Your Identity

Compared with other blindspot areas, your identity is the least fixed part of you. If you're a parent, think about the moment you laid eyes on your brand-new baby. You became a mother, or a father—you took on a new identity. Your priorities shifted. You started evaluating things in terms of how they affected your child and started paying attention to all the things that a good parent does. Baby food commercials suddenly became engrossing. The way you saw the world changed, and the way you saw yourself changed. Circumstances shift our identities frequently. You get married, you change careers, you take on a new hobby, you move to a new country.

The identity blindspot arises when circumstances change—or, as in Elizabeth's case, goals change—but your identity *doesn't* shift.

Imagine moving to a new country and trying to barrel forward doing everything the way you'd always done it. You wouldn't get far if you didn't learn the language, adopt the customs, and adapt to your new surroundings. Or imagine becoming a parent, but still seeing yourself as someone without the responsibilities of child-rearing. You'd be frustrated every time a diaper change interrupted a work call; you'd plan exotic vacations and then sulk when you realized you needed to get back to the hotel room for your baby's midday nap; you'd resent that your home office was now a nursery.

Many of us probably do know people who embody exactly that kind of identity blindspot—they seem like they're being dragged reluctantly through every aspect of childcare—and, sadly, we're not voting them Parents of the Year. But we also probably have some sympathy for them, mindful of all the ways people's lives have to change when they have kids. You can love your children and still acknowledge that there's a loss to taking on this new identity as a parent.

Evolving your identity is a difficult process. It's not just a simple choice you make, but a true change, and a change that often hurts. This pain is what holds people back—we're used to ourselves and how we see our identities in the world—but it's something you must overcome if an identity blindspot is getting in the way of success. It's hard, but it's not impossible.

Sharon, a midlevel manager in a consulting organization who wanted to advance her career into upper management, had a core identity as someone who spoke truth to power. This made her highly effective in her role and deeply trusted by her clients. Straight-talking, no-nonsense, and unafraid, Sharon was the person everyone sought out when they had a grievance with leadership, or a policy proposal they wanted to be taken seriously. When a decree came down that unused vacation time would no longer be rolled over to the following year, it was Sharon who cornered the CEO and made him revert to the old system. "It's not fair," she argued, and, without the company giving any warning to the people about to lose their banked vacation days, she was right. It wasn't fair, and the new rule was changed.

But how do you retain your identity as a fighter when you want to progress into the roles of the people you've been fighting against? Sharon had no growth potential unless she moved into management, and she wanted the added responsibility—and the salary increase. Told she was on a short list for promotion, she began working to figure out how best to position herself to be chosen. Nothing clicked as a clear opportunity for change until we started talking about her identity as a fighter. She loved that about herself—and it was only with a good deal of conversation and then introspection that she was able to realize this was an identity blindspot. Now that it was visible to her, she was going to have to find a way to align her desire to fight with her career aspirations. By becoming aware of the blindspot, Sharon was able to more consciously make decisions about how she would behave. She didn't give up fighting back entirely, but she was more careful, she chose her battles, and she restrained her impulse to speak up in meetings, instead approaching leadership in a friendlier, more private way, behind the scenes, using political capital to get things done.

Sharon stopped thinking in terms of "us" and "them" and instead started thinking of herself as already a part of upper management—advocating for change from the inside rather than the outside. Her identity shift caused her behavior to shift; she began to see the reasoning behind management decisions, and she became the "explainer" of management choices rather than the voice against such decisions. Acting as if she were already a member of management caused others to see her as a member of the executive team. Indeed, adopting a new identity before you even take on the new role can allow you to begin practicing the behaviors associated with the shift. In doing so, you communicate your new identity to others—you change your brand.

Sharon did get the promotion, and while her new position is not a perfect fit with the fighter identity she still embraces and values, she has been able to make it work because it's no longer a blindspot. Rather, she's now very aware of the choices she's making. I don't want to minimize the loss: Sharon had to come to terms with the fact that she wasn't going to get that same emotional gratification that she had felt being a fighter, but, perhaps unlike Marcus, unlike Fernando, and unlike me, she was willing to make this trade-off in service of career advancement, and the different kind of gratification she would get from that.

Elizabeth Becomes the Senior Leader

Elizabeth, the natural number two, had sought help at a pivotal moment in her career. As it turned out, her company, Admiral, was being acquired, and there was going to be a new organizational hierarchy, with a new set of leaders at the top trying to work through who would stay and who would be ushered out. Elizabeth had a chance for a fresh start; she could rewrite her personal brand with new bosses and colleagues. We needed a plan for change.

First, I asked Elizabeth to think about what she would do if she had her boss's job—if her role had already changed, and she were trying to catch her identity up with it. What issues would she think about that she wasn't spending a lot of energy on now? What kinds of decisions would she have to get more comfortable making? And what behaviors could she exhibit, acting as if she were already in the role she wanted? (Acting as-if is a great technique to begin the identity-change process.)

Elizabeth mulled those questions for a few days before our next session and came back with a fairly comprehensive list of answers. A number of big, strategic issues were taking up her boss's time that she hadn't needed to think much about in her current role. She explained that if she were in her boss's role, she'd be trying to gather information about those issues from a wider range of sources and build relationships outside her division so she could work with leaders throughout the organization. She also said she'd be speaking up more at meetings, contributing her ideas in public instead of in one-on-ones with her boss.

As Elizabeth ran through these ideas, I asked what was holding her back from implementing some if not all of these strategies right now. She was senior enough that she didn't need permission to set up meetings with other leaders in the company. And she was already attending many of her boss's meetings, so there was no reason why she couldn't start speaking up. She had been mostly observing from a seat on the perimeter of the room in those meetings, like the support person she saw herself as. I encouraged her to take a seat at the table, literally, and contribute when she had something valuable to say. Not to step on toes, but to make it clear to the people in the room that she had strong ideas and wasn't just someone who could execute.

From a tactical perspective, I've found that asking questions is often the best way to thread the needle between showing you're engaged and seeming like you're trying to do too much. "What if we thought about it this way?" rather than "I think we should do this." Or "Have we considered trying this?" rather than "I have an incredible idea."

I pushed Elizabeth to act more like her boss—deferentially, of course—and to start adopting the identity she wished to embody. With identity, practice really works. When we force ourselves to perform a certain way, our identity will adjust in response. Remember how I mentioned that becoming a parent almost always changes someone's identity? It's not instantaneous for many of us. But the acts of changing diapers, of feeding, and of caring for an infant can gradually make you embrace and embody the new role at a more internal level. Playing the role helps you assume the role. That's what Elizabeth needed to do for herself.

It worked, largely because Elizabeth already had the right skills; they just weren't being deployed in the way they could have been for her to be seen as a member of executive leadership. None of what Elizabeth started doing was too far outside of her comfort zone. Had she been too introverted to speak up, or too anxious to make suggestions—or had her ideas not been very good—these may have been more complicated fixes. It may have turned out that she was not in fact the perfect person to lead the organization, and was deluding herself based on *trait* or *emotion* or *intellect* blindspots that we will explore later in the book. But this really was purely an *identity* blindspot for Elizabeth, and, once she was aware of it, changing how she presented herself was not that hard.

Six months later, as the acquisition was finalized, Elizabeth's boss was given a retirement package, and Elizabeth was promoted into the leadership position she had wanted for years. She had overcome her identity blindspot and made herself into the leader she aspired to be. She mitigated the risk for the company because, now that she was acting more like a leader, people could see how she would lead—and it turned out she was quite good at it. Elizabeth was excited about her new leap forward. "Realizing I needed to shift my identity completely changed the way I talk about myself, my story, and my experiences—and that translates to a shift in the way I see myself."

Her identity now? She is the leader she always wanted to be, with a brand where her colleagues still see her as organized and thorough, and as a person who can get things done, but where they are also able to see the side of Elizabeth that steps out from behind the shadows and takes charge.

. . .

How to Find *Your* Identity Blindspot

Perhaps some of the stories in this chapter have resonated, and you see a mismatch between how you are presenting yourself and the needs of the role you are in. Perhaps you are wondering about your brand. Maybe you are concerned that something about your identity is interfering with your achievements. Even if not right now, perhaps you are worried about the future, as your identity may have to shift for you to continue progressing in your career. At the end of each chapter, I offer next steps for you to dig deeper into the associated blindspot area, starting with *awareness*, to help you determine if there is a blindspot at play, followed by *action*, to take steps to resolve the problem and grow as a leader.

Awareness

The first step is to figure out your own identities, with particular focus on the ones attached to your work. How many different ways can you finish this sentence: *I am a* _____. Look at the list you just created: What does it say about what you pay attention to and what you don't?

Make a list of what you love doing in your job, what functions you spend the most time and energy thinking about, planning for, and measuring your success against. Write down what identity or identities you would ascribe to someone who behaves the way you do. Think hard about the choices you make as to where you put your energy and honestly assess if there are elements of your role that you dismiss or ignore. Make a new list with those. Are any blindspots coming to mind as you make these lists?

You may want to ask the people around you about your personal brand or you may simply want to reflect on the parts of your job you get most excited about, the way you talk about your job to others, and, more concretely, where you spend your energy. Look back at your calendar for the past three months and analyze how you have been dividing your time. Or do a time study looking forward, over the next couple of weeks. Track your activities and see what it is you are doing each day.

Next, map these identities and the way you spend your energy to your current job—and to a role you might want in the future. Write a description of the priorities for success in your present role, and for the next role you aspire to grow into. What would a dispassionate third party hiring for the job want to see as far as priorities and, more specifically, the behaviors that demonstrate attention to those priorities? Where would someone ideally expect a person in the role to spend their time and energy? Are these activities that you enjoy, consistent with your strengths, and that fit with how you see yourself? Do these activities align with your career?

When you map these against your own time and your own identities, is there a mismatch? You'll know if there's a mismatch if the top identities on your personal list don't line up with the top identities on your current or future work-role list. Are you perhaps in the wrong role, or is it possible you are embodying the wrong identity? What are the points of friction, and are there obvious ways to resolve them?

Elizabeth didn't prioritize speaking up more in meetings until she understood that showing up as a senior leader instead of a number two meant speaking up more—and then she was able to adjust how she presented herself. Do the disconnects feel fixable to you, or is there discomfort? Is it possible that this exercise is highlighting, as in Helen's case, that your identity blindspot led you into a career path that's wrong for you? Or are you in a situation more like Sharon, whose brand was speaking truth to power, but who was able to moderate her identity impulses to thrive in management, even if the role wasn't a perfect fit?

These are the kinds of questions to ask as you sort through the possibility that an identity blindspot—a misalignment between identity and role—is holding you back. Once you become aware of the blindspot, you can take steps to resolve it.

Action

Changes in identity are relatively easy to make, especially if you are motivated. As happened with Elizabeth, these changes can lead to profound jumps in one's work productivity and career opportunities. Identity adjustments can feel like small shifts, but they unlock us in ways that can drive truly transformative growth. As you change how you see yourself, you change how you behave, and that changes how others see you. Suddenly, your impact on the world is vastly different—and the opportunities that flow to you can be vastly different as well.

One of the most important things you can do is try to embody the new identity you are aiming to shift to, even if you're not yet feeling it. Think about the changes that someone shifting identities would need to make, and then, one by one, make them. Start speaking up more in meetings, for instance. Take on a new initiative at work. Do whatever it is someone with that identity would be doing.

If you feel like a new identity may be needed in the future—if you are nearing a transition point in your role—what is most needed is preparation. Put yourself in the shoes of the person whose role you are transitioning to—and make sure you have a full understanding of what is important in that role, and what skills and personality attributes are the keys to success. If you wait to prepare your identity shift until you are actually promoted into the role, then, like Elizabeth, you will probably not even be considered for the promotion. Even if you get the job, you risk failure as you take the time needed to wrap your head around the role and finally make the identity shift.

You may want to seek out role models who appear to embody the identity you are looking to have, and watch what they do. Take inspiration from them and shift your activities to more closely track theirs. Be honest with people around you and tell them that you are working hard to grow in certain ways—and then follow up with them as you try to shift your identity, asking them if it's working, and if they've been noticing any changes. You may find that your brand is in fact changing more quickly than you expected.

As you go through all of these questions and think about any mismatches between your identity and your role, it may be that identity is not an area of concern for you—in which case, we move on. In the next chapter, we will look at the *motive* blindspot, at the core of the model and the core of our souls, to figure out how our deepest desires may be driving us in ways we don't fully realize. Motive is the hardest blindspot area to change, but once we identify a motive blindspot, there are ways we can compensate so that the motives we've been blind to aren't holding us back as leaders.

CHAPTER 2

MOTIVE

ARE YOU BLIND TO THE CORE FORCES DRIVING WHO YOU ARE?

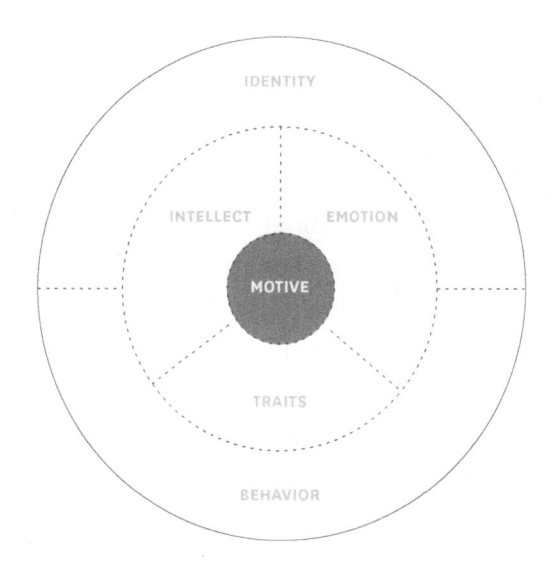

Motive refers to the drivers deepest in our soul—why, at the most fundamental level, we do what we do. As the innermost layer of the self-awareness model, it is the element most hidden from our conscious awareness and thus the most difficult to change. And yet, if we can gain greater awareness of our core motives, we can see how they inform almost everything about how we present ourselves to the world. With that

awareness, we may not be able to alter our motives, but we can certainly implement tools and systems to move us from instinctual responses to more conscious and considered alternatives. We can be more in control of how our motives show up in our behavior, and thus more in control of our business career.

"I'm beginning to plan for my retirement," said the voice on the other end of the phone, "and I need some help." Don had been the CEO of Midwest Grocers for nearly two decades, expanding and stabilizing the company, and now seemed to be the right time to begin the process of turning it over to his successor. The regional supermarket chain had treated him well, and Don saw it as his duty to leave the company in the most capable hands he could. He had been grooming three internal candidates and wanted a coach to help with the succession plan, work with the three candidates, and share with Don and the board of directors observations about their leadership potential.

The three executives couldn't have been more different. First, there was Craig, a lifer in the business who had worked his way up from store manager to the head of operations for the entire chain. Craig was universally respected as a hard worker and effective manager, but with technology transforming the grocery business—in domains ranging from inventory management to dynamic pricing to the customer experience—it was unclear on first reflection if Craig was too steeped in tradition to have the innovative ideas or agility to be the right leader for the current environment.

Next was Wanda, who had excelled running the company's most profitable store region. She had developed unparalleled relationships with vendors and suppliers and introduced many high-margin products. Wanda also invested heavily in the local community, working with schools and nonprofits to make a difference and ensuring that her stores reflected local input and tastes. People—including

Don—loved the work she'd done but weren't sure if she had the necessary focus on the bottom line needed to lead the entire organization.

Finally, Salvatore had skills and experience across the business, from operations to finance. He was a technology whiz who was considered by Don and others to be a strong thinker well-positioned to figure out how to move the company into the future. Sal had in fact spearheaded a recent successful initiative that landed Midwest Grocers a series of awards and profiles lauding the company's understanding of where the supermarket business was heading.

Going in, having read those profiles, I suspected Sal was the candidate to beat. And then I met him.

Motive Is the "Why"

What directs us comes from deep within, and isn't always obvious, either to others or to ourselves. At a basic organism level, humans are driven to move toward pleasure and away from pain—but what defines pleasure and pain is different for different people, and different in different circumstances. The psychologist Abraham Maslow gained fame for his 1943 paper describing a hierarchy of human needs: physiological needs (air, food, water, shelter, clothing, sleep), safety (employment, health, security), love and belonging (friendship, family, connection), esteem (respect, status, recognition), and self-actualization (the desire to be the most that we can be).[1] We start with the need to satisfy our most basic requirements, and from there we advance to higher and higher levels. If we are well-fed, safe, loved, and praised, we get to the final level, where we look to feel as if we are living up to our greatest potential. But what it means for each of us to fulfill our potential is different—and those differences are driven by our deepest motives, which are often hidden from our conscious awareness. In other words, they can become blindspots.

Motives in business come in different varieties. The first set to think about contains the three universal, shared motives that the

Harvard organizational psychologist David McClelland has said drive all of us: the desire for achievement, the search for affiliation, and the quest for power.[2] How those translate to the business world: achievement is success for success's sake—launching a new innovation, making people's lives better, or accomplishing something difficult; affiliation is social connection, recognition, love, or fame; and power is control, or the freedom to act as one wishes, often represented by money. While these universal motives are likely present in some amount for each of us, the weights we give them, how we prioritize them, and how they show up in our behavior signal to others what is most important to us.

I often think about a client and friend named Robert, who commands pretty much any room he enters—tall and handsome, with a deep baritone voice. Phenomenally smart and creative, with extreme interpersonal warmth, incredible storytelling skills, excellent business acumen, and a decisive presence, Robert would seem from the outside to have every ingredient necessary to be an effective CEO. Indeed, Robert has launched perhaps twenty different companies over the years. Investors never hesitate to put him in charge, yet Robert has a long résumé largely filled with surprisingly small returns and disappointed stakeholders.

Why? Though he insists (especially to investors looking to write him a check) and genuinely believes that he cares about making a profit, Robert's behavior, time and again, reveals that he has a motive blindspot. His core drivers are achievement (innovating to change the world) and affiliation (working on a rewarding team), not the pursuit of financial success. When it comes to money, Robert has every reason to care, every intention to care, every desire to care—yet he simply doesn't.

It's not for lack of knowledge. Robert is well-versed in the world of finance—and in fact his comfort talking about his companies' cap tables, balance sheets, and financial goals is part of what makes investors so eager to go on the journey with him. But Robert wakes up every morning far more excited about his products and his people and invests his energy there. He's happiest when trying to solve a problem, with a team of gifted all-stars around him. He wants all-hands-on-deck meetings, strategy sessions, audacious goals, world-changing products, and broad ambitions. Those are the elements of business building that motivate him. The financial objectives are left aside. Until they can't be anymore, and another venture bites the dust.

This isn't to say that Robert is a failure. He has led a life of excitement and has achieved a great deal in terms of innovation and product breakthroughs. And he has built a community of loyal friends and colleagues who would drop everything to follow him anywhere, knowing that his companies will be incredibly fun, rewarding, and inspiring places to work. But his investors have lost millions of dollars, and Robert lives almost paycheck to paycheck—because even though his motivational blindspot was pointed out to him long ago, Robert loves his life and doesn't crave financial success enough to actually make a change. Robert's push to achieve something new and interesting every day has driven him to create product after product, company after company—but that motive has also made it hard for any of those companies to succeed long-term.

Similarly, as much as Marcus, the tech CEO from the introduction, would never have admitted it, part of his problem was that his desires for fame (celebrity friends and glowing press) and achievement (to truly change the world) dwarfed his desire for a giant bank account, too. Don't get me wrong: Marcus loved the high life that money brought him. But that wasn't his measuring stick, no matter how important money was to his investors. That's part of why his attention could never seem to land on the operational problems that were holding back his company. He was likely unaware of this: a true motive blindspot that was standing in Marcus's way and keeping him from changing his behavior in a way that would have helped contribute to longer-lasting financial success.

My own business struggles came in part from a similar motive blindspot. I was never about maximizing wealth, and wanted, above all, to be creatively solving hard problems and working with people

I liked. I didn't understand that about myself until much later in my career, but it helps explain why I was never driven particularly hard to extract the best deal in a negotiation, or why our ultimate sale—at a lower value than we'd reached at our peak—didn't particularly gnaw at me.

Interestingly, I don't think Robert, Marcus, and I are alone. Over the course of my career, it has surprised me how many people in business, a field where success is in fact measured almost entirely by financial results, are driven much more by other factors than by the bottom line.

Are You a Robert? Or Are You a Jeannette?

Maybe a lack of desire for money and power isn't the issue for you. Perhaps, without realizing it, you're low on the affiliation motive. In that case, you may be burning bridges and failing to invest in relationships in a way that is going to pay off in the end.

Jeannette is a real-estate agent I worked with who prided herself on getting the most out of every single deal, purely from a dollars-and-cents perspective. For the sellers who turned to her for help, she was the best choice they could have made—at least when the market was hot. She was shrewd, savvy, and relentless, innovative in staging and publicizing her houses, aggressive with the agents she negotiated against, and willing to get creative with deals—as long as when they closed, she knew she hadn't left a penny on the table.

Jeannette sought help because suddenly she found herself in a sales slump, and she wasn't quite sure why. Initially, she was focused on concerns that she might be depressed. She wasn't sleeping well, and her husband and kids said she'd become more irritable and distracted. She was finding it harder to exercise and thought all of this was leading to poor performance at work. "I need my mojo back," she told me. But the more we talked, the more I realized that this was not depression. I asked Jeannette what had changed in her life, aside from her mood. "Well, you know the whole housing market is in a major slump," she said, almost as an aside, "but if anyone should still be killing it, I'd think it would be me." Jeannette was critical of agents who were too "soft," who prioritized relationships, or who accepted less than the absolute maximum they could extract. "I don't even want to do those kinds of easy deals," she admitted. "The fun is in the negotiation, in winning, in getting the most money for my clients."

And yet—those agents doing "easy" deals were exactly the agents who were still busy and succeeding. The change in the market meant that Jeannette's motive to always secure the best possible deal was no longer the way to win. As soon as I pointed this out, Jeannette saw what I was seeing—a motive blindspot. Getting the best deal was what drove her, even in an environment when trying to get the best deal wasn't the right approach. Looking at it through this lens, she realized she was finding it harder to get other agents on the phone or engage in the kinds of hardball negotiations she was accustomed to. More and more agents were reaching out to each other through back channels, leveraging friendly and robust preexisting relationships, trying to connect buyers and sellers directly, and closing quick deals that satisfied all sides. Jeannette's brand as the tough negotiator made her the last person other agents wanted to call. Jeannette was out of the loop and didn't really understand why the tactics that had worked for her for so long were now ineffective—until we hit on the affiliation blindspot that was holding her back.

Jeannette could now see that she hadn't built a business for the long run, one that could be sustained through the market's ups and downs, and that her focus on "winning" the negotiation was getting in the way of success. She needed to rethink her motive and draw on a different internal driver; she needed to prioritize relationships so that she could change how other agents experienced her.

Fortunately for Jeannette, this wasn't an impossible adjustment. Jeannette had plenty of friends, a loving marriage, and a strong relationship with her kids. Building relationships was something she could do; she just hadn't been motivated to do it at work. She thought the fun of the job was about making money, but now she could shift her behavior to find reward in the other elements, helping sellers achieve their goals and building productive bonds with other agents so that she would have partners to turn to when she had inventory she wanted to sell. Slowly, she altered her business tactics and found just as much success even when money wasn't the only consideration.

It's important to note that money didn't drop out of the equation entirely. *Of course* Jeannette still wanted to get as much money for her clients as she could. She didn't need to supplant one motive for another, but rather she needed to balance motives. And with visibility into what was really driving her, she could make the active choice to adjust. When she could draw on a fuller range of motives, and shift among them as needed, it made it easier to function in changing market conditions and remain agile no matter the business circumstance. Jeannette could add value in more ways and remind herself that there was not only one route to the goal.

Balancing Motives

Robert, Marcus, and Jeannette were all suffering from the same type of motive blindspot: the domination of a universal business motive they were unaware of, which was overpowering all other motives and leading them to act in certain ways, regardless of whether those ways put them on the best path to success. But not all motive blindspots are this straightforward, in part because the three universal business motives (the desire for achievement, the search for affiliation, and the quest for power) are not the only ones we experience. As I said earlier, there are different varieties of motives. Aside from the universal, there are also our unique individual motives—drives to satisfy our own personal needs. Not recognizing how these are impacting our behavior often leads to blindspots just as powerful as when we are missing insight into the three universal motives. Among the most common personal motives are:

- The need for approval
- The need to prove significance
- The need for independence
- The need to win
- The need to fit in

This is just an initial list, and, indeed, we often have a number of individual motives lurking beneath the surface. Looking at our motives does not mean boiling it all down to one element that drives us. We have many motives, and we are continually balancing how they show up in our behavior. In a well-functioning situation, we are aware of what is driving us, and we can consciously choose how to behave. We are often trying to balance opposing motives, vacillating between choosing one or the other. Do we eat that extra piece of chocolate to satisfy our pleasure, or do we resist the pleasure because of concerns about our health? Do we fire a legacy employee because of poor performance, or retain them because of loyalty?

When seeing our motives clearly, multiple motives are not a problem. When we understand we have choices in how we respond, we can make sound decisions—and though we may regret our choices later, this isn't a blindspot issue. Instead, the blindspot occurs when our motives are unclear to us, or when we don't deliberate on our multiple motives and act instead—instinctively—on a single motive that doesn't match the moment.

One motive may in some cases be so strong that it pushes all other motives to the side—and as we find that motive being frustrated, our behavior becomes so focused on realizing it that we act counter to our best interests and the best interests of our business.

This was the case with Thad, a new chief technology officer for a large public company. Thad had a sterling résumé and was bringing the rigor and structure the company needed in technology ops, but he was quickly earning a reputation as being incredibly difficult to work with. When I was called in to coach him, I was told by the chief people officer that the company was experiencing "organ rejection." Thad was dominating his new colleagues and pushing his ideas through in a way that meant he was never going to get buy-in and succeed in the role. Basically, people couldn't stand him.

I expected to find Thad uncoachable, but when we met, he couldn't have been nicer. As soon as I walked in the room, he mentioned that he'd heard a colleague had worked with me recently and had nothing but good things to say. That wasn't what a difficult individual would tend to lead with. Thad was delightful, smart, engaged, and agreed with the frustrations people had with him. He knew he was being impatient and difficult, but tried to defend himself. "I need to get things turned out—and fast," he said, "so while I regret how people are feeling, I unfortunately don't have time to be sympathetic and understanding. We have big changes to make, and I need my team and others in the organization to make them."

I asked Thad to think back over the past few days, looking for specific interactions where he knew he was responding in ways that weren't ideal, but that he just couldn't avoid. The first couple of stories were unsurprising: One colleague had engineered a thoroughly convoluted system for handling expense reports, and Thad needed her to pivot to a different system . . . and he didn't have a lot of patience for explaining the problem to her. Another colleague hadn't yet updated her division's annual technology budget, and it was holding back Thad's firmwide analysis. She claimed she was too busy to get it to him urgently, which wasn't an answer he was happy to accept.

"I needed them to focus on these issues, and they kept wanting to tell me why they couldn't, or what else was getting in their way. The executive team agreed on these priorities, and I needed them to understand that, agree to get their task done, and let me move on to my next meeting."

Thad's tone changed as he told me these stories. I could see how exasperated he was in situations where he felt like people were wasting his time or keeping him from staying on schedule. Even as our meeting got close to its scheduled end time, I noticed him watching the clock, fidgeting with his phone, and seemingly trying to will me to leave his office.

"We're not going to run over," I assured him, "but I'm curious to ask: Do you find that this impatience is a problem in your personal life, too?"

Thad thought for a moment, and then chuckled. "Well, my wife told me the other day that our neighbors think I hate them because I'm never friendly. But they're always trying to engage me as I'm rushing into the house. I'm carrying twelve bags of groceries, fumbling with my keys, and they want to talk about the weather. I just want to get in the house before I drop the bag with the eggs and have to clean up a mess!"

I gave him a look as I packed up to leave. "Do you think your drive for efficiency might sometimes be getting in your way?" I could tell Thad was already thinking about his next appointment. "Just something to reflect on before we meet again."

When I came back a week later, Thad couldn't contain his excitement. "I have to admit, I rolled my eyes as soon as you left last week," he told me, "but then I mentioned our session to my wife, and she said that trying to be efficient all the time is exactly my problem, and why—her words, not mine—no one wants to be around me. I'll drive around and around a parking lot just to get a spot right in front of the store. I load up my arms to carry all of my bags in one trip instead of wasting time going back and forth. It drives me bonkers when anyone else loads the dishwasher or packs a suitcase. I will not be late to anything. No matter what."

At work, this motive blindspot—this unrealized need for perfect efficiency—played out exactly how one might expect. As the new CTO, Thad was back-to-back in meetings all day, every day, all critical meetings, with interdependent objectives driving Thad's priorities. But his mind was always on the clock. He had to work through his agenda, tell people what he needed, get them to agree to do it, and move along. There was no time to indulge, to explain, or to build relationships, at least not in Thad's mind. And while efficiency might feel like more of a trait than a motive—we'll get to trait blindspots in the next chapter—for Thad, this drive was so innate that it really was what was motivating everything he was doing and the reason why he was so difficult to work with. When strong, uncontrolled emotion emerges, in a situation where you might wonder whether the emotion is necessary, it is a clue that a motive is being blocked, not a trait being expressed. For most of his career, Thad's efficiency motivation had been a superstrength, leading to tremendous impact at his previous jobs. Laser-focused on corporate objectives, he rebuilt technical teams and reinvented businesses to serve customers far better—but now his need for efficiency was driving his behavior in ways that were extremely destructive.

For Thad, there was a solution. Once his efficiency motive was out in the open, no longer a blindspot, he could take action. He needed to reduce the negative impact that resulted from his motive consistently being blocked by preventing those blockages in the first place. In other words, he needed to engineer his calendar so that he could give people the time and attention they needed, but also feel like he was still being efficient. The motive wasn't going to change, but Thad's behavior could. He decided to rework his schedule so that he could satisfy his need for efficiency without making everyone around him an enemy. Rather than scheduling back-to-back meetings, Thad reorganized his days to build in ten-minute gaps. This way, meetings could run over without Thad panicking, and he would have a few minutes to gather his thoughts before the next appointment. Also, he made more of an effort to communicate his expectations in writing before each meeting so that the other party would know the agenda and come in understanding how the time together was going to be used.

Thad asked for a clean slate with his team and established much better relationships with his direct reports. It was a total turnaround. He still believed himself to be right all the time (and he usually was), but he was able to be mindful about the language he used and the emotions he expressed, and became much more enjoyable to work with. It was fully solvable with self-reflection and a system in place—because Thad had the interpersonal skills, which were clear in our meetings from the start... at least until we got close to the end of a session. When he started to panic, the fight-or-flight reaction emerged. When anxious, we fall back on instinctual behaviors, even when they're not right for the situation. Thad just needed to release the hold that his efficiency motive had on him, to be able to use his interpersonal skills to positive effect.

His team likes him now and understands the value he brings, rather than wanting to see him fail. With awareness of the motive driving his behavior, Thad was much more able to make considered decisions and not get in his own way.

Motive Blindspots Emerge at Times of Greatest Stress

Thad's anxiety—and anxiety in general—deserves a closer look. More than a few puzzled venture capital investors have told me about companies that were going gangbusters until suddenly the founder-CEO "blew up" and everything became a mess. As sudden as these blowups seem, they never really are. They have inevitably been building for months as the CEO has continued to do what they've done before—driven by an underlying set of motives that match the company's needs at the time—with everyone cheering them on... even as circumstances are shifting. The blowup happens when things have shifted enough that there is now a mismatch between how someone's motives are driving them to behave and what continued success requires them to do. The people who were on your side suddenly wonder why you're flailing. They turn against you—and you have no idea why.

In retrospect these motive blindspots may seem obvious. In hindsight, *of course* Jeannette should have realized much earlier that her motive needed to shift in a changed economy. But it is particularly hard to think clearly during times of stress. And, indeed, when extremely strong motives—like Thad's need for efficiency—

are frustrated by circumstances, people who are used to succeeding tend to double down and push even harder to realize their desires. Until the manufacturing issue crept up, for instance, Marcus from the introduction was moving with great speed toward unbelievable success, powered in large part by his unique combination of the urge to innovate and the desire to spread his innovations to the world. And then, although circumstances shifted, Marcus kept on barreling forth. He got stuck pursuing his motive to keep innovating, despite needing in that moment to be driven by something else. He didn't understand his true motives, and they became a problematic blindspot. Marcus didn't see that his desire for breakthrough technology and the fame that would accrue was causing him to make decisions that didn't make sense in the face of the company's manufacturing issues. He was blind to the bigger picture that his company's existence was threatened and he needed to switch gears.

Anxiety narrows our focus and our thinking. We crowd out complexity. Instead, we dig in and go on a kind of autopilot; our strongest instinctual motives take over. The executive who would normally understand that her drive for fame needs to be balanced with other considerations starts to imagine that one more magazine profile will make all the difference, and she chases press, blind to why she's really doing it. If we're confronted, it only makes the problem worse, and we dig in deeper. Think of medical emergencies, or times when you haven't slept well—suddenly it's so hard to take a breath and think through the best approach. We yell at our kids; we send the ill-considered email. Marcus was surely under stress as his company was failing; Jeannette was under stress as her client pipeline dried up; Robert was under stress each time his investors threatened to pull their money. Many of us are under stress a lot of the time, unfortunately—and that's when we lose the ability to check and see if our motives are pushing us in the wrong direction. Instead of thoughtfully juggling our many motives, we instead act to our detriment. With increased motive clarity, we have the opportunity to consciously choose whether or not to pursue what is driving us. Understanding their motives certainly would have helped Craig, Wanda, and Sal at Midwest Grocers calibrate how they behaved as they sought to be Don's successor at the top of the company.

The Race for CEO

Craig was the first of the three to begin the coaching engagement. He introduced himself by asking where I tended to shop, and proceeded to run through the pluses and minuses of my pick's biggest competitors. He explained how Midwest had plans to beat them all, and how he expected the company would go about winning in the long run. By opening with this discussion, Craig was communicating an identity that appeared to be very much merged with the business and its success—a good sign that identity was likely not a problematic blindspot for him. His motives, too, seemed to be very much aligned with the business and its success. As I sat in on Craig's meetings with Don, I did not notice much in the way of unique personal motives driving him. Instead, I saw the three universal business motives play out in their conversations. For instance, they would discuss new initiatives, and Craig would be pushing for the company to take action (achievement motive), while leaning on his relationships (affiliation motive), and making it clear that he was very much interested in being a leader (power motive).

"I've looked at the proposals for the new back-end system for the mobile app," Craig would say, "and it's clear from pricing and capabilities which vendor is best. Our current system is so outdated. I think we should do it." (Achievement motive.)

"But do we really have an internal team with the capability to follow through and make the most of the app once it's up and running?" Don would reply, trying to push Craig to ensure the investment made sense.

"I think we can invest in training our people; I'd love to see them have the skills that will not only pay off here, but make them more valuable wherever they go, and loyal to Midwest for the rest of their careers." (Affiliation motive.)

"I don't know, Craig. It seems like a big expense."

"I know, Don, but you put me in charge of operations, and I think this is a reasonable bet that the business should make. I want your guidance and advice, but I also think it's an area in which you should feel comfortable empowering me to make the final call." (Power motive.)

These were fun meetings. Craig and Don would talk through operational issues like this one and figure out how best to solve them. Craig respected Don as a leader, but clearly saw himself as a leader as well. Craig pushed back when he didn't agree with Don's ideas but was also open about the areas where he was still learning and eager for Don's guidance. If nothing else, Craig was clearly the "safe" choice for the business. His motives were aligned with business needs, and no red flags emerged. It was not clear to me that he was driven to be seen as an industry innovator or to change the grocery world in some profound way. But he cared about the people in the organization, and I believed that he could very capably run the business.

My introduction to Wanda began on a completely different note. The first thing she asked me was whether I had noticed the group of developmentally disabled adults who were on a tour of the company's facility, being educated about how to grocery shop. She was proud of this program and spent quite a bit of time telling me about it. Her deep interest in this initiative made me think her prime motive in her work likely had something to do with altruism and doing good, even if she wasn't consciously aware that this was driving her behavior.

This idea continued to show itself throughout the meetings I sat in on. While Craig was eager to engage in the issues that were in Don's sweet spot (Don had also come up through the operations side of the business), Wanda kept steering their discussions to the bigger picture of what the company could do better for all stakeholders—employees, customers, and the community. Wanda was full of ideas and demonstrated the passion and organizational skills to bring them to life. Her motive became clear: she did want to change the grocery world, and make sure that the company was doing everything it could to impact lives in a positive way.

"Don, you know that five of our stores in the region have high schools within walking distance," Wanda would say, "and we've seen an uptick in theft during the lunch hour. We've added more security—but I'm wondering if we need to go in a different direction."

"Oh, boy, here we go," Don would answer, chuckling just a bit.

"No, I'm serious. We have the opportunity to help mend the social fabric in our region. The thefts may not be reckless behavior—some of these kids may be poor, malnourished, hurting."

"And?"

"We can be a resource. What if we brought some healthy snacks into a corner of our sit-down area, hired a social worker or community organizer to spend a couple of hours a day supervising, and redirected the kids from stealing our stuff to getting some free food and a place to hang out?"

It wasn't that Wanda didn't care about making money; Wanda ran the numbers for every initiative she brought to Don and was convinced that her ideas made sense not just in terms of impact but also in terms of the financials. But it was hard for Wanda to exhibit the same passion when she and Don were talking about the nuts and bolts of the core business. She was eager to learn—and respected Don tremendously—but it was clear that they had different interests and different motivations for doing the work. I started to worry about two things as I listened to their conversations: first, that Wanda's clear identity as a world-changer wasn't a perfect match to the board's vision of the CEO role, and second, that I would have to be conscious of my own personal motives when giving advice to the board. I identified very much with Wanda: I wanted my work to make a positive impact on society as well. But my job wasn't to let my own motives interfere with those of the client I was supposed to serve. It's a broader point worth making when you are in a position to evaluate or hire. As important as it is to understand the motives of the people you're judging, it is also important to know your own motives and make sure they don't interfere in inappropriate ways.

When I talked to Don after a few of his meetings with Wanda, I asked him directly about the tension I sensed between his motive—to leave the business in the strongest possible hands—and Wanda's desire to make a positive social impact. He said he respected Wanda tremendously, but was also cautious. "I know the board has relatively modest goals. I can imagine Wanda's ideas leading to amazing opportunities for the organization and its stakeholders, but I don't know if the board will feel comfortable with someone who's driven by something other than the bottom line."

When I brought it up with Wanda, however, she was dismissive of the issue. "The business succeeds by doing good," she told me. "It's really not a conflict for me." It was clear she had a blindspot when it came to how much she was being driven by her motive, and I worried that this might doom her ability to effectively lead the company.

Sal's meetings were harder to unpack than Craig's or Wanda's. They would start with the same kind of productive discussion that Craig had with Don—a back-and-forth focused on improving the business—yet Sal was gifted with an innate strategic sense that Craig was still developing, and, like Wanda, he also brought big and audacious goals to the table. Don liked that Sal looked to him for mentorship, and also liked that Sal had a terrific handle on the business as it stood now, and a vision for where it could go.

In fact, with his deep knowledge of new technologies and how they could potentially change the business, Sal would end up spending lots of time during these meetings teaching Don and inspiring him to investigate new opportunities for change. In turn, Don would push Sal on how to bring his ideas to fruition and navigate the internal politics of the organization and the industry.

Yet there was something a little forced about the conversations. While Don listened to Sal's vision, it wasn't clear that Don was receiving Sal's ideas with the same enthusiasm with which Sal was delivering them. Similarly, as Don would offer suggestions and guidance, Sal would become quiet, listening but not really engaging.

Inevitably, each meeting would fall apart at some point, often over the tiniest of issues. In one meeting, Sal had just finished a well-reasoned and well-researched proposal as to how Midwest could partner with a set of very popular third-party apps to add more flexibility in how customers could pay for their groceries.

"Interesting," Don responded, "and I see the promise, but there are a lot of internal functions that would have to adjust to make this possible. And the amount of internal training would be significant."

Sal became slightly red in the face and ratcheted up his speech in speed and volume. "Don, how do you not see the advantages here? We'll reduce costs by outsourcing some of the payment infrastructure to third parties *and* we'll be more relevant to a younger market cohort. It's a slam dunk."

"Maybe . . . but Sal, I know our people and how much change they can take, and even something that feels small can be a big deal when rolled out across the entire company."

Around and around they would go, each becoming more adamant and at the same time more distant from each other.

Don's meetings with Craig and Wanda were predictable and calm; his meetings with Sal were emotionally fraught in ways that didn't make immediate sense to either of them, or to me. After watching Don and Sal become emotional with each other several times, I could see something big was getting in the way of Sal and Don being able to have productive interactions—and getting in the way of Sal deserving a recommendation for the CEO role.

The "something" that was getting in the way, despite both men being intellectually engaged and often aligned on the business, was a clash of motives. Sal had a blindspot as to what was driving his argumentative behavior, and until (and unless) he could see it and address it, the tension between him and Don would remain unresolved.

Personal Motives Can Get in the Way

I couldn't see Sal's motive at first. As I processed the meetings afterward with Don, he didn't see it either. Don told me that he didn't understand how or why the meetings with Sal always seemed to turn negative. He didn't know why they would end up bickering, and what it was about Sal that made things turn so emotional for them. Don was known throughout the company as a good mentor and an easy person to get along with—and I saw it in his meetings with Craig and Wanda, certainly. He would pose thoughtful questions, get them to think about things in new ways, and support them as they came up with solutions. He wanted Craig, Wanda, and Sal to succeed. Yet something about Sal's approach was consistently pushing his buttons.

"He gets arrogant," Don said to me. "It's like he really wants me to agree with him, but I'm not there to agree with him. I'm there to help him learn and grow."

For his part, Sal didn't dispute Don's characterization. "I do want him to agree with me," Sal admitted. "He invites my ideas, but then challenges them rather than acknowledging how much I am contributing." This was causing Sal to dig in and force a confrontation—and it never went well.

After the first meeting, I found myself taking a more active role bridging the gap in their communication. When things began to get tense, I would ask Sal what he was trying to achieve, and I would ask Don to rephrase what he was saying . . . but nothing quite seemed to click. I started to feel a bit like a marriage counselor, as Sal and Don would fall into the same traps meeting after meeting, Sal pushing Don to tell him that his latest idea—often a wonderful one—was beneficial for the company, and Don refusing to give Sal the satisfaction of unqualified approval, instead pushing Sal on how to execute on the idea or get past the inevitable obstacles. Nothing either one of them said was objectionable on its face, but somehow it still led to conflict.

I empathized with Don as we debriefed after each meeting, because if I was being honest with myself, for as much as I believed Sal should have been a very strong candidate for the CEO job—and as smart and driven as he clearly was—I found that I didn't like Sal very much, almost from the moment we met. Just as I needed to make sure my own favorable bias toward Wanda's altruistic motive didn't color my recommendation to the board, I also had to keep any personal feelings about Sal out of my evaluation. That doesn't mean I ignored my gut response to Sal; in fact, I used it as a clue to dig deeper. I wanted to figure out where my feelings were coming from, and whether they had emerged from something idiosyncratic inside of me—and irrelevant to the board and the role—or whether they indicated something more about Sal.

I kept coming back to a moment in my very first conversation with him. Sal had found a way to insert the fact that he had gotten a perfect score on the SAT into an entirely unrelated conversation. There's nothing *wrong* with getting a perfect score on the SAT—but the fact that he thought this was important to assert thirty years after the fact, with no natural reason to do so, was curious to me. Not to mention, this was in a context where Sal's value would be based entirely on his job performance and leadership skills, both in the past and in a predicted future, and not on how he was able to perform on an exam more than half his lifetime ago.

As I went through my own blindspot checklist, some possible issues emerged. The SAT score spoke to Sal's identity, certainly—he very clearly wanted to be seen as a smart person, even if he had to say it rather than show it. And Sal was definitely overindexing on the trait of persistence, causing him to miss Don's cues that he needed to move on when the conversation was exhausted or at a stalemate. Sal was so convinced of his own rightness—an intellect blindspot that caused him to ignore the emotional impact his tone was having on Don. And both men were getting frustrated beyond the point of professional appropriateness, without fully realizing it, an emotional blindspot for sure.

But it was the strong emotion coupled with the combination of these other areas that led me to motive. When a problem situation isn't getting better and there is strong emotion surrounding an unsatisfied need—think Thad and his drive for efficiency—motive blindspots are often the place to look.

Emotion Is the Flashing Red Light That Points to a Blocked Motive

Strong emotion that we can't explain can be one of the most puzzling things we experience as individuals. Think about a time you met someone and had a visceral dislike that you couldn't quite put your finger on. Or when you found yourself getting angry at your partner, and you didn't really know why. Conversely, recall when you've been unexpectedly happy at some new development or piece of news; or found yourself really enjoying something in a way you never anticipated; or tearing up unexpectedly at a scene in a movie. It is likely that the explanation for what is happening behind the scenes revolves around motive, usually a strong motive being blocked (in the negative case) or an unrecognized motive being satisfied (when something feels unexpectedly positive).

I remember an incident when I was a partner at RHR, and one of the manager partners (a role senior to mine) stopped me in the hall. "Marty, I need you to pick up this project at Bow Engineering for me," he said.

"Sorry, Jason, but I really don't have the time right now," was my instant reply, and it was true. I couldn't take on a whole new client and wasn't sure why it seemed like he was telling me and not asking me.

"Marty, you are a member of this firm, and you need to step up and contribute now and again."

The nerve of him! I became immediately furious, with thoughts of how much I was contributing, in ways that Jason wasn't even aware of. I wasn't one to advertise my contributions, but I also didn't understand why he was acting like my boss when . . . well, I guess as someone senior to me, he kind of *was* my boss.

I held my tongue and we worked out a suitable arrangement, but in hindsight I realize this was a motive blindspot driving my emotional reaction. I wanted to see myself as being my own boss, in charge of my own time, rather than working to satisfy others in the organization. That motive was being challenged, and I didn't like it, even if I couldn't put my finger on why.

Similarly, Don and Sal didn't know why they were upset with each other. And that meant they couldn't fix the problem. Relationship change can only happen when you discover your motive blindspots and give yourself and the person you are frustrated with the conscious opportunity to respond and adjust.

Leveraging Motive to Help Us Succeed

Tracy, the CEO of a growing startup, wanted to get ahead of a possible problem in the future. She knew she was going to have to expand her senior leadership team, and she wanted to make sure she had a good understanding of the strengths and weaknesses of everyone already in place. She called in help to do a 360-degree feedback analysis for everyone on her senior team and to give her some feedback on her own leadership.

Tracy's results were consistent. "Good human being." "Trustworthy." "Righteous, principled person." "Filled with integrity."

Integrity was in fact the single most common word in all of her evaluations, and it bubbled up in nearly every story I was told about her. I often ask CEOs to tell me the stories people tell about them, and I ask people throughout an organization what stories they tell others about their workplace. Stories are extremely powerful indicators of motive—and ways to identify motive blindspots that might otherwise go undetected. If everyone is always telling the story, say, about the time the CEO decided to fly the whole company to Las Vegas after a stellar quarter, and how it was so *out of character* for him to want to celebrate with his team that way, it should make you think: Why was it so out of character? Maybe affiliation—relationships and team bonding—isn't a strong motive for this CEO, and that's why the story stands out. On the other hand, if the story is told as just one more example of how incredibly the CEO treats his people, then it tells you something else about his motives, and that he is quite strong in terms of affiliation. The CEO himself may not realize this is what is driving him, but if you listen to what people say about someone's behavior, motives can become more readily apparent.

Building on that, a particularly savvy leader can be on the lookout for stories that communicate the motives they want to be associated with and try to propagate those stories throughout the company—by highlighting them in communications, for example. Consistently sharing stories of moments when employees helped people in the community will send a different message about what drives the leaders of the company than sharing a similar set of stories about breakthroughs in corporate efficiency or photos of the executive team with celebrities around the world. Thus, motive can be used strategically in this way— once you figure out the kinds of behaviors you want to drive.

The most powerful story I heard about Tracy concerned a time when the company had gone through some financial difficulties. While Tracy had made a promise to pay bonuses to several layers of employees, the finance and HR leads were insisting that it couldn't be done. "Circumstances have changed," they told Tracy, "and we need to communicate that to the employees, explaining we can't pay the bonuses now, but we'll try to make it happen as soon as we can."

Tracy refused to take their advice. A promise is a promise, she said, and insisted they figure out a way to make it work. Through some maneuvering they found a way, and it was to Tracy's credit that the bonuses got paid—fully and on time. The power of the retelling of that story as it cascaded throughout the company was phenomenal. People were driven to go above and beyond for Tracy, stay late when needed, or come in on the weekend. Their trust in her paid off in enhanced performance.

"We can rely on her word," was the message that came across, and in talking to Tracy, what struck me is not only how that filtered its way through everything she did at the company, but also how she was entirely unaware that this made her special.

Tracy had a motive blindspot that actually played out differently from the other stories in this chapter. Tracy's motive—to always tell the truth and act with integrity!—was *helping* her, not hurting. It made her easy to work with, because, as one employee said, "What you see is what you get, and you never have to spend time and energy wondering about her intentions." She had weaknesses, for sure—she wanted control over details that she probably should have delegated; she was not particularly effusive with praise—but because everyone trusted that Tracy meant what she said, those negatives were mitigated to the point of not affecting her employee relationships.

My advice to Tracy was the reverse in some ways of my advice to Thad. She needed self-awareness about her motive not so she could overcome it, but so she could embrace it and even advertise it. She needed to share stories like the one I heard and help make sure employees, customers, and investors understood her very special "brand" as a truth-teller, motivated by integrity above all else. I helped give Tracy the self-awareness that she could deliberately and strategically use this motive to become a more effective and powerful leader, supercharging her personal influence and even winning over new customers and new hires, excited by the idea of working with a company and a leader who would never let them down.

Tracy had an underleveraged leadership opportunity. Self-awareness allowed her to lean into this strength that was so natural to her. She had no idea how rare and valuable it was. Recall from the introduction that we don't tend to recognize when we are at an extreme in some element of our personality. Tracy imagined everyone else was as honest as she was. She didn't see her integrity as a superstrength or something that made her stand out. She did not recognize how much so many people struggle with keeping their promises or living up to their commitments. Since it would have never occurred to her to behave any differently, she lacked the insight and self-awareness to know how different it made her. Sometimes, rather than change your motive, you just need to lean into it.

Sal's Motive Takes Over

I didn't know after sitting in on a few months of meetings whether Sal was the best candidate to replace Don as CEO of Midwest Grocers, but I absolutely knew that he would never be seriously considered if he couldn't fix their relationship. It was in one of our final sessions when Sal inadvertently let something slip: "I do wish, just once, that Don would tell me how smart I am and how valuable I am to the company. No recommendations, no advice, no hypotheticals to push back on my ideas; just give me the satisfaction of knowing I impressed him. Why is that so hard for him?"

In that moment, I flashed back to when he told me his SAT score in our first meeting. He had wanted a response from me—"Wow, you are so smart." Or, even more than wanting the response, he *needed* the response. He needed validation, and that's why he was driven to advertise himself in such a way. He wanted to feel that pat on the back—"You, Sal, are a wonderful person." And when he didn't get that, he felt intensely frustrated and lashed out.

As a psychologist, I was tempted to ask Sal about his relationship with his parents, and whether this need for approval had something to do with his childhood. It seemed, after all, that Sal was looking for Don to be a father figure and give him the support and attaboys that would fill whatever hole was inside him. Instead, I tried to remind him that this was a work relationship, that Don was his boss, and that Don was doing his very best to train Sal to be a better leader. The validation Sal was looking for was unlikely in just about any workplace scenario, at least in my experience, but it was certainly unlikely with Don, who was not wired to give praise in the way that Sal was seeking it.

Indeed, when I went back to Don and told him how I suspected he could fix their relationship, Don laughed. "I'm not going to tell him he's smart. He should know he's smart, and if he doesn't, then he's probably not that smart."

This motive for validation couldn't be articulated by most people who interacted with Sal, but it was felt under the surface and hurt the impression people got. If Sal would have been aware of his needs—if he could have seen his motive blindspot—then perhaps he could have corrected for it.

At the board meeting when I presented my findings, it became clear that Sal never stood a chance. "There's something that bothers me about Sal," one board member said, "but I can't quite put my finger on it." Everyone who'd met him nodded in agreement. They couldn't put their finger on it, but there it was, his motive blindspot: overshadowing any concerns about driving the business forward, about power and status, or about money, Sal craved approval. And he didn't realize it. This motive blindspot was blocking his success, even though he had many of the skills that the board was otherwise looking for.

Chasing approval, it should be said—independent of whether the decisions you make are the right ones—is a terrible motive for a leader, especially if they're unaware of it. A leader who is chasing approval will chase the wrong priorities for the business and will never have the backbone to make the hard decisions that inevitably disappoint some of the people around them. Leadership so often is about making decisions in the face of stiff disapproval.

Sal's personal motive didn't match the leadership role he was seeking. It was clear to me that he had reached his ceiling at the company and would very likely go through the same cycle elsewhere, at least until he gained self-awareness about his blindspot and made a correction.

The board in this case was worried about Wanda as well. "I love her vision of our stores being a force for good in the community," one director said, "but I worry that down deep, making a difference is more important to her than the actual financial success. I don't want to be at a board meeting where she is insistent that we improve community relations at the expense of the bottom line." They had exactly the right read on her, and while I thought Wanda did a tremendous job balancing her motive with the realities of what she needed to do in her job, it probably wasn't the best fit. If you want to be a leader, as simple as it sounds, the most effective motive you can have is to be someone who wants to lead.

Craig's motives, on the other hand, were entirely aligned with what the board was looking for. When they looked at Craig, they saw their next leader—but what they were really seeing were his achievement, affiliation, and power motives, balanced in a way that made him a safe and effective choice, able to step right into Don's shoes. He got the job not only because his knowledge and skills were a fit, but also because his motives were clear to all—including himself. That's how leadership hiring decisions work in the best scenarios. The knowledge and skills have to match the needs of the role, but the "intangibles" often boil down to motive: Are you seen as someone driven by what the business needs, or do you seem like you might be pulled in other directions by other forces deep inside you? Those forces, of course, are your motives. If you don't see them, others will, and even if you can't change them, at least you can be more in control of how they show up in your behavior.

Midwest Grocers continued to thrive under Craig's leadership. I would have imagined Wanda to have taken the news hard and moved on to an organization more receptive to her motivation to change the world, but to Craig's credit, he carved out an executive position for Wanda where she was able to focus on the initiatives that moved her, and both the company and the community benefited. Sal left the company soon after the decision to pass over him was made.

. . .

Do *You* Have a Motive Blindspot?

We don't always spend sufficient time examining our own motives and seeing how they play out in our careers. But it's important to understand your motives so that you know why you're feeling the way you feel and why you're acting the way you are.

Awareness

Start your investigation of your motives by turning back to my point about stories. What are the stories you tell people about your job and your career? What are the moments that make you proudest, and the ones that frustrate you to an extent that it's hard to even know why?

When my company was sold, I found myself telling friends not about the size of the deal or even the impact we were making, but about how I, as merely a psychologist, had been able to learn all kinds of new skills to build a company, and had done so in a way that enabled us to grow something that a *Fortune* 50 business really wanted to buy. It was clear from the way I told the story—if I took the time to think about it—that I was driven by the learning, the growing, and the possibility for impact more than anything else.

Think about the choices you've made along the way in your career and in your life. What motivated you to make those decisions? Why did you take the jobs you've taken? Why do you live where you live and do the things you do? Can you identify patterns, if you really think about it? Tell these stories to yourself and others. Write them down if you need to. Mine them for those deep motives.

Along similar lines, have there been moments of strong—unexpectedly strong—emotion in your life or career, both positive and negative? If there are experiences that stand out ("I didn't think I'd care so much about _____" or "It got me so surprisingly angry when _____"), these may be clues to motive blindspots that you are not fully recognizing.

After looking back, you need to look forward. If you fantasize about wild success in whatever you're doing, what does that look like to you? Does it involve money? Fame? Excitement? Impact? What are the two or three sentences you'd want to be able to say about what you had accomplished, and do those sentences bring you close to an understanding of what drives you? How would that wild success impact your day-to-day life? Are you looking for more freedom? More opportunity? More knowledge? What would you spend your time doing if you had an unlimited amount of it? What do you want your legacy to be? Does answering those questions bring you any new insights into what drives you and why you do what you do?

Pose to yourself a set of "Would you rather?" questions. You can start with the ones that speak to organizational psychologist David McClelland's three core motives: Would you rather be rich or famous? Would you rather be known superficially by a billion people or known intimately by just a handful? Would you rather be in charge of a risky project or follow and support a leader on their own journey? Would you rather win the lottery or find the cure for the common cold? If you did win the lottery, what would you do with the money?

Then, you can move on to more-specific questions that get at your own personal, idiosyncratic motives. There is no master list of possible motives, though I included some to start with earlier in the chapter, and again in the appendix. There are more. Before meeting Thad, I'm not sure I would have thought someone could be so motivated by pure efficiency that it would drive everything they do—but then I got to know him. Is there a through-line to your life, or your career, that people wouldn't necessarily expect?

All of these questions should lead to some commonalities. Taking all of it together, what drives you? And, just as important, do those drivers match what you're trying to accomplish? If not—if you have needs that are being overexpressed or unfulfilled—you may need to take action.

Action

Motives, as I've said, are very hard to change. But that doesn't mean we can't—with awareness—alter how they show up in our behavior. As you think about your motives, are there mismatches between what drives you and your role? And are there changes you might want to make?

For instance, if you're motivated by money and working for a nonprofit where success is measured by impact, that may not be the perfect fit. Similarly, if you're motivated by spending time with people you care about and you work from home, alone, on projects that keep you isolated, that may not be right, either.

Are there ways you could shift your job responsibilities to better reflect what drives you and give you more fulfillment and reward? Are there people at work whose motives match yours and who might be worth finding ways to collaborate with? Wanda, for instance, could have formed a team of altruists to help her look for the next great opportunities for Midwest Grocers to make an impact. Are there ways you could get your motive needs met outside of work so that you don't need to bring your mismatched motive into the workplace? Perhaps Sal could have found another way to get validation from people in his life so that he wouldn't have needed quite as much of it from Don.

In the next chapter, we turn to *traits*. Each of us has our own unique blend of strengths and challenges, and the way these play out is different for everyone. Our innate personality traits can either support our efforts or detract from them—and investing too much in the things we are good at, while ignoring the areas that require more work, can often lead to serious blindspots.

CHAPTER 3

TRAITS

ARE YOUR SUPERSTRENGTHS ENABLING UNSEEN WEAKNESSES?

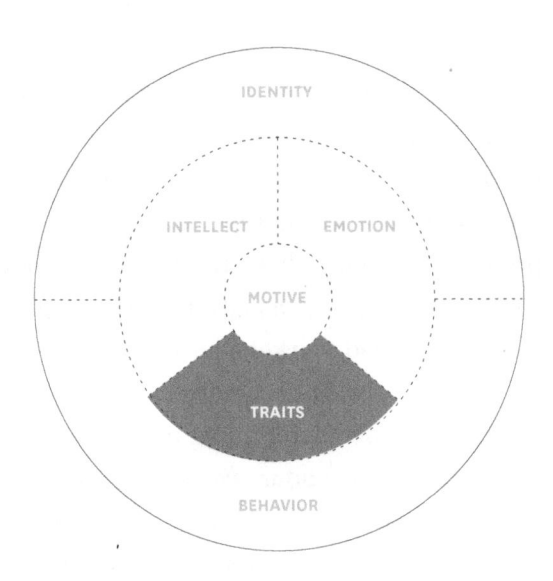

In the middle layer of the self-awareness model are blindspots that emerge as our core motivations are filtered through our traits, intellect, and emotions (before they eventually come out as identities and behaviors). Our traits are the features that make us unique, not just physically—our eye color, the shape of our nose—but in our personality. They can feel so intimately connected to who we are—extrovert versus

introvert, flexible versus rigid, etc.—that we often don't see when they block our success. In this chapter, we open our eyes to traits, and how we can become aware of when they lead us down the wrong path.

"We shouldn't be dealing with this," said the board member on the phone. "I mean, our CEO is great, and the product is terrific. The company is a rocket ship—the fastest-growing investment we've got, the one we parade out when we're meeting with founders. Everything is amazing . . ."

There was a telling pause before the inevitable *but*. After all, if you're calling someone like me, there's definitely going to be a *but*.

"But our heavily recruited chief marketing officer just quit, and she's not the first member of the senior team to walk away. Our cofounders are great with each other, but it's like they can't let anyone else in."

The board member explained that Brendan, the CEO, and Miguel, the head of product, had been best friends since childhood. Together, they had launched ClassU, a platform in the digital education space that had rapidly gained market share and appeared unstoppable. Miguel was technically brilliant, creative, curious, and ambitious. Not only were his ideas spectacular, but he could execute—he got things done. I was told that Brendan was kind, responsible, and collaborative, with terrific judgment (he had navigated the company through crisis after crisis), but that somehow the two of them were driving others away. The board had sufficient distance from day-to-day operations that they didn't really know what was happening—and needed a coach to step in and figure out what was going wrong.

I sat down with Miguel and Brendan for a get-to-know-you session. I would conduct my assessments soon, but first I wanted to have a sense of what I was dealing with. I found the two of them delightful to interact with and could see their close bond on display. They joked easily with each other, and even finished each other's sentences as they told me story after story about the company's founding. "We stayed up forty-eight hours straight before our initial investor pitches, fueled by caffeine and ramen—" Brendan said.

"*Homemade* ramen," Miguel interjected. "I had been obsessed with this ramen place downtown and for some reason got in my head that the biggest week of our lives in terms of the company was also going to be the week I was going to figure out how to make authentic Japanese noodles from scratch. It was amazing—"

"And so much work that he never did it again," Brendan laughed.

In between bowls of soup, they finished coding their prototype, and investors practically begged them to take their money. They ended up with a rapid funding round that landed them three times as much investment as they were seeking, and it had been off to the races since then. Already from the ramen story, I had a sense of Miguel's extreme traits—his intense curiosity, his persistence, his endurance, and his bias to action. They had served him well as both a founder and a kitchen adventurer.

When I asked about the quick departure of the company's new CMO, Brendan and Miguel suddenly grew quiet and looked at each other with a bit of embarrassment, like two pals who'd been sent to the principal's office for goofing off in the back of the classroom. "She didn't really like us," Brendan admitted, holding back a bit of a smirk.

"She didn't like *me*," Miguel clarified. "I disagreed with her marketing plans, and I let her know."

"I told him it wasn't his place," Brendan clarified.

"And I pushed anyway," Miguel admitted. "Brendan and I argued about it—"

"In front of her—"

"And I think she probably thought Brendan didn't have her back," said Miguel.

"I was trying to make everyone happy," Brendan responded.

"And he knew I was right."

"I did not know you were right," Brendan pushed back. "In fact, you were probably wrong, but you don't like it when people tell you that."

"I wasn't wrong, but I probably should have backed down."

Brendan rolled his eyes. "Here we go," he said to me, "Miguel admitting after the fact that he should have backed down when we both know full well that he'll do the same thing again next time."

"And I'll be right."

"He probably will be, Marty," Brendan admitted. "He's really smart."

I went into the engagement thinking that Miguel and Brendan were going to need help with their communication skills—something like the marital counseling I had done at times in my psychotherapy practice—but as I talked with them, I realized their interpersonal relationship was fine. Something else was going on. The problem was that their supertraits—Miguel's curiosity and persistence; Brendan's agreeableness and loyalty—were turning from positives into negatives, and they didn't see it. They had trait blindspots that were deeply hurting the company.

"I think with some work, I can help make it so the next CMO sticks around," I told them, as our initial meeting came to a close.

"And that's a good thing?" Miguel asked, only half-kidding.

Character Traits Can Define Us—and Destroy Us

Of all six blindspot areas, traits is perhaps the most familiar—and the category we turn to first when we think about the building blocks of what makes a person. We should first distinguish a trait from a skill or a state. States are transitory characteristics in response to a particular environmental influence—you're in a state of anxiety while you're waiting to be seen in the emergency room, for instance, or you're in a state of euphoria after finding out you've landed your dream job. That doesn't mean you're necessarily an anxious person more generally, or a euphoric one; it's situational. Skills, on the other hand, are developed aptitudes or abilities, the using of our learned knowledge or life experience to do something we otherwise couldn't, like knitting a cozy blanket, writing genius code, or giving an amazing presentation.

Traits are distinct from both of these things, the adjectives we use to describe people and their personalities, stable and consistent across our lifespan. Someone who has the trait of confidence may have moments when they don't feel confident, but for the most part they are confident in a wide range of situations. Someone who is organized or empathetic or extroverted may certainly have times they feel otherwise, but true traits are labels that stick and apply no matter what we're doing.

When I began as a coach and started to hear people talk about the strengths and weaknesses of the people they work with, I took their answers at face value. If an executive was praised for their confidence, I'd make a note of it and look for other areas that might need to be worked on instead. After all, strengths are good, I reasoned. It's the weaknesses that we need to worry about.

But after a little while, I started to notice a surprising pattern. Often, if an executive was praised for his confidence, that same reviewer might also mention his arrogance. The friendly extrovert would have trouble leaving people alone to do their work. The same individual would be described as both persistent and stubborn—and the more persistent she seemed to be in some people's eyes, the more stubborn she seemed in the eyes of another. The visionary would have trouble with execution. The understanding boss was quick to agree with everyone, leaving no one quite sure where they stood. The calm, unflappable CEO never signaled when he was upset, causing people to guess what bothered him. The "curious, out-of-the-box thinker" seemed to always get "easily distracted by something shiny and new."

My realization: strengths are *not* unqualified positives. Instead, our challenges often emerge from investing *too* heavily in our strengths—the superstrengths become supernovas and tip over into the qualities that most frustrate the people around us and get in the way of our success. The list goes on. My attention to detail might feel to others like micromanagement; an orientation toward action can look a lot like a lack of strategic thinking; conscientiousness becomes perfectionism; critical judgment becomes a lack of interpersonal sensitivity.

And because these strengths are often the qualities we are most proud of, the things we like best in ourselves and have heard positive feedback about over the course of our lives, the idea that they can become our biggest weaknesses is a serious blindspot. Most of us simply won't be able to see when that happens.

Esther was a great example of this. She was the CEO of a small pharmaceutical company started by two medical researchers with little interest in running a business. They figured Esther, an experienced pharma exec, could help steer their company through an IPO and beyond. She had an incredible reputation as a conscientious and careful leader, traits that had served her well when she was a senior-level executive at a large, established pharmaceutical company, where diligence was prized over boldness. Her references had spoken glowingly of her "flawless judgment," "strategic genius," and "capacity for avoiding undue risk in an industry where one mistake can mean bankruptcy."

The board was overwhelmingly in favor of this move, delighted for the scientists to stay in the lab and let the company be run by a seasoned professional. They loved that she felt like a safe and reliable choice for an enterprise that did not have a lot of business expertise at the highest level.

The board chairman called me nine months later because things hadn't taken off as the directors had hoped. "Growth has been surprisingly slow," he told me. "We brought in this new sales guy. And it's helping, a little . . . but the sales guy keeps telling me we need a new CEO. We like Esther—we want to make it work. Can you figure out what the problem is?"

I reached out to Esther to set up a meeting. She asked if I could connect her with a few references—perfectly appropriate and reasonably commonplace. Two weeks passed before I followed up. Esther said she still hadn't had a chance to reach out to one of the references. Another three weeks passed, and I figured this was never going to happen.

Until, to my surprise, she reached out and said we were good to get started.

Two weeks later Esther and I met at the International Terminal in the San Francisco airport, the only place and time she could find that worked for both of us. It was not an ideal location for a substantive meeting, but I was able to explain my process—interviews, testing, a report, a plan. She seemed amenable, and I found her to be pleasant and polite. No red flags.

Except the pace of the follow-up remained glacial. Esther gave me limited access to her team, making the process slower than normal. She also kept putting off her testing. When I had gotten about three-quarters of the way through the process—now a full three months after I had initially reached out to her—the board chairman called me and asked for a progress report. "Do you think she can get better?" he asked.

"I hope so—but I'm not sure. I have to admit, I haven't even begun coaching her yet."

"You've got to be kidding."

I paused for a beat. "I'm sure Esther is coachable. I just—"

He cut me off. "I think you've given me what I was looking for," the chairman told me. "We're going to let Esther go. She's great, but just isn't a fit for a startup. We have to move fast, and, like you've seen, she can't."

This was a trait blindspot affecting Esther's success, illustrated perfectly. Her superstrengths were of tremendous value in her old role. The problem was that the new role required something else, and by continuing to lean into her superstrengths—being cautious and deliberate—Esther was failing. She couldn't see the problem because it had never been a problem for her before. Being cautious and deliberate brought her great success ... until it didn't. If we'd gotten further, I would have tried to help her and the board come together to bridge the gap. Even before that, I would have tried to get Esther to gain the self-awareness to understand what her blindspot even was. I believe that with awareness and a plan, she could have fixed this. But she ran out the clock, and her extreme traits cost her the career opportunity she'd been so excited to earn.

The Traits That Matter

As with identities and motives, there are a seemingly unlimited number of traits we might possess, and it takes some focus to figure out which ones are the most likely to lead to blindspots. I have no doubt that many of you have taken countless personality tests, whether for fun or for work—Myers-Briggs, Enneagram, and others. While these tests are fun to take and yield findings that are interesting to explore, the Big Five traits—see table 3-1—are a particular set that have been developed and refined by research psychologists over the past seventy years.[1] Numerous teams of investigators using robust statistical methods have agreed that there are five traits that show remarkable stability throughout our lifespans and across cultures and contexts, and are orthogonal to each other, or statistically independent. One advantage of the Big Five is to codify the range of human experience to give us a common language to describe and compare the kinds of people we see around us, and they are a good place to start in any discussion about traits—and trait blindspots.

Psychologists believe that a bell curve exists for each of these traits. Many of us are somewhere in the middle on a trait—somewhat extroverted; not too extroverted—but then there are those of us who fall on the extremes, and that is where we run the risk of falling victim to a blindspot on the opposite side. What do I mean by that? You think your superstrength will always be the right approach, even when it isn't. If you are very extroverted, you will be at a loss when being introverted would be the optimal trait for a particular situation. If you are extremely open to new experiences, you won't be able to adapt to a situation where what's needed is deep focus on one domain without the opportunity for change.

A client named Mila, for instance, had experienced an exceptional rise at one of the most successful B2B companies in the world. She was known in the industry as a rock star: supersmart, incredibly

TABLE 3-1

The Big Five traits

Extroversion	When someone finds energy in the company of others (introversion—comfort being alone—is on the other side of the spectrum)
Openness to experience	Curiosity and an eagerness to do and learn new things (as opposed to someone who thrives with routine)
Accommodation	Agreeableness and trust (while people low in this trait are comfortable with disagreement and in environments where they may have to play politics or manipulate others)
Conscientiousness	Discipline as we push toward goals (with relaxed spontaneity and a willingness to multitask at the other extreme)
Neuroticism	Anxiety and irritability (as contrasted with an even mood and generally sunny disposition)

driven, and a key leader with a legendary ability to focus and quickly devise elegant technological solutions to problems. Expectations were high when she jumped to a prominent startup and found herself elevated to CEO after an unexpected resignation. The marketing team was delighted to have a reason to get Mila's name out in the world even further, wanting to book her as a keynote speaker at conferences around the world. The technologists couldn't wait to see one of their own shining in a broader, more public-facing role than she'd ever had before. The sales team was thrilled to have her in the top spot at the company, because they knew her name would mean something to customers, and their ability to bring her in to help close deals would give them a competitive advantage.

That is not how things played out. Mila was aware when she took the job that she was quite high in terms of conscientiousness—she was, like Esther, slow and deliberate at times. She liked to spend time holed up in her office working through problems, and her previous role made it possible for her to do that. Unlike Esther, she knew that wouldn't work as a CEO. She was pragmatic and had a strong bias to action, so she forced herself to act more quickly, to rely on her team, and to make big decisions on perhaps less data than she might have hoped for.

Still, the role of CEO has few day-to-day requirements and is shaped by the person who occupies it. There were more decisions to make in the job than she'd faced in her previous role, and even with her conscious effort to speed up, she still found herself wanting more time alone, time to focus, to recharge, to think. She was friendly and charismatic when forced to interact, but left to her own devices, she tried her best to keep her schedule free of what she saw as social distractions. She told her team, "There's lots of work to do, and I need the time to do it."

There was no one to force Mila to add things to her schedule that she would rather avoid, so, as much as possible, she sidestepped what made her uncomfortable. Salespeople had to ask her again and again to come to a closing to answer a client's questions, or even just to say hello and lend some of her star power to the transaction. The marketing team got her to agree to one keynote when they would have wanted to book her for a dozen.

One-on-one, Mila was warm and caring, but she did not take advantage of opportunities to rally the team in big ways, to give inspiring speeches, and to stand in front of them as their fearless leader; she became almost an invisible presence. Her internal leaders were exceptionally frustrated that they had to spend time convincing Mila to do the things that they thought she should have naturally been seeking out and genuinely excited to pursue.

When I was brought in and interviewed her team, they were baffled. "Why do we have to beg our CEO to be the face of the company?" they asked. One of her senior leaders even confided in me, "It's like Mila only wants to do the hard work. Getting interviewed is fun! Giving speeches is fun! People would love her. And she wants to look at spreadsheets all day???"

This was, as it turned out, an easy one. Mila didn't realize, nor did her team . . . she was an introvert in a job that required the behavior of an extrovert. This was not an issue of identity or motive, or any of the other blindspots to come. The simple reality was that for Mila to leave her comfort zone (to meet with clients, lead company meetings, talk to the media, etc.) was exceptionally challenging. She coped with the stress of extroverted activities not just by avoiding as many as she could but also by convincing herself that these tasks were extraneous, and that simply focusing on strategy and execution would be enough. She was blind to the reality that her innate introversion was holding her back as the company shifted from product development to commercialization, when a CEO needs to be external-facing—a clear trait blindspot.

Traits are hard to change, and I don't intend to argue otherwise. Any attempt to change them is likely to end in frustration and failure. We are, for better or worse, who we are, and rather than fighting our instincts, it is almost always more productive to become aware of our traits and then manage around them or find a role where we can thrive not just despite who we are but because of our unique gifts and abilities.

Mila was never going to be the life of the party, but at the very least, if she wanted to be a successful CEO, she needed to become aware of her blindspot, and then adapt and figure out ways to compensate for her innate introversion. To some degree, she needed to push herself out of her comfort zone, but she could also compensate by building a team around her that could own at least some of the tasks she didn't want. I advised her to hire a chief of communications and inspiration to own some elements of the role that she didn't feel comfortable with, and we worked on ways to strategically harness her limited tolerance for meetings by using her in only the most important sales closings. While Mila was uncomfortable being on stage in front of large groups, I could see that her genuineness, warmth, and industry credentials made her quite charismatic in small group situations. I encouraged her to schedule monthly sessions—"Friday breakfasts with Mila"—and invite four employees at a time from different parts of the company to join her for a meal. She used these meetings effectively to connect with employees as individuals, inspire them about her vision for the company, and show them how much she appreciated their contributions.

She also worked with sales and marketing to help them shape her identity to the world as a brilliant, compassionate, introverted leader. This allowed her to stay in her comfort zone as much as possible while adjusting the world's (and the company's) expectations of who she was and how she might behave. Finally, she leaned on her extroverted CFO to take a more central role during board meetings in order to relieve her of the responsibility of "performing" for the board, letting her focus instead on building the one-on-one relationships.

Through understanding and accepting her trait blindspot, Mila was able to make changes that felt like a relief, and with help, she blossomed as a CEO and found success. Her introversion was a blindspot she had to address, not a fatal character flaw. Rather than trying to pretend certain parts of the job weren't important, she needed the self-awareness to know what she could and couldn't do, and strategies to overcome the problems.

Do We All Have the Traits to Be Leaders?

I suspect some of you were thinking ahead while reading Mila's story, wondering how she could possibly have been the right match for the role. Isn't it obvious, you might ask, that an extrovert is going to be a better leader than an introvert?

As Mila's company moved from developing the product to commercializing it, the answer was yes, but I wouldn't make the case that this—or any trait—is universally valuable in every situation. I have seen CEO roles where deep thinking matters most, and the nature of the business doesn't require the kind of robust presence that Mila's team wanted from her. There may be leadership traits that prove useful in many cases, but even more important is the fit: Which traits are useful in the particular context?

To the extent that there are traits associated with being a successful leader, I'm cautious about giving them too much credence, in part because it's hard to identify what those traits are, but even more because those traits, just like the Big Five, run the risk of tipping over into problems, causing blindspots as we rely on them so extensively that they prevent us from seeing other traits that may be more suited to the problem at hand.

Many have tried to distill leadership down to a set of particular traits. A quick Google search of leadership traits results in perfectly legitimate publications and websites offering 10 qualities of a leader; 16 leadership characteristics; 12 necessary leadership traits; 6 characteristics of an effective leader; and endless other links providing somewhere between 3 and 101 crucial traits for leaders.[2] Some of these lists fail to distinguish between traits and skills, some are contradictory, and some are well-meaning but entirely incomplete when they don't consider the context.

Some of the most commonly referenced leadership traits can be seen in table 3-2.

The first column lists twelve characteristics of strong leaders identified by the Center for Creative Leadership—where I spent the early part of my consulting career. These are important, and it should be no surprise that I would make the case that the first one on the list, self-awareness, is the most critical of all. But it is absolutely the case that good leaders should strive to act with respect, compassion, vision, and the rest—and that when those traits are innate for a person, that person is likely to find the journey toward leadership to be more natural.

The second column focuses on entrepreneurial traits specifically, as they are somewhat different from general leadership traits. An entrepreneur needs to behave in certain ways that are not necessarily needed or desired in an established company. Building from scratch requires a bias to action, comfort with risk, vision, perseverance, and more. Mila, as you might recall, possessed a number of these traits. But sometimes, as she found, one trait blindspot ends up overwhelming all else, and the rest of the package doesn't really matter.

I've found it interesting over time to discover that trait blindspots do tend to rear their head for entrepreneurs more than leaders who have moved up through the ranks in a traditional corporate

TABLE 3-2

Leadership traits

Leadership	Entrepreneurial
Self-awareness	Resilience
Respect	Perseverance
Compassion	Confidence
Vision	Bias to action
Communication	Owner mindset
Learning agility	Comfort with risk
Collaboration	Abundance mentality
Influence	Vision
Integrity	Passion
Courage	
Gratitude	
Resilience	

Source: "12 Essential Qualities of Effective Leadership," Center for Creative Leadership, July 3, 2024, https://www.ccl.org/articles/leading-effectively-articles/characteristics-good-leader/; Michael Lorusso, "4 Traits of an Entrepreneurial Mindset," Fleishman Center for Career and Professional Development, Binghamton University, August 27, 2024, https://careertools.binghamton.edu/blog/2024/08/27/4-traits-of-an-entrepreneurial-mindset/.

environment. The collection of traits needed to build is very different from the set of qualities required to lead. Successful leaders in established companies are often described as "well-rounded." They have filled a number of different roles along their career journey, and significant trait blindspots end up weeding out many of the contenders on the move up the hierarchy; you simply don't become CEO if you don't have the right mix of traits or learn how to adapt to your own particular set. To the extent there are weaknesses, they are known and managed around, not blindspots.

Entrepreneurs, on the other hand, succeed not because they are able to thrive through *everything* but because they are exceptional at *something*, maybe vision, maybe resilience, or maybe none of the leadership traits at all, but they have an innovative idea or an ability to execute that is so beyond the norm that people are willing to overlook their challenges. Think about the stereotypical brilliant founder with no people skills, where employees accept that he's difficult and leave him alone to do his magic. People fear pointing out the issue because of the possibility of an adverse reaction, denial, or defensiveness. Some entrepreneurs, when confronted with evidence of their gaps, may argue that others are exaggerating the impact since they are still achieving great results. There is a ceiling to growth when someone has an unaddressed trait blindspot standing in their way. Once the demands of the job shift to encompass far more than just product development and rapid growth—once the founders must become managers of people—they're exposed as fundamentally flawed CEOs. They are "spiky odd-shaped polygons," as I like to put it, and they don't fit as leaders in a more established enterprise.

When you are struggling, one of your first questions should be whether you are missing a particular trait, but the very next question should be whether one or more of your inherent traits are actually hindering you rather than helping you achieve results.

When Self-Awareness Isn't Enough

Miguel, who had founded ClassU with his best friend, Brendan, was more than happy to sit down with me one-on-one and dive deeper into the company's issues—at least once I could find time on his calendar. It seemed like he was constantly flitting from department to department, jumping in and out of meetings, pulling people into special projects, and acting like he ran the place. It wasn't that he was trying to usurp Brendan's ability to make decisions, but his intellectual curiosity and enthusiasm for learning, his excitement over the details, and his vision for what the company's product could be were making him a one-man wrecking ball when it came to the agenda laid out by the board, by Brendan, and by senior leaders throughout the organization.

There was a set of employees who were incredibly devoted to Miguel, who wanted to be on his team and continue learning from him. They were drawn to Miguel and would drop everything when he called—and he called quite often, with ideas and projects that would take valuable contributors away from their regular duties for hours, days, or even weeks. Others wouldn't be able to rely on their teams because people would be off helping Miguel instead. He would come into meetings and change the agenda, convincing people his ideas were right—which they often were. He would tell employees that the tasks others had given them weren't as important as what he needed—and they would end up agreeing and reprioritize. To them, keeping up with Miguel—and where his brilliant brain was taking him—was worth the ride. On the other hand, to leaders like the departed CMO, he was a distraction and an annoyance.

Every leader strives to cultivate the kind of people who would follow them anywhere, and Miguel had done that. Except that rather than serving the broader aims of the company, this created chaos. Miguel admitted that Brendan would sometimes have to show up at board meetings and explain to investors that they hadn't hit their objectives because Miguel had other goals in mind. The board would set a strategic direction and find out weeks later that their dictates didn't matter unless Miguel was also in agreement.

"But Brendan's good at that," Miguel told me, "and trust me, everything I'm doing is good for the company."

Miguel was at the extremes in a number of traits: extreme in the Big Five's openness to experience; extreme in his confidence and perseverance; extremely low in his accommodation. This worked well for his brilliant programming breakthroughs and product advances, but they made him ineffective in collaborating in situations where there were competing priorities. His curiosity, persistence, and bias to action really *were* superstrengths, but Miguel was blind to the possibility that they weren't always leading him in the best direction for the business, despite what he claimed. He did not see how his curiosity led to a lack of practicality; he did not see how his persistence meant he didn't know when to back down; he did not see how his bias to action resulted in the disrespectful abuse of people and company resources.

Often, my conversations with leaders are eye-opening as together we discover their blindspots. Miguel actually had a tremendous amount of self-awareness. He was completely aware that he was restless and driven, and that the elements of the product he would dive deeply into weren't necessarily the ones the board wanted people to be focused on. He acknowledged that he was guilty of wandering in and out of projects. But he did not believe he was doing anything wrong.

"I'm not stopping anyone from saying no to me and doing their job," he insisted. "If I have a better approach, I'm not serving the company to keep it to myself. But if you want to tell people they should ignore me and do the less important things they're assigned to, I'm not stopping you."

Miguel was being honest—with me, and with himself. If he had been the CEO, or looking to move back up in the leadership ranks, I would have told him that his traits were standing in his way, and that his overreliance on his strengths had become a blindspot that would keep him from being a productive team member and working effectively with the board. But Miguel didn't care. He was confident—tipping over into arrogance—that he was right, and that the company would be worse off without him. He saw no issue in continuing to pursue the projects he wanted to pursue, regardless of whether or not the investors understood.

"But for the good of the company—" I started to say, but Miguel cut me off.

"The board is worried about what's good for the company in the short term," he said. "I know that, and it's important, but I'm looking at product breakthroughs that will ensure our long-term success. I'm also looking at what's going to get me up in the morning. To keep the work interesting, I have to follow my passions and instincts. Keeping the board happy is Brendan's job. I'm trying to make sure that our products remain cutting-edge, which will make us a great company and a sustainable company, whether or not the board can see it."

The more I pushed, the more I realized—Miguel did not want to change, which meant that he was never going to. As it turned out, the trait blindspot I needed to deal with to help this company wasn't Miguel's. Miguel had self-awareness. His issues weren't blindspots, at least not once he understood that his traits were getting in the way of the company's success. Instead, they were active choices Miguel was making to be more difficult than he needed to be. Instead, the blindspots I had to tackle were Brendan's.

As Situations Change, You Must Change Too

I sat down with Brendan and explained what I'd observed. He listened attentively and validated that nothing I'd uncovered was news to him. Brendan's reaction fit with everything I'd been hearing about him from his team: He was indeed kind and thoughtful. He was measured and calm, "a real gentleman," as two different people had said, independently. And the description fit. Others had described his "bull's-eye judgment," and in fact the only place his judgment seemed to be lacking was when it came to Miguel and figuring out how to rein him in.

"You're right," he told me. "I probably do have a blindspot when it comes to Miguel." And then Brendan filled in some more of the story.

Brendan explained that ever since middle school, he had seen himself as Miguel's protector. "He never had many friends," Brendan said, "and I think it was because he was just too smart for other kids to really 'get' him. He'd become passionate about something or other, it would turn into an argument, and the other kids would walk away. He's never been in a serious romantic relationship. He's never held a job at a company he didn't create. And he's never been able to moderate his feelings to fit in. Heck, he almost failed out of Caltech because he couldn't bring himself to fulfill the humanities requirements. His adviser had to invent an independent study just for him, just to get him the credits he needed to graduate."

I could see tears welling up in the corners of Brendan's eyes. "Miguel went into a pretty major depression after college when he was kind of floundering and didn't know what to do with his life," he continued. "I was working at a consulting firm, and was not looking to start a business—but Miguel came to me with the idea, and I could see how much he needed me. Heck, I needed him too. I never would have taken the leap without him, and I'm grateful every day."

I passed Brendan a tissue and maintained eye contact, encouraging him to keep talking. "I honestly don't know what to do," he said. "There are board members who are so frustrated that they want me to fire him, but I can't do that. He's fragile, even though it doesn't seem that way. I'm actually losing sleep over it. I've fired people before—it was hard, and I waited too long almost every time—but I will not fire Miguel from his own company, I just won't."

I appreciated Brendan's honesty and explained to him what I was thinking. Just like Miguel had superstrength traits that were interfering with the company's success, I was seeing similar issues with Brendan. His traits of loyalty, responsibility, and agreeableness had served him incredibly well as the company had grown, and were continuing to serve him in his relationship with Miguel. But as the situation with Miguel had worsened, and senior leaders were leaving the company, these traits were becoming problematic at times. Though loyalty and responsibility were Brendan's superstrengths, they were keeping him from doing what needed to be done. He had a blindspot when it came to these traits, and how they were no longer serving him well. Brendan was risking his own job if the board did not see some change—and it certainly wouldn't serve Miguel if Brendan ended up being pushed out as CEO.

"Is there any kind of special project where you could direct Miguel's energy?" I asked Brendan. "Maybe something to keep him out of everyone else's way but still harness his talents for the company?"

"He won't be steered," Brendan pushed back. "And it's not like he has anything else to spend his energy on but the work he's already doing. The only thing he even thinks about besides this business is the one afternoon a week he goes back to Caltech and mentors undergrads. He loves it, actually."

This gave me an idea, and together with Brendan we came up with a plan. Brendan reached out to the university to engineer a transition that would preserve Miguel's value at the company *and* give him an opportunity that could take advantage of his amazing skills. When Caltech reached out to Miguel to offer him a chance to start his own research lab, working closely with a team of students, he went right to Brendan. "I'd love to do this, but I don't want to let the company down," he said.

They worked out an exit that allowed Miguel to stay on as a consultant, working directly with Brendan on strategy and product development without interfering with the work being done by others. And Brendan felt reassured that his excellent judgment had helped him navigate this difficult situation and allowed ClassU to dodge a bullet that would almost certainly have curtailed its success.

"Just One More Thing . . ."

Overcoming a trait blindspot is hard, because it forces you to acknowledge that the way you are wired is less than ideal for your success in a given situation. This is a challenging thing to do. Brendan was able to shift with just a bit of awareness and advice. Anneke needed more help than that. As the general counsel for a private equity firm, she was the most exceptional negotiator I had ever met. Anneke would push the CEOs of the companies her firm was acquiring on every deal point, resulting in agreements where nothing was left on the table. Within the firm, and outside of it, Anneke was known for her persuasiveness and her strategic brilliance.

I was called in by the private equity firm to work with Anneke to round out her leadership skill set beyond her obvious negotiation strengths. To that end, we embarked on sessions focused on people leadership and the softer skills she would need as a manager. After one of our sessions, Anneke's boss pulled me aside. "This may be unorthodox," he said, "but I'd like to engage you for a bit of coaching myself. I'm negotiating Anneke's next contract, and ironic as it sounds, it's not so easy being on the receiving end of her talents." He chuckled, but admitted that he really did need my help.

It felt like a bit of a conflict of interest, so I talked to Anneke and got her blessing to work openly with the two of them on the contract. At first, I would hear updates from both sides about the negotiation process. Usually they went something like this:

Anneke: "We're mostly done, but there are just a few more sticking points."

Anneke's boss: "She's torturing me over every last detail."

Just like she did in her normal course of work, Anneke couldn't resist getting the very best deal for herself. She wanted a larger bonus, more stock, all kinds of extra incentives that were atypical for the industry: percentage of deal flow revenue, added retirement benefits, extra perks. It was all on the table, and there was always one more element worth discussing. Weeks passed. The offer on the table at that point exceeded Anneke's initial expectations, but the more she got, the more she wanted to eke out every last bit of value. She couldn't stop herself.

"Every time Anneke calls me," her boss confided, "I have to pull off the road if I'm driving, because I get so angry. I swear I am ready to fire her because she won't even let us finish the contract."

Anneke's boss wanted me to get Anneke to accept the deal before things got past the point of reparation. Anneke, on the other hand, was still in no rush. She was missing the cues that her boss was at the end of his rope.

"I know I'm frustrating him by not wrapping up my contract, but I can't stop until it feels completely finished to me," Anneke admitted.

I explained to Anneke that her superstrengths—persistence, negotiation, strategy—were not helping her here. She had a blindspot when it came to those traits, and it was affecting her relationship with her boss. She needed to stop herself, but couldn't figure out how. She was never going to change who she was, but she was open to finding a way to force new *behavior*.

Knowing that both sides wanted a resolution, I got Anneke's boss to issue an ultimatum: negotiations had to stop on a certain date, and there would be no extensions. Wherever they were at that point would become a take-it-or-leave-it deal. Anneke could respect that there was a firm end date, and—after a full year of working on the contract—they did reach an agreement.

The work wasn't done, though, because the more we addressed her leadership skills, and as I talked to some of her clients, it became clear that Anneke's master negotiator superstrengths were starting to morph into toxicity in the field, too. The same frustrations Anneke's boss felt over the contract negotiation were being felt by some of the company executives who needed to negotiate with her over their purchase agreements. They felt bullied and exhausted by Anneke's insistence on pushing every deal point as far as she could. They liked Anneke; she was quite friendly and personable. But they would also regret how much she had gotten them to sacrifice, and they didn't want to return for repeat business. Better—and easier—deals were sometimes available with different private equity firms. Anneke's tough negotiations were hurting the company in the long run to a greater degree than they were helping short-term.

Anneke's blindspot was showing up at work just as it had shown up in her own contract negotiations. Just as she benefited from a deadline for her own contract, Anneke needed a forcing mechanism to stop her from pushing CEOs over the edge with her natural traits. So Anneke was told she wouldn't be part of deal closings anymore. She would get to 95 percent of a deal and then offload the finalization to her M&A lead, who would take over at the end to get everything signed. She knew she would never stop trying to get an extra edge and needed to build in a safeguard to protect her from her own instincts.

Did Anneke change? No, not really. But she had the realization that she needed external intervention to make sure that her own personal traits didn't sabotage her.

Coming to Terms with Your Traits

What do you do to figure out your own superstrengths and whether they are serving you or holding you back?

Awareness

The first thing you need to understand is who you are and what core traits define you. Fortunately, in this blindspot area more than any other, there are tests that can tease these out. Personality tests, like one to measure where you stand on the Big Five traits, do not provide the whole picture, but they can be a useful place to begin.

Looking at your results, do a gut check. In which categories are you at one extreme or the other, and how does that play out in your life? If any of these traits were overused, how might that negatively impact you? I look back at my own extreme agreeableness and how it nearly sabotaged me as an entrepreneur. Like agreeableness, consolidation and focus are seen as unmitigated virtues, but not when they impact speed, as in Esther's case. Miguel's openness to new experiences was great when his company was still finding its footing but was a huge problem when focus on the existing elements was needed. Everything can be taken to an extreme, and that's the insight we need in order to catch our trait blindspots before they become intractable problems. Looking specifically at the Big Five and how they play out in leadership scenarios, it is easy to see how being at either extreme for any of the traits can be harmful.

When it comes to neuroticism, if you are too reactive, you will be unlikely to maintain your equilibrium through the endless pressure and the ups and downs of business. You may be too unpredictable to your colleagues and subordinates. Being too calm, on the other hand, has the potential to make you appear as if you are unaffected by difficulties, and others may doubt that you are taking problems seriously enough.

As far as openness to experiences, if you are too imaginative, it becomes toxic to productivity, but if you are too conventional and cautious, you can't move at the required speed.

Pure extroverts may lack the internal focus to put in the solitary efforts that are sometimes required on the road to success, while introverts may not be able to handle the social and interpersonal demands of any career that involves interaction with others.

Being too agreeable can affect potential business gains, while being too critical can harm needed relationships.

Being too high on conscientiousness may lead to a discomfort with risk and ambiguity, while being too carefree can lead to mistakes.

Leadership traits beyond the Big Five also need to be investigated. If we think back to Marcus and his company, Aesthetics, we can ascribe a whole set of hugely positive characteristics to his behavior—tremendous perseverance, an owner mindset, a comfort with risk and failure, self-confidence, and a high level of passion. But these traits all added up to arrogance when things got tough, and an inability to self-correct.

Ask yourself the top adjectives others use to describe you, and then reflect on what happens if you modify them with the word *too*—are you *too* smart, *too* energetic, *too* selfless? These are probably things you like about yourself, but that's what makes them even more dangerous. If you are proud of these facets of yourself, you are less likely to try to extinguish them or control them. Who wants to act less smart, for example, or less careful?

You may not be able to see all of this yourself—and in fact you probably can't. Ask others to help. How do they perceive you when it comes to the Big Five and other leadership traits? How would they describe you, and, if asked directly, what do they say you are *too much* of? Do you have a trait blindspot—an overused strength or a critical gap—that needs addressing?

Action

After identifying your traits, you need to examine whether they match your current context. Within an organization, you know the landscape better than I or any other coach ever could: Do you find your traits bumping up against expectations in ways that are holding you back? Where are you consistently finding yourself struggling, and does it come back to an area where you are too much of something, or where a different trait is needed?

You might ask yourself to think about the people succeeding in your organization or your profession, and whether they embody different traits than you. Do the truly persistent individuals around you seem to be getting things done in a way that you're having trouble with? Does that mean persistence is a helpful trait here, and is that something you might be willing to grow within yourself, or might it mean you are in the wrong role?

Are there mechanisms you can put in place to guard against relying too heavily on any aspects of yourself that you are overrelying on? If, for example, you have too much of an ownership mindset, can you force delegation and outsourcing so that you mitigate your inclination to do everything yourself?

There are no universals here; as the stories in this chapter have revealed, different traits are useful in different roles. Your default responses may be perfect, or they may need some adjustment.

For Esther, whose caution ended up being a blindspot that caused her board to force her out, there could have been a three-step action plan to address the problem:

1. Recognize that your superstrength (in this case, caution) is a blindspot in your current context.

2. Ask yourself—can you shift? Do you even want to shift, or is a role where, say, speed is prized above deliberation the wrong fit? (You can swap in whichever specific blindspot you are contending with.)

3. Find a solution. Coming forward with honesty about her strengths and limitations could have prompted a discussion between Esther and the board about how to move forward productively. Perhaps she could have convinced the board that the company didn't need to move as quickly as they believed, and that her more deliberative style was a benefit in an industry prone to missteps. Perhaps she could have brought in a number two to own some of the decision-making that depended most on speed and yet still have given herself the space to focus on the company's larger strategy. There wasn't necessarily a right or wrong answer, just the opening for a discussion that could happen only once Esther recognized her blindspot. There are often solutions like this no matter what trait blindspot you are trying to manage.

In the next chapter, we turn to *emotion*. While we are usually aware of our traits, our emotions are sometimes more hidden. We don't always understand why we are responding in the way we are, yet those responses are critical to our success. We have all acted in ways we later regret because of the emotions roiling inside of us. Those blindspots are critical for so many of us to examine.

CHAPTER 4

EMOTION

ARE YOUR FEELINGS MANAGING YOU OR ARE YOU MANAGING YOUR FEELINGS?

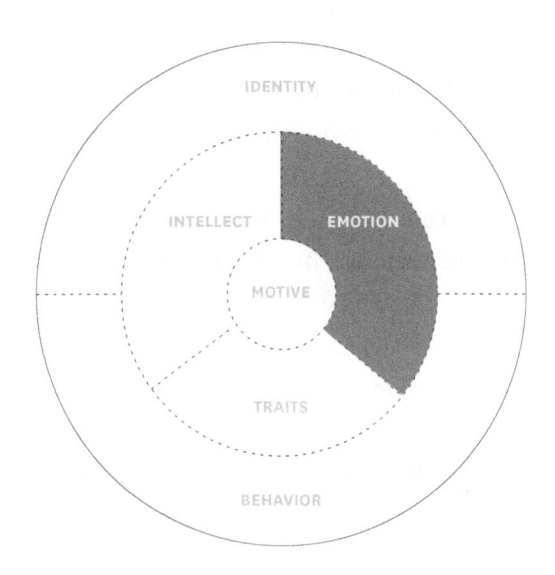

As we continue in the middle layer of awareness, we get to what we can think of as the blindspots that emerge from our heart: our emotions. *Some executives act as if they believe a good leader should never show emotion, but that couldn't be further from the truth. Beyond the fact that experiencing emotion is unavoidable, a true leader recognizes that*

emotions are data—and there is potential for this data to be effectively deployed for maximum impact. Being emotionally facile—and recognizing and addressing your emotional blindspots—is critical to success.

Kimball wasn't exactly a menacing physical presence—he looked more like a guest on a sailboat than a guy at the gym—but sometimes he spoke with a coldness that made me uncomfortable to be alone with him. He wasn't always discomfiting; he was smooth when he needed to be. But in his tiny conference room, with his chair blocking the door so there was no easy way to leave, I felt surprisingly nervous as he went on a long rant. "Those suits are not going to take the company away from me, I promise you that, Marty," he said with alarming intensity. "I'm the only one who can lead this company, and we both know it."

He seemed ready to explode, to leap across the desk and squeeze the life from me, and although he kept his hands to himself, I wasn't entirely confident in my safety. In my time doing emergency psychiatric consultations, I was trained to always have an exit path; I hadn't thought that would be relevant to my work coaching executives, until now.

I had no doubt that Kimball believed what he said, but after just a few days interviewing him and his colleagues, I wasn't terribly sure he was right. The board of Platforma—a startup in the financial-technology space that had recently raised a series B round led by four of the top VC firms in Silicon Valley—had called me in, but they were not quite certain what they wanted me to do. Suddenly the confident, commanding CEO they thought they had gotten into business with wasn't returning their calls. They wanted input on the company's strategy, and Kimball wasn't sharing it. They wanted reports, and Kimball didn't seem to have them. They wanted to be included in the decision-making, and Kimball seemed hell-bent on keeping them out.

This wasn't at all what the board had anticipated. Kimball, they believed, was a trustworthy player who had cofounded Platforma along with Simon, a rock star among a niche group of computer scientists, Simon's reputation having been built on the extraordinary work he had done at one of the big tech giants. I was told that when Simon left to become an entrepreneur, he recognized that he was never going to be the business guy. It didn't interest him, and he knew he needed a partner to handle that part of the job. When he found Kimball, Simon quickly ceded all power to him, except when it came to the technology itself, for which Simon had gathered a small team of engineers and decamped to Salt Lake City, away from the bustle of Platforma's San Francisco headquarters.

On paper, or at least the papers I was given access to, this plan had been a triumphant success, and the company was in great shape. Simon's tech was cutting-edge, the funding round had been extraordinary, and the business was growing. Which made Kimball's antagonistic turn all the more baffling. The board had not set out to make Kimball their enemy; everything had been friendly, until it wasn't. They were perplexed, even vexed. "What he talks about as strategy isn't a strategy," a board member told me, "so we need you to convince Kimball to open up."

I wasn't having any success getting Kimball to open up. I wasn't even sure why he was angry. "There is not a problem," Kimball kept telling me. "Everything is good, and I'm not going to let the board replace me."

No one had been talking about replacing him.

But if Kimball remained this defensive, this paranoid, this angry, then they were going to have no choice but to send him packing. As I walked the halls at HQ, it was clear that people were reflecting Kimball's demeanor. Everyone was cordial, but cold and uncommunicative. When I had first met Kimball earlier in the week, I found myself waiting outside a conference room where I couldn't help but overhear him berating an underling—in front of perhaps a half-dozen other employees. I couldn't make out the words, but the tone was unmistakable, and what I heard, plus my own frightening experience, added up to an executive who was either not in control of his emotions or who had, for some reason, decided that he wanted to seem as scary as he could.

Expectations can be high at a young, growing company like this, and CEOs can and do get frustrated, but there is never a good reason for a leader to lose control and disparage an employee, especially in front of others. Incidents like the one I was half-hearing inevitably reverberate throughout an organization. Trust evaporates. Who would ever admit a mistake or show weakness if they thought a scene like this would be the result?

The employees I spoke with expressed loyalty to Kimball and to the company, but it was loyalty driven by fear—which is unusual to see, especially in this stage of growth, with fewer than fifty employees and the business model still developing. Companies like this are typically filled with early-career professionals, eager and mission-driven, with energy to spare and something to prove. The hours are long, the halls filled with easy banter and casual dress, the CEO right there in the trenches with everyone else.

Platforma was different, except for the long hours. There was silence in the space. Eye contact was limited. And the button-downs and khakis were unusually formal for the environment. It felt more like a high-strung corporate law firm than any of the dozens of other companies at this stage I'd previously worked with.

I asked Kimball about the culture, and he told me he'd always imagined running a tight ship if he got the chance to lead. And about dressing down one of his employees? "Look, business is tough," he told me. "You have to threaten sometimes, get in people's faces. Only the strong survive, Marty. Maybe *you* weren't strong enough."

He laughed off his dig at me, and I did too, but I can't say it engendered any warm feelings for the man. When it came to actual information about the business, Kimball stonewalled me the same way he was stonewalling the board. "Proprietary info," he kept repeating, hoping I would give up, I suppose. But the board didn't want me to give up. They suggested I talk to Kimball's cofounder, Simon, and wondered if he might actually be more suited to the CEO role and open to the board engineering a coup.

I flew out to Salt Lake City hoping to find a leader, or at least a cofounder who wasn't plagued with the same worrying set of emotional issues.

Emotional Blindspots: The Five Stages of Emotional Mastery

Kimball was suffering from a set of emotional blindspots driven by a lack of emotional mastery. He was blind to his own emotions and those of others, and to how to use emotion strategically in the workplace. To uncover these types of emotional blindspots, in ourselves or others, it is useful to understand the five stages of emotional mastery and see where emotional awareness or control may be lacking. I should add, before we get to the stages themselves, that mastery does not mean perfection. Each of us can surely point to moments in our lives when our emotions overtook us and caused us to say or do things that we didn't understand at the time and later regretted. Many of us have reacted with too much emotion at work—crying when we know we shouldn't be; screaming when we know we shouldn't be; making cutting remarks driven by unstoppable feelings, not logic; making impulsive decisions driven by emotional instincts that turned out to be entirely wrong. What keeps these from being blindspots is that we recognize them—ideally in the moment or, if not, shortly after the fact. We can't let those moments pass by without looking deeper into ourselves and our pasts; we want to use them to understand our emotions rather than remain blind to them and their underlying causes.

The work I do as a coach is very different from psychotherapy, but I mention our pasts because it is not the case that the past is always irrelevant to the situations in which we find ourselves struggling in the workplace. In the course of our conversations, countless clients have revealed emotional moments from long ago that lingered in their minds years later. Those moments could generate surprising levels of emotional intensity when they came up in our conversations, even if it had been years or decades since the particular incident. They would start crying, for instance, and often not be able to articulate why. It's remarkable that feelings can be detached from time, so powerful that they overwhelm the reality of current circumstances; suddenly, as a memory comes flooding back, you're no longer the fifty-year-old CEO but rather the eight-year-old child getting scolded by your father.

To that end, I remember interviewing a CEO who was telling me how he needed to manage an upcoming conversation with his board: the company had missed its revenue targets, and the CEO knew the board was going to pressure him again about replacing the chief revenue officer. He suddenly got quiet, his eyes opened wide, and he said to me, "Wow, that was weird. I just flashed back to my father yelling at me for taking the car without his permission."

Beyond our own emotions, it is critical to understand how the things we do will affect others. Leaders know that it's inevitable that sometimes people will react to what we do or say in ways that surprise us and are entirely inconsistent with our intent. Sometimes this is because others are struggling with their own emotions; sometimes it is because we fail to understand the emotional impact of our actions or because others may be experiencing something different than we are.

When I was CEO, I knew well before everyone else that we were going to be selling the business. I had time to deal with the inevitability of it. But our team—two hundred employees by the time we sold—hadn't been on that same roller coaster of ups and downs as I had. They had no idea we were already in talks to sell. The annual holiday party for employees and their families, a big deal at the company, was the night after my partner and I flew back from what we thought were our final negotiations (although that particular deal ended up falling through and we ultimately sold to a different buyer). We were wrestling with sadness, pride, happiness, all of the emotions—and also the reality that our news, once revealed, was going to change the lives of

EMOTION

everyone at that party, some changing roles, some perhaps losing their jobs.

I needed to put my emotions aside and be the leader people expected at a holiday party, not the one sitting on potential news I wasn't yet allowed to share. There was a huge difference between my emotional state and theirs. I needed to understand that and manage my emotions to do my job effectively. Had I been suffering in that moment from a lack of awareness of my emotions (one emotional blindspot) or from a lack of empathy for the emotions of others (another emotional blindspot), it may have created a significant problem. I needed to be able to juggle what I was actually feeling—excitement about selling the company—with an understanding that my employees didn't know anything about what was going on and simply wanted to have a fun party to celebrate the year.

Emotional blindspots are so impactful because emotions are the currency of interpersonal relationships. People who are emotionally open and aware are attractive to us and make us want to be around them. Similarly, people who are emotionally closed-off or who fail to connect on an emotional level cause us to be cautious and hold back. Facility with emotions is necessary to build and maintain relationships—not to mention that we pick up a tremendous amount of information through nonverbal cues. People forget the words we say and remember the emotional content.

The psychologist and writer Daniel Goleman became famous in the mid-1990s for his book *Emotional Intelligence*, and his work defining EQ, or emotional quotient.[1] This term has become ubiquitous in the corporate world and effectively defines the emotional and interpersonal skills necessary for success. Business leaders who are highly aware of their own emotions and the emotions of others—in other words, leaders who lack emotional blindspots—can use that awareness to develop strong relationships, immense trust, and loyal followers. True masters can strategically use their understanding of people's emotions to achieve greater success for themselves and their teams. On the opposite end of the spectrum, those who are blind to their own emotions and to the emotions of others suffer, especially when situations get stressful or they need to rely on others. It is often said that people get hired for their hard skills but get promoted for their soft skills. Being in tune with your emotional life and the emotions of those around you is highly correlated with moving up the ranks in an organization and achieving success.

There are five stages of emotional development that an ideal leader must master with sophistication and elegance. Failure to recognize your struggle at any of these stages indicates an emotional blindspot that can sabotage leadership and performance:

- *Awareness of personal emotional bandwidth.* Some people have a broad range of emotions that they experience and understand, from delight to empathy to anxiety to humility to doubt to contempt to disgust and perhaps hundreds more, while others live much more limited emotional lives, where they mostly feel one way or another: happy or sad, glad or mad, relaxed or anxious. Those who don't experience the broad range of emotions themselves often don't realize that these more subtle emotions even exist. They are unable to appreciate deeper feelings and see any emotion in the workplace as merely getting in the way. These leaders may act in ways they believe are logical and direct, and may be utterly baffled when others react emotionally.

- *Awareness of your personal emotions.* We may experience a broad range of emotions, but if we don't understand how and when those emotions are showing up in our behavior, we are suffering from a different kind of emotional blindspot. Not recognizing that we are angry, and that this is manifesting in our behavior, for example, is an emotional blindspot, one that made Kimball such a challenging client to work with. I remember I once said to him: "You seem angry." And he tersely replied, "I. Am. Not. Angry. I'm just a bit frustrated. No big deal." But no matter his words, his face turned red and he clenched his fists and it was very clear to anyone watching that it was a big deal indeed, and he was, by any definition, angry. Others can often read our emotions even when we can't, and our lack of awareness can persist even when feelings that are obvious to others are brought to our attention.

- *Emotional self-regulation.* Being unaware that you are not managing your emotions effectively is another potential emotional blindspot. In an ideal scenario we should be able to control how we react even in stressful circumstances and also deploy our emotions to influence others, turbocharging our ability to achieve objectives. It would have been only partly sufficient for Kimball to have controlled his anger and reined in his tendencies toward intimidation and menace. To fully demonstrate an ability to emotionally self-regulate, a leader needs to use their emotions to move others. Imagine a leader who strategically demonstrates anger at a competitor during a companywide meeting in order to motivate her employees to race to meet a deadline, or who knows that some added kindness and warmth to a colleague struggling with something in her personal life will yield benefits in their working relationship. This isn't manipulation; it is being aware of your feelings and expressing them to maximum effect—full control, as opposed to a blindness to how we are using our emotions.

- *Awareness of the emotions of others.* Beyond knowing your own emotions, you need to develop a level of empathy that lets you "read the room." The failure to recognize the emotions of others, especially in fraught moments, is another type of emotional blindspot. Kimball did not recognize the fear he instilled in his employees, even as it was obvious to others. He simply couldn't see things from their perspective and understand how his behaviors were affecting others on an emotional level.

- *Awareness of the downstream impact of your emotions.* This is the "chess game" aspect of emotional mastery, the strategic ability to think several steps ahead, anticipating others' emotional reactions and then adjusting your actions as needed. Even if you become skilled at managing emotions in yourself and in others in the moment, you may have a blindspot if you can't see how those emotional moments may play out down the road. For example, a leader may recognize that while demonstrating anger at their competitor at a companywide meeting—as discussed above—might inspire short-term hard work to meet a deadline, in the long run to be seen as someone who gets angry might not be great for team morale. Far better, perhaps, to reveal that anger only to a core group of internal leaders, who can then use their own emotional mastery to get their individual teams to perform.

Not everyone proceeds through these stages in exactly this order, or necessarily completes their development in one stage before moving onto the next, but the stages are roughly ordered from basic to more complex, and generally if people achieve competence in the final stage, they have already mastered the ones prior. The failure to recognize your gaps in these five elements defines your emotional blindspots, and only the leaders who excel across all five demands are fully capable when it comes to the emotional domain.

It is accurate to take away from this discussion that the most successful leaders in the emotional domain aren't just aware of emotions but of how they use emotional techniques—drawing on people's empathy, anger, and joy, for instance—to motivate and inspire.

On the other hand, when someone suffers from an emotional blindspot, it can destroy any attempt to act strategically and can doom a leader even if they are otherwise doing everything else right, as the executive in the next story eventually realized.

More Than Just an Empty Suit

Vincente had risen to become CFO for one of the largest consumer snack brands in the world. He seemed to be the complete package: honest, likable, friendly, and well-spoken, with good judgment and capable decision-making. Which is why an industry competitor, Yum Bar, was trying to poach him to become its CEO and inject fresh energy into the company.

He took the job, and within twelve months after Vincente started his first CEO gig, the board chair called me. "Something isn't clicking," she said, "but we're not sure what it is. Everyone seems to like him, but some of our best team members are starting to leave the company. Can you help us figure out why?"

I showed up at Yum Bar headquarters, and Vincente offered me one of the company's newest snacks. I found him pleasant and engaging. He looked the part of CEO, neatly groomed and dressed nicely in a well-tailored suit. He was friendly to people we passed in the halls, and they seemed friendly in response. We went to an executive team meeting, which was ordinary, if a bit uninspiring. There were no immediate red flags—and, certainly, I felt more welcomed there than I had in the conference room with Kimball.

But when I spoke to some of the executives in the meeting afterward, they were surprisingly negative. "It was a waste of time," one told me. "I didn't even bother bringing up my most important issues, because I knew nothing would get done."

"Vincente says all the right words," someone else shared, "but I never get a sense of what he's actually feeling, so I don't know if what I'm working on is important to him."

"We spend so much time on issues that we all agree on," a third executive told me, "that we never get to the hard stuff. I leave these meetings totally dispirited about the state of the company. It's like we're just going through the motions."

A full 360-degree evaluation painted a remarkably consistent picture. "I don't feel like I know him." "I don't really have a clue what upsets or excites him." "We talk, but I never feel like he's truly listening and understanding; if I had a problem, I don't know if he would care enough to have my back." "If I could use one word to describe him, it would be *distant*."

Vincente's blindspots were clear: he lacked an emotional repertoire himself, and lacked an awareness of the emotions of others. And even though he had perfectly reasonable emotional self-control, his failure to read the room and connect with his team was making success impossible.

When dealing with someone who has an emotional blindspot, it is hard if not impossible to convince them that dealing with emotions is "actual work" and that emotions are important. One of the most consistent research findings on executives who take on new roles is that when you ask them what they would have done differently in their first hundred days, they say that they would have prioritized getting to deeply know the key people rather than jumping right into the work. It is harder to get things done when you don't know and understand people and they don't know and understand you.

But Vincente didn't get that. He had a lot of useful skill sets: he was analytical, results-driven, accountable, and strategically aligned with the board. But his emotional blindspots made people feel unheard, unappreciated, and unmotivated.

This is why his team members were leaving the company. Vincente wasn't an abusive leader like Kimball—far from it—but he was an emotionally shallow one, without the ability to connect, and that made good, emotionally intelligent people frustrated and not want to work for him.

When I brought this analysis to Vincente, he listened carefully. "I know none of this is good," he said, "but what am I supposed to do? I can't read their minds, so if they don't tell me these things, how am I supposed to know?"

He was concerned about the feedback, but he didn't know how to fix it. "I don't want to run bad meetings," he told me. "If people aren't getting their needs met, something needs to change." As a coach, I knew that for someone with so little emotional understanding, it was going to be nearly impossible to give him the *awareness* he was missing, but I could work with his *behavior* and hope that would be enough.

As with many blindspots, even if the deeper layers don't change, behavior can change, and that can have a tremendous impact on how others perceive you and on your ultimate success. The question was whether Vincente could change his behavior enough to be the leader his coworkers needed, even if he didn't connect with why emotions were important. He needed some tools to manage around his gaps.

We put together a behavior change plan: first, Vincente needed to let others run meetings, others who would be able to respond to social cues and move the agenda in ways that would be useful for the entire team. He could still give a CEO's report, but otherwise I wanted him to take a back seat, literally. I told Vincente not to sit at the head of the table. I also suggested he rotate who runs the meeting so that he would hear how a range of other leaders would manage the conversations. I helped him to designate his CHRO as the meeting facilitator, whose job it would be to monitor the emotional tone of the meeting.

I hoped that by watching others, Vincente might pick up on some of their emotional skills himself, but over time it became clear that this was just not an ability Vincente had. When I dug further, I learned that Vincente's emotional blindspots affected far more than the internal team meetings. His people weren't loyal to him, or even interested in how he felt about their work, because they had no relationship. He started having one-on-one meetings with his direct reports, but the interactions were so bland that both he and his team began canceling them.

Relationships with important customers had also started to suffer, and he was missing opportunities to engage productively with government regulators. He found the company being left out of the kinds of important stakeholder discussions the previous CEO had always been invited to.

The board, while recognizing the progress Vincente had made, began to hear comments from big customers, who felt they weren't getting adequate attention from Vincente. One frustrating call from a key strategic account—a complaint about a pricing mistake that Vincente hadn't responded to with sufficient emotional concern, it seemed—pushed the board to action. They replaced Vincente after less than eighteen months on the job. His emotional blindspots doomed him, and it was not enough for me to try to tell him what to do. He needed to understand it himself because I couldn't be by his side at every meeting giving him instructions.

Vincente's story illustrates that it is not enough to have a social skill set. You can be a great storyteller and a pleasant colleague and perfectly polite at a cocktail party, but if that's as deep as it goes, you're in trouble. Vincente had functioned quite well in roles that allowed him to use his strengths and ignore the emotional side of things. When he was CFO, no one was necessarily expecting him to build external relationships beyond what he could do with his social niceties, or to engage with customers and the community, or to motivate a team. He needed to make sensible decisions and manage the financial portfolio, which he was entirely capable of doing. But when his portfolio expanded to sophisticated people leadership, he failed entirely. This also, of course, points to a blindspot on the part of the board—who hired him for his professional skill set and neglected evaluating his emotional facility.

Emotions as One More Type of Data

Vincente's avoidance of emotion doomed him. If he could have validated his customer's feelings rather than move past them, he might have saved his job. Consider another example: imagine your direct report walks into your office and asks, "How are the sales numbers?" You answer in a logical, rational way—you provide the data she asked for—and she leaves. Later, you hear that your entire team is upset and anxious, and worried about layoffs. But you didn't mention anything about layoffs. You ignore the gossip and continue to focus on the work. After all, there are no planned layoffs, and even if the sales numbers were lower than expected, you know that the best way to improve the situation is to make more sales, not coddle people's feelings. Your team shouldn't be assuming there's a problem if you haven't said anything, right? Their fears are on them, not on you.

Are you being a good leader in this situation?

The answer is no. The initial mistake was the result of an emotional blindspot. You answered the question about sales numbers without thinking first about the tone of voice in which it was being asked—or reflecting on why the question was being asked at all. Was there anxiety, hope, fear, concern? A good leader would first acknowledge whatever emotions were coming through, and perhaps then ask, to be sure, "Why are you inquiring?"

A good leader would also think through the emotional consequences of the answer. Will it be surprising in a positive way or a negative way? Do you need to offer reassurances? Surely you should offer some context and try to manage the emotions that will undoubtedly emerge. People have thoughts, ideas, and feelings independent of what you directly tell them—thoughts, ideas, and feelings you can't necessarily control, but that doesn't mean you can't and shouldn't try.

A blindspot for many of us is to assume logic should rule above all else in the workplace, but that's a flawed assumption. Emotions are present in every interaction, even if we don't announce them out loud. To believe, or pretend, that they are not a factor is a major emotional blindspot. This is hard for some leaders to hear, especially when they have been taught to value results and data above all. One way I've successfully convinced leaders of the role emotions play is to suggest that emotions are another kind of data. Executives who don't take emotion into consideration are leaving out an entire data set. I ask these leaders how they might rework a particular course of action if they added the emotional data to their analysis.

Without accounting for emotions, leaders seem like "Teflon executives." They don't show any emotion, positive or negative, and think that equals effectiveness. They don't celebrate wins, don't recognize the need for emotional bonding when times are tough, and don't show empathy and understanding when others are struggling. They assume there is nothing under the surface for others because, for them, there may not be. Or at least those feelings may be too difficult and ambiguous to acknowledge. Alternatively, they may feel that whatever is there should not affect business.

Some people even consider emotions dangerous. Why dangerous? Some people are afraid that emotions will take a conversation in an unproductive direction. They worry that they aren't prepared to handle an emotional response and that the resulting interaction will spin out of control, with adverse consequences that they would be responsible for causing. They worry that if they acknowledge and uncover emotion, they won't be prepared to deal with the aftermath—in other words, it's best not to stir the hornet's nest. This is not the right way to approach leadership.

Because my background is as a psychologist and I trained first as a therapist, I am comfortable with emotion and, when I became a coach, I knew that true progress could only be made when leaders made emotion part of the equation. (Surprisingly, a lot of executive coaching is ineffective because it ignores emotions or treats them as unnecessary or counterproductive in the workplace—these coaches treat coaching as advice only. But advice is worthless if it ignores your emotional state.) "High maintenance" employees are seen as negative presences when in fact they can be strong contributors—as long as they are skilled at managing and regulating their broad emotional range.

Good leaders overcome the please-no-emotions blindspot by embracing emotions with sophistication and being strategic about their use. What employee doesn't appreciate a warm inquiry about how their family is doing, or a note of congratulations after a job well done? If someone experiences, say, a death in the family, a good leader isn't just tolerant of that employee taking time off, but in fact uses it as a moment to deepen their emotional connection, reaching out to check in, assuring them that they don't need to worry about anything at work until they're ready. These moments of outreach and connection—done well—are what create loyal relationships and the bonds that will keep people motivated and inspired to do their best. In nearly all of my engagements with successful leaders, I hear a story like this: "When my mom died, the CEO not only called and told me he didn't want me thinking about anything work-related, but he sent a personal card. That meant a lot. My family still talks about how great my CEO is."

True emotional sophistication couples an openness to emotion with a compassionate ability to set boundaries around it. Emotionally skilled leaders respectfully honor the emotions of those around them and believe that the emotional state of their employees is equally as important as their own emotional state. They treat others in this respect exactly as they would want to be treated, with kindness and an acknowledgment of their shared humanity.

How to do this? A leader should be transparent about the things they are struggling with emotionally, and should personally rally employees and support services when a team member is having a crisis. Everyone at the company will remember a moment when a CEO shares what a difficult weekend he had, breaking down when describing a serious accident involving his child, for example, or when the EVP of operations hears that one of her direct reports suffered a house fire and arranges for temporary housing, meals, and donated furniture to replace what was lost.

Looking for Emotional Connection in Salt Lake City

I wasn't sure what to expect when I left Kimball in San Francisco and met Simon and his engineers in Utah. Kimball was frustrated that I was even going. He told me that Simon was "an idiot," "a loser," and, most alarmingly, "a drug addict" who wouldn't be able to tell me a thing about the company. "I know why the board is sending you out there," he said. "And if you end up thinking Simon would be a better CEO than me, well, that would just be proof that you don't know a thing about tech companies."

Trust me, I liked Kimball just as much as you do.

Simon, in comparison, was a joy to be around, an open and easily excited engineer who couldn't wait to walk me through the company's technology and show off his ability to make me a terrific tuna sandwich.

Simon's team loved him and was excited to continually improve the company's tech. It all seemed idyllic—until I got Simon alone. Simon was warm and engaging, and wanted to help, but it was not long before I could see that he had no idea how to run a company. More to the point, he had no deep interest in his company's business strategy—it's why he was in Salt Lake City in the first place, to get away from the hubbub of headquarters. He was excited about his company, but lacked curiosity beyond the technical challenges, and didn't have all that much to say about his business partner, Kimball, though he acknowledged that he would run the company with a different attitude, certainly. But tech was Simon's passion; running a business was an uninteresting necessity he'd rather not engage with.

With a different pair of cofounders, this situation might have worked. As it was, it did not. Simon was not so much a leader as he was a playmate. He, and the entire tech team, had the energy of fourteen-year-olds committed to winning an endless game of Dungeons & Dragons. They worked late into the night fueled by pizza and beer. They hung out together on weekends. They barely had a life outside of work—and when problems came up, Simon shrugged his shoulders and trusted his people to solve them.

In terms of his emotional depth, he was available at a friendly level and superficially aware of how other people were feeling, but he preferred to avoid emotions rather than engage with them. While Kimball was unable to regulate his emotions, it was unclear whether Simon experienced emotions at any level of depth. He was happy, sure, but I couldn't find any emotional words to describe him beyond that.

Simon deferred questions about the business to Kimball, and his team knew better than to bother trying to reach out, so their questions usually went unanswered. They were happy enough when things were going well, but as employees they were a bit at sea, disconnected from the company they worked for, unsure of how to add value or how the business was even doing.

Of course, there was no mutual trust between Simon and Kimball, or any real interest in building it from either one. Simon and Kimball hardly talked, and when they did, nothing meaningful was said. Simon was aware that Kimball ran the company differently than he would have, but he did not feel entitled to challenge Kimball, nor did he entertain any idea how he *would* challenge him. He preferred not to think about it. The board had engaged Simon to talk about their misgivings with Kimball, but Simon had used these meetings to ask about the product and came away with lists of new product features to build and no point of view on the alignment between Kimball and the board.

This is not to say the board didn't like Simon, because they did—the board in fact loved Simon because he was making real progress with the technology in ways that could lead to significant breakthroughs, and he was doing so in a hard-working, creative, and joyful way. He was receptive to the board's ideas and strategy; he liked being part of the team and was happy to engage. The problem was that he wasn't a leader or a strategist and had no interest in becoming one.

This was why he had needed Kimball in the first place, and why, even though Kimball was clearly a terrible leader, a coup to put Simon in as CEO wasn't the right move for the board. Both Kimball and Simon had fundamental blindspots in how they dealt with emotion. We've already talked about Kimball's blindspots with self-regulation and awareness of his own emotions and the emotions of others. Simon was unaware of the range of emotions, unaware of his own emotions—incapable of communicating any feelings he may have had beyond excitement about the technology—and completely unaware how to strategically use emotions or what the downstream effects would be. While he himself was emotionally regulated, he was not deploying his emotions in any kind of useful way.

Simon was unaware that his hands-off leadership was making the employees under him feel anxious about the future of the company and unsure where they stood. And he certainly wasn't trying to use emotions to motivate behavior. Indeed, he was doing the opposite, trying to avoid emotions and unwilling to acknowledge feelings about anything at all—making it impossible to ever have the honest and productive conversations with Kimball that would have been needed to put the company back on track.

One of the biggest problems I recognized with both Kimball and Simon was that they had no relationship with each other independent of the company. This is a huge problem for cofounders who find themselves in arranged marriages like this, which are reasonably common in new companies. You often end up with the innovative engineer-type who has an idea and builds a technology, but needs an entrepreneurial partner on the business, financial, or sales side to make it all work as a company. They—and investors—imagine that the complementary skill sets will lead to success, but the emotional piece of the puzzle is set aside and ignored, or actively discouraged. We assume that in success, these things will work out, but fail to recognize that success is very hard, and the road to success is made much more difficult when there isn't a positive relationship to build on, mutual trust and respect, and a genuine warmth for each other. Add the high-stress environment, with existential risk around every corner, which would test any relationship, and the need for a real bond becomes even clearer. This closeness cannot be manufactured, and while sometimes you can luck into a situation where cofounders do like each other and grow to make the relationship work over time, in many cases you end up with situations like Kimball and Simon's, where indifference grows into dislike and eventually the relationship falls completely apart.

In the traditional corporate world, there is sometimes an attempt at co-CEOs, which leads to similar issues. There are all sorts of political and skill-related reasons why co-CEOs get chosen, but the relationship piece is not given the attention it deserves. Co-CEOs must have that preexisting bond and be able to trust and depend on each other—and emotional blindspots can hamstring their ability to maintain the relationship and grow as a team. They need to be able to resolve differences behind closed doors and either present a unified front or use conflict strategically as a driver for productivity.

At Platforma, Simon was choosing not to engage emotionally, but that wasn't really a solution to the company's issues, just a coping mechanism. He assumed that because he knew he was not going to be the right leader for the company, his obligation as cofounder was to stick to his area of expertise and ignore the rest. He felt he didn't have to think hard about Kimball's effect on the culture and on the people, since that wasn't his domain. Kimball instead needed a strong co-founder to rein him in and help him keep his emotions in check—and Simon was not going to be that guy.

I knew that I did not have an easy answer for the board. The two men didn't work well together, for sure, but it was just as clear to me that neither should be the leader on his own. Was there a solution? Could I train either of them to correct for his emotional blindspots?

If you recognize yourself as a Kimball or a Simon, you will either need to do some work on your emotional mastery or figure out a way to pair up with someone who has tremendous skill in this area—and defer to them when it comes to all things emotional.

The Power of Getting It Right

For every Kimball and Simon, there is a Lauren, whom we can use to demonstrate what it looks like when you avoid emotional blindspots and achieve mastery. Lauren was not an original founder of VR Box, a virtual-reality startup, but was brought in as CEO by the board, replacing one of the founders, to help shepherd the company toward an IPO. Like Kimball, Lauren was an experienced executive. Unlike Kimball, Lauren was not plagued by emotional dysregulation or a set of emotional blindspots. Rather, she was a balanced, emotionally intelligent leader who impressed me from the moment I met her.

Lauren herself, not her board, reached out to me after nine months on the job. "I want to be as effective as possible," she told me, "so I want a full 360. I want to understand my gaps and have you create a report that I can bring to the board to justify my asks when we next review my compensation package." Strategically, Lauren sensed that an outside perspective would improve her case for an increase. She trusted that my observations would be positive—and knew I would be found credible by the board since they had referred her to me—so she was happy to give me full access to herself and her team.

This could have been a fraught situation, with a CEO coming in and taking the reins from a founder. The company had initially been built by three engineers. One had already realized the business world wasn't for him and moved onto other pursuits (while keeping equity in the company). One had gotten excited by a new idea and agreed, in exchange for a board seat, to move on to start his next company. The third, Geoffrey, was the one who had preceded Lauren as CEO and also had a board seat. I expected that when I talked to him, he would be very negative about Lauren. After all, she had been brought in to replace him.

Instead, I got an instant glimpse into just how emotionally aware Lauren was: Geoffrey described her in glowing terms, explaining how she had won his support during the interview process by telling Geoffrey that she was reluctant to take the job if he didn't stay on. Lauren convinced him that they could work well together, and that his involvement would be comforting to many employees. She wanted him to remain a senior executive at the company during the transition and beyond to help make it all run more smoothly for her, giving her the institutional knowledge she needed and helping her get up to speed on how to effect change at VR Box.

It was incredibly savvy of Lauren to value Geoffrey's experience and want him to stay on the team—but to have the emotional tools to pull it off and make him excited to cooperate was truly impressive. In doing so, she demonstrated a real sensitivity to other people's emotions (the fourth stage of mastery).

"Once the board told me I was out," Geoffrey revealed to me, "I was so ready to move on, but Lauren really tried to understand what had made me love the company and was committed to carving out the perfect role for me."

Lauren told me that it was about more than just getting the benefit of his guidance; she understood there were people at the company and outside who looked up to Geoffrey tremendously, and that keeping him in the fold would demonstrate to them that this was a new regime that would honor the past and value their contributions. She was afraid that if he angrily left, many valued contributors would follow him—and she had no interest in seeing that happen. Her deft reading of the situation helped lead her to a series of decisions that seemed very likely to pay off in the future. Here, she showed a strategic grasp of the downstream effects of emotions (the fifth stage of mastery), understanding the long-term message she would be sending.

Lauren acknowledged that she knew other leaders might feel intimidated to have their predecessor—especially a cofounder of the company—hanging around, but she trusted that she could manage the situation. She also felt that she would be able to put aside whatever feelings she had about wanting to be considered the company savior and sole hero (showing an awareness and control of her own emotions, the second and third stages of mastery).

In meeting with Lauren's senior executive team, I realized that the diversity of the company's leadership, on pretty much any dimension I could think of, was remarkable. Many executives fall into the trap of hiring people just like themselves, in terms of age, functional expertise, personality, and other characteristics, because those are the kinds of people they feel most comfortable around. Lauren saw value in filling her team with people as different as possible, with a range of perspectives, and knew she had the emotional dexterity to manage the inevitable conflicts that would emerge. (This was an indication that she respected and understood the wide range of emotion, the first stage of mastery.)

There were people new to the industry whom she had brought in as outsiders, and others who had deep industry knowledge. There were people she had brought in from her former companies, loyal to her, and others she had decided to keep from the previous regime, and still others she had gone out and hired fresh to fill gaps. There were people of all cultures, identities, and educational backgrounds, and this was done deliberately to get the broadest range of views incorporated into her decision-making.

I asked Lauren if she was worried about factions developing—the people loyal to her versus those who were loyal to the original founders, for instance—and she dismissed my concerns immediately, confident that she had the right people in place and could manage through any conflicts. Indeed, she expected her direct reports to manage through the conflicts themselves and embrace the diversity of thought, experience, and decision-making that existed among the leadership team rather than fight against it. To that end, I noted that there were few emotional gaps among her key leaders. The one commonality across the people she hired, almost without exception, was that they were all emotional masters like she was, and that she would simply not let someone with emotional blindspots be promoted to a senior level in the company.

I said *almost* without exception, because there were in fact two exceptions, and one of Lauren's biggest challenges was in figuring out what to do with those two people, whom she had inherited from her predecessor. One was her head of marketing, who would typically have been counseled out due to what was seen by everyone as a lack of senior executive experience. But Lauren recognized strong emotional intelligence in the woman—and an eagerness to learn and improve—and decided that she was trainable. Lauren invested time and energy into growing her as a leader, and within a year she was winning the company marketing awards and becoming a star.

The other was the head of finance, who was smart and well-liked but resistant to training and had blindspots regarding his own emotions and the emotional reactions of others. His resistance to getting better was incompatible with becoming a member of Lauren's leadership team, but Lauren worried that losing a well-liked executive would hurt morale, so she deftly hired someone above him, who had public company experience and experience with the IPO process, keeping the head of finance at the VP level but framing the situation as a career learning opportunity in such a way that he didn't see it as a demotion.

Because of Lauren's facility with emotions, people in the company adored her and saw her as powerful and decisive even though she was not someone with a big personality. She was appropriately social, but she did not command a room in the way we might imagine a charismatic leader doing. Nevertheless, the goodwill she built one-on-one and in small groups made it possible for her to exert tremendous positive influence even without all of the traits that one might associate with leadership.

Lauren spent significant time coaching her senior leadership team and invested a lot of resources into growing them as leaders; this ended up paying off both in terms of their loyalty to her and in their effectiveness, allowing her to focus on strategic issues rather than personnel problems. A diverse team with emotional mastery allows for constructive conflict. Team meetings are productive, and difficult issues get resolved efficiently with a feeling of interdependence and mutual accountability.

More than any other leader I worked with, Lauren had an excellent handle on the strengths and weaknesses of her team members, to the point where it was clear she hardly needed my analysis of them at all. There was one moment in my time working with her that really crystallized her emotional strength. At a board meeting, she and Geoffrey got into a rare disagreement, and he made some comments that Lauren felt were inappropriately harsh. Board meetings are rarely the right time to air grievances, and in this case Geoffrey really did seem to cross a line.

Lauren could have demanded that Geoffrey give up his operating role in the company and stopped listening to his counsel. She had enough credibility with the rest of the board that I believe they would have backed her up if she asked. But she chose not to react in the moment, and not even to react in the aftermath. She reflected on it and realized that her best strategic move was to ignore it and let Geoffrey grapple with what to do with his outburst, which he did—and in fact he soon apologized to Lauren in private. That she didn't throw it in his face, and allowed him to come to the realization on his own that he had overstepped, showed incredible self-regulation.

Lauren craved my feedback, and because she was so emotionally secure, she was not defensive when I brought up her gaps. She wanted to address them and was confident she could. My evaluation revealed, for instance, that her sales team was struggling with the demands she was putting on them in the lead-up to the IPO, and that her risk-averse CTO was focusing too much on the current product, missing potential new opportunities. She immediately acted on that and used me as a coach/partner to figure out how to motivate her CTO to expend additional resources on new products rather than continue to fine-tune what was already working. The sales team ended up meeting its goals, the IPO was a wild success, and Lauren convinced the board to give her a substantial increase in her next contract. She is quite possibly the most emotionally astute leader I ever worked with, and it paid off for her in every respect.

Culture Issues Are Really Emotional Gaps

Lauren's company was praised throughout the industry for its extraordinary culture, and she was frequently invited to speak on the topic. Many attribute good culture to having excellent people, but it's more than just the people themselves. When we talk about culture, we are really talking about the emotional life of a company, and that emotional life starts with the leadership. Emotional blindspots are problems for individuals, certainly. They lead to diminished influence, diminished ability to motivate, and an inability to develop a strong team around you. But emotional blindspots are also problems for corporate culture more broadly.

The culture at Platforma was clearly suffering under Kimball's iron fist. As a leader unable to regulate his emotional responses, Kimball had lost his leadership power and was at the whim of where his anger was taking him. His decision-making had become clouded by his own frustrations, and he found himself ignoring input more and more often because he didn't trust the people around him. He was paranoid that everyone was a spy sent by the board, reporting back about his failures. This became a self-fulfilling prophecy, as that paranoia led him to fail.

As I thought about what I would recommend to the board, I recalled another company I had worked with, in the gaming space, where the atmosphere was ... sad. That's strange in an industry where most companies are high-energy, chaotic, and cheerful. When I first met with the CEO, he was distracted. The company had "hit a rough patch," he said, but would get through it. He didn't sound like he believed it. The company had been on a meteoric rise just two months prior. He had been the "golden boy," not just as CEO but at every stop in his career, living a life where he kept exceeding even the highest expectations. No one was surprised that in his early thirties, he was the CEO of an exciting startup; they just kept expecting success, and it appeared that he did as well. The current situation was the company's first stumble. His depression over it was palpable, and the corporate "culture" reflected it. Everyone else was as sad as he was. His inability to self-regulate his emotions coupled with a lack of strategies for dealing with adversity had created a company that was nervous like he was, much like how Kimball had created an office culture driven by fear.

I encouraged this CEO to acknowledge his anxiety and allow himself to experience the struggle rather than fear it and push it down. That would, I hoped, free him to reach out and rely on those around him to pull him and the company through the difficult period. He needed to get past his fear and belief that everything was doomed.

He was willing to change. Kimball, as I found out when I asked him directly in our final meeting—"Would you be open to some coaching?"—was not.

Kimball or Simon? Simon or Kimball?

My report back to Platforma's board was simple: neither one of these "leaders" was emotionally equipped to lead, and if the company wanted to survive, a new CEO was needed immediately. The board knew Kimball and Simon were ineffective, but they couldn't put their finger on why until I labeled it for them: emotional blindspots. These were people with serious emotional limitations, and that is why things would never get better.

I told the board that there would never, as far as I could tell, be a solution that involved either one of them in power. I recommended that they exit Kimball and keep Simon restricted to his role in the technology effort, without any further leadership duties.

Instead, the board decided to hire a chief operating officer under Kimball. They hoped to get the communication that Kimball was blocking, and imagined that with a COO of their choosing, they would regain the leverage they needed. They sold this idea to Kimball and Simon by saying that it would bring the two halves of the company together, and planned to gradually transition Kimball out of the CEO role. I warned them that Kimball was likely to see any new hire as a threat and undermine that hire's authority in order to keep power and avoid being pushed out. "It would be easier to get rid of him now," I said, but they didn't listen.

The COO did his best, but he ended up having to work much harder than necessary because so much energy was spent controlling Kimball instead of preventing the company from going off the rails. Kimball eventually told the board to decide who was in charge, and the board responded, finally removing him. But it was too little, too late. Opportunities had already been lost, and the board ended up selling the company to a competitor at a steep discount. Platforma's superior technology was not enough to survive the enormous negativity of a toxic CEO full of emotional blindspots.

. . .

Finding Your Emotional Power

How do you figure out if you are being crippled by an emotional blindspot?

Awareness

First, you need to ask yourself where you are on the bell curve of emotional bandwidth. You can start with a self-assessment, but these issues (like many) are often seen best by the people around us. Ask your family and trusted colleagues: How does your emotional range, your awareness of others' emotions, your self-regulation, and your strategic use of emotion compare with others? Ask them to describe you emotionally in just a few words. Does it match how you see yourself? Sometimes we have a different picture of ourselves than the reality of how we are coming across to others, especially in the emotional realm.

Next, what emotions are you most aware of within yourself? How often are you aware of what you are feeling, and when are your emotions sometimes a surprise? Are there emotions you rarely feel? What feelings are you comfortable with—used to—and what feelings are less familiar? There are people who live in a state of anxiety and unease; while these can be unpleasant feelings to experience, those people get accustomed to them, and may know how to recognize them in others more than someone who is positive and comfortable all the time.

Do you believe that feelings are critical for being a good leader? Or are you skeptical? If you are skeptical, why?

Finally, can you think of any situations where emotions got the best of you—and of any situations where you saw emotions get the best of someone else? Emotional meltdowns we witness in the workplace often stick with us for a long time, and certainly our own do as well. It's important to analyze these situations closely. What happened? What triggered the issue, and if it was your own struggle, what do you wish you would have done in the moment? If it was someone else's struggle, can you imagine how you might have handled it differently?

Similarly, think of times when you effectively managed your emotions. What made those situations easier or possible? Are there certain emotions you are more comfortable managing than others?

In reflecting on all of these questions, do you see an emotional blindspot—a gap or lack of awareness when it comes to any of the five emotion elements, or an overemphasis on one emotion element while you ignore the rest?

Action

First, think about your current role and what emotions are needed. Write an "emotional job description" for your position, and then reflect on whether it matches your typical emotional state. Is there a gap between the kind of person you would advise someone in your job to be and the kind of person you are? If so, might that be the cause of any issues you are having at work?

Keep a journal of your emotions. Every week, review to find any patterns. When were you happy, sad, or mad? Report on the emotions of others as well. What emotions are you seeing displayed around you?

Identify an emotional superstar colleague or friend, who seems to be an expert like Lauren in managing and strategically deploying their emotions. Observe them, and see what you can learn. If you are in a position where you can interview them about their emotional life, how they self-regulate, how they understand what others are feeling, and so on, then that can be a useful exercise.

Finally, ask yourself: If you could be better at one thing in the emotional realm, what would it be? Then, go find someone good at that and try to learn from them.

Next chapter, we turn to *intellect*. Many of us overindex on our intelligence, assuming that smarts is the only thing that matters in the workplace. By now, you probably realize that there are many things that get in our way, regardless of our raw intellectual horsepower. You probably also understand that there are different kinds of intelligence, valuable in different ways depending on your role. If we aren't thinking carefully about what kind of intelligence we need in the moment, or if we assume that being the smartest person in the room will solve all problems, then we may well be falling prey to an intellect blindspot.

CHAPTER 5

INTELLECT

ARE YOU SMART ENOUGH TO REALIZE THAT BEING SMART IS NEVER ENOUGH?

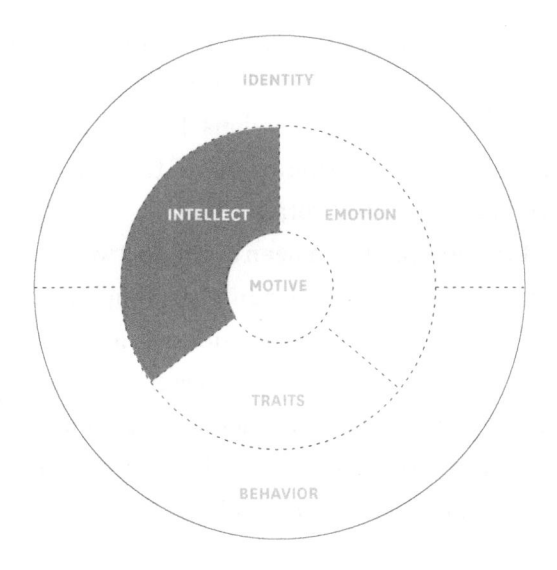

As we finish up the middle layer of self-awareness, we arrive at the blindspots in our head that relate to our intellect. *The general wisdom from the business world—and to an even greater extent in the business coaching world—is that the smarter the executive, the better. But smart can mean many things, and being the "smartest person in the room" is*

neither a meaningful thing by itself nor an excuse to ignore the other facets of good leadership. When we fall into the trap of thinking our intellect will compensate for weakness elsewhere, and fail to see that it can't, we are succumbing to one of the most common blindspots there is.

A few years ago, Patricia, an old college classmate, called me. I had stayed in occasional touch with her over the years. She was part of the fifth generation to run her family's specialty-foods business. It had started out as a local farmstand in the early 1900s and grew to become a nationally recognized brand of upscale jams and condiments, with a robust online business, coast-to-coast distribution, and relationships with many grocery businesses that white-labeled her company's products for their own store-branded versions. Patricia had been CEO for a number of years before transitioning out of the role when she turned sixty. A slightly younger cousin rotated in.

This is what the company had been doing for two decades, since the death of Patricia's father, who'd run the company for more than twenty-five years. Patricia, two of her siblings, and three of her cousins all had board seats and each had spent some time as CEO since her father's passing. Now, as the fifth generation approached retirement, they faced a decision over what to do next and how to pick a successor-leader from the sixth generation to modernize the company and bring it into the future.

Patricia convinced the rest of the board to bring in a coach to consult, meet, and assess the four top sixth-generation candidates and then make a recommendation. "We need an outsider like you," she told me, "to give us an objective opinion. After all, these are our kids, our nieces, our nephews. We still think of them as babies!"

I was happy to help, especially since my pantry had remained stocked with their incredible raspberry jam for decades. At company headquarters, Patricia, her brother Scott (a past CEO; now chairman of the board), and the rest of her family gave me a rundown of the people I was about to meet.

First, there was Ethan, who I was told was unassuming but "wicked smart" and had the pedigree to prove it: two Ivy League degrees, a tour as a management consultant, and experience as operations chief for the family business, where he had shown tremendous aptitude in cutting costs and streamlining systems. He was a problem solver and a respected leader, but Scott and Patricia both confided to me that he was "better with data than people," and maybe not the best public ambassador.

Next, there was Leila, who had a fine résumé herself and was now head of the partnerships division of the business, brokering strong deals through top-notch negotiation skills. I was told that where Ethan favored deep, rigorous analysis, Leila, in comparison, could rapidly consume vast amounts of information and consolidate it into articulate analyses and plans. However, too often she shot from the hip. She was quick in the room, but also sometimes spoke over people and lost them with the machine-gun fire of ideas and information coming from her brain.

Third was Jasmine, an unexpected contender to lead, given her lack of formal business training. But she had shown surprising talent as the head of marketing—and had led the company's digital transformation, turning it into a true online player and pulling talented individuals from throughout the business to contribute innovations that had probably done more to generate top-line revenue than anyone else's efforts had. Beyond that, Jasmine had a fun, free spirit, and everyone loved her.

Finally, Rohan was perhaps the dark-horse candidate, a college dropout who had started on the factory floor and had a way about him, an intuition for people and for products. Rohan was the one they brought in for the final interviews when hiring new executives, and the person who seemed most in tune with what new offerings would sell, where they would sell, how to price them, and how to avoid costly mistakes. Patricia told me how Rohan—whose role at this point was barely defined, leaving him a jack-of-all-trades who floated among divisions—had pulled her aside when they were about to sign a lease for a second factory and asked if they'd taken a look at the floodplain map. It turned out that they were about to commit to twenty-five years in a site below sea level—a site that ended up flooding just six months after Rohan convinced them to walk away. "Why was he even thinking about the floodplain?" Patricia asked me. "He has some kind of magic," Scott added.

I decided to initially meet with the four contenders for a group dinner. I wanted to see how they interacted with each other as well as how they would interact with me. The briefing proved generally correct. Leila, as I had been told to expect, did much of the talking, but didn't dominate in the way that I feared she might. In fact, the four of them were able to demonstrate to me that they each had interesting ideas, were committed to the company's success, and would quite possibly all make fine choices as the next CEO. I liked them, and even more important, they clearly liked each other.

There was a refreshing openness to the conversation, and a general sense that they all wanted to cooperate with the process and figure out the best leader who would keep the company thriving. That isn't to say that each of them wasn't ambitious for the job themselves, but in a multigenerational family business like this, the children are typically taught early on that the business only survives if individual ambition remains in check, petty grievances are cast aside, and all eyes remain on the goal of preserving the family legacy for subsequent generations. None of the four wanted to be the one to sink their great-great-great-grandparents' enterprise, and the common goal that bonded them was to build the business to even greater heights of success.

It was going to take some work for me to figure out whom to recommend to the fifth generation, but after the dinner, I had reason to feel confident that the process would be a productive one, and that I could figure out who was the best kind of "smart" to lead the company.

What Does It Mean to Be "Smart"?

Many in our society fetishize intelligence and treat it with a kind of obsessive focus. They let this one element determine how to assess behavior, decisions, and even someone's overall value as a person. I can't count how many times I've been told someone is the smartest one in the room, as if that's a ticket to success on its own, or, worse, a license to make uninformed decisions, bully to get one's way, or even mistreat others. I've repeatedly seen people excuse bad behavior by a leader because they're *just so smart*—and if a lack of people skills, or intuition, or humility, is the price to pay for getting the benefit of someone's raw intellect, then isn't it worth it?

I usually find myself wanting to make the case that it isn't worth it, and that we are missing a lot of important information when we focus too much on a very narrow, often incomplete measure of an individual. One of the biggest blindspots I see in leaders who are building teams is an overwhelming focus on finding people with the highest IQs. People who look exclusively or almost exclusively at IQ-type intelligence skills are failing to understand the full scope of what intelligence is and what success in business means—it's a blindspot that comes up quite often.

In that spirit, while my background as a psychologist is an advantage when looking at many of the blindspots covered in this book, it might get in the way with this one. Psychology, after all, is a discipline very much concerned with intelligence, starting with the development of IQ testing more than a hundred years ago.[1] Still today, psychological testing often starts with an IQ test, even though we know that there is so much more to someone's intelligence and abilities than what that test measures.

Statistical correlations show that IQ tests do a good job of measuring someone's fitness for traditional academic success—but academic success is not the same as success more broadly in life, or even in business.[2] An IQ score—and indeed, a degree from a top academic institution—is a poor measure of a broader notion of intelligence, which includes street smarts, business acumen, creative thinking, social skills, intuition, and nuance. It is useful to know that someone went to, say, Stanford, Harvard, Yale, or Princeton, for sure, but it is not nearly as meaningful a piece of information as knowing what they were able to do with that degree, and the kinds of real-world achievements they have effectuated.

In my work with executives, I think of intellect in a more nuanced way, as something that comes in four types. You need—or at least a well-functioning business needs—all four. As we take a closer look at the four types of intelligence, you may well recognize Ethan, Leila, Jasmine, and Rohan—and you should also notice aspects of yourself:

- *Horsepower.* This is where we end up with incredibly high IQ scores and descriptors like "wicked smart." As shorthand, we can think about horsepower as represented by someone asking, "What else?" They simply want more. Horsepower involves the ability to retain and synthesize huge amounts of information, to learn new ideas and concepts and incorporate them into existing frameworks, to connect details and separate the meaningful from the noise, and to cogently express conclusions.

- *Processing speed.* Distinct from those with raw horsepower, people who lead with processing speed can marshal their intelligence quickly and spit back solid answers to questions or challenges on the spot. The shorthand question here is, "Can we move on?" People with this strength are three steps ahead and ready to keep going. They tend to dominate meetings and conversations, but sometimes leave others asking, "Is what he said really the full picture?" Speed is often important in business, but sometimes the first answer isn't the right one.

- *Creativity.* Creative intelligence is about nonlinear thinking and seeing connections where they may not so obviously exist. The question being asked here is often, "Why not?" Creative thinkers can look past conventional wisdom, across seemingly unrelated sources of information, and pick out ideas that connect in surprising ways. They don't just ask *what* and *how*, but venture beyond, in search of brand-new ways of doing things outside of typical constraints. These are the people who aren't just thinking outside the box but wondering why there even needs to be a box at all.

- *Street smarts.* This is where "How come?" is the animating question. Street smarts are about having an intuitive feel for the underlying levers and drivers of people and of business. People strong in this area are attuned to *motive*, see around corners, toggle between taking a big-picture view and mastering the details, and are able to predict how individuals will react to something or how the world will move. It is hard to know if someone has this kind of intelligence until you see it in action. It's also one of the most valuable in business. Faced with someone with incredible intellectual horsepower but an inability to predict how the world might unfold in response to a particular stimulus, it's hard to envision their success. At the same time, some of the best business leaders I've encountered were probably not gifted with the highest IQs in the room, but they had the ability to look at the big picture of a situation (the "thirty-thousand-foot view"), spot the places where something just didn't seem right, and dive down into the details.

All of us have different amounts of each of these types of intellect, and the fundamental intellect blindspot is failing to see that they are all distinct, and that they are all important. Many of us naturally overindex on the type of intelligence we see as our strength and fail to recognize that the others are valuable and necessary as well. We assume that everyone thinks the same way we do, or at least that they should—but that's false. We are all wired differently.

When you have multiple strengths in your intellect, it is sometimes hard to tease out which type you lead with. So, failing to see yourself in any of these descriptions may not be a negative; it may instead mean you are relatively well-balanced, which can be a huge gift when it comes to leadership. The greatest leaders, I believe, are either high in all four types of intelligence or they understand very clearly where their own gaps are and work to proactively fill those gaps by bringing people with the other types of intellect into their closest circle and relying on them. Great leaders are not blind to the existence of different types of intellect or the degree to which they possess each type. They have respect for all four and don't have the arrogance to think that their way of understanding the world is better than any other. Poor leaders fall into the trap of assuming they know best.

If Speed Is Good, Is More Speed Better?

Sophie was a partner at a top venture capital firm, whose colleagues came to me for help. "She's brilliant," they said, "but she tends to derail meetings. She grasps the logical flaws in founders' pitches incredibly quickly, but then jumps on them, causing the founders to get defensive." Her quickness, they explained, is a really valuable skill, but not when it derails the rhythm of the pitch, keeps the rest of the team from understanding the business, or prevents the founders from telling the rest of their story. "And she won't hold back!"

The partners admitted that Sophie was often right in her quick assessments—so they didn't want to completely muzzle her—but they also needed her to understand that her attack-mode style was pushing founders away and keeping the rest of the team from making fully considered, careful decisions about their investments.

I realized immediately when I sat down with Sophie that this was going to be a difficult engagement. Just like she did in the room with founders, she started interrogating *me* on my methods. "How are you assessing me? What is the framework you're using, and how has it been shown to be valid?" I was restraining myself from becoming defensive even before we really began. I explained to Sophie that this wasn't about judging her or even trying to change her, but that I merely wanted to get a sense of her approach and then try to coach her to use her skills more effectively.

"We need to get through hundreds of pitches a year and move faster than the competition," she said, "and this is how I do that."

"But aren't there great founders who won't necessarily thrive with this kind of rapid-fire questioning?" I asked.

"This is how I pressure test an idea, Marty. If an idea can't hold up to scrutiny, it's useless to us."

"People aren't robots and companies are more than ideas," I replied, not imagining I was saying anything controversial. "Don't you sometimes want to slow down and take the time to find great people, even if the idea isn't there yet, trusting they will have the ability to iterate until they land on a winner?"

"No," she said, surprisingly, seeming ready to walk out of the room. "People don't matter. We need great ideas, and we need them now. Monkeys could execute on world-changing products. People are just coin-operated machines. Put enough change in, and they'll get the work done."

We went back and forth, but Sophie could not be moved. There was of course an emotional element to her blindspot, as she seemed to lack empathy for the people she was investing in—but the bigger issue, I thought, was that she was absolutely convinced that her way of seeing the world, with her kind of processing-speed-driven intellect, was the only one that had value. Her intellect blindspot left her uninterested in being coached, and eventually her partners lost patience and counseled her out of the firm.

But Which Type of Intellect Makes the Best CEO?

So, you might be thinking, processing speed isn't the perfect type of intellect for a great leader to have as their strength. But that would be the wrong lesson to draw from Sophie's story—or at least only a partial lesson. The type of intellect you are strongest in doesn't matter as much as your awareness that other types of intelligence are valuable. More of one type of intelligence cannot compensate for a deficiency in the other areas. Sophie was fast, but she would never be fast enough. She needed more range. The key to avoiding intellect blindspots is understanding what you bring to the table and where you may need some help.

At the jam company, Patricia and her board were hoping that even with the disparate ways of thinking that Ethan, Leila, Jasmine, and Rohan brought to the table, I would be able to find one of them who could lead successfully and not be held back by intellect blindspots. I needed to see if they had the self-awareness to know who they were and understand the gaps that they would need to fill if they were to be the next CEO.

Ethan was clearly high on horsepower, and it showed in our one-on-one. I could tell right away that he understood the business and would be ready with plans from the get-go. "I'm very confident we could increase profits by 15 percent if we built a new shipping facility closer to the East Coast," he told me, "and set up a satellite office there to deal with our national accounts." He had the numbers to back him up and a clear road map for achieving significant gains. But when I asked him what he might be missing, he didn't have a clear answer, and when I pressed him on how he'd convince some of his best employees to relocate to the new facility, he blew off the question. "If we need to train new people, we will," he insisted. "This is about the unit economics, that's all, and if you let me walk you through the data again . . ." The more we talked, the more it was clear that Ethan was so focused on the numbers that he might be missing the street smarts to understand how human beings operated and the creativity to get beyond the data. He believed that his analysis was airtight and not up for debate—and I worried that relying too much on data-driven conclusions would hurt him.

Meanwhile, Leila was a speed demon, barreling forth with ideas of her own, from new products she envisioned, to which employees she'd jettison, to her half-developed thesis on how the color of a product label is more important than anyone gives it credit for being. She was engaging and personable, and clearly loved the business—but it was exhausting to talk to her and hard to get her to stop and listen. I floated Ethan's idea about the new shipping facility. Immediately, she decided it wouldn't work, firing off half a dozen reasons why—all reasonable hypotheses, but not necessarily correct, and when I tried to push her to ask more questions, or to stop and think for a moment about whether there might be a way to address her concerns, she didn't see a reason to. She wanted to get straight to the decision and not waste any more time. I worried that the success she had achieved by thinking quickly made her intolerant of other approaches to decision-making. Her ideas were sometimes creative, but like Ethan, she didn't seem to have the street smarts to understand people, and I feared that would doom her in the end.

Next, I tried to dive deep with Rohan, who had more than enough street smarts to make up for what his cousins were missing. He described what he felt was one of his biggest triumphs at the company: "I noticed one of our suppliers suddenly becoming easier to work with, for no good reason, seeming to want more and more of our business even if it didn't make obvious economic sense," he said. "No one could figure it out—until it hit me: they were clearly angling to gain knowledge and at the same time disrupt our other relationships so that they would be in a better position to launch their own consumer brand and undercut our market position. I realized that if they were doing this to us, they were likely doing it to our competitors as well. I worked with Leila—head of partnerships—to develop a strategy to take advantage of the opening our supplier was giving us. We let our competitors take the opportunity to give this supplier more of their business, and instead we beefed up our other supplier relationships so that we would be in a stronger position if this one supplier launched a brand of their own. I saw it coming, and so when they did launch their brand, we were well-positioned to not just avoid a loss in market share, but to actually gain 15 percent as our biggest competitors scrambled."

Rohan was an expert people-reader, both externally and internally, giving me the rundown on every executive in the business and their strengths and challenges. He explained how he loved Ethan, Leila, and Jasmine, but worried that they lacked the savvy to lead, that Ethan was often too data-driven, Leila was sometimes too quick to reach conclusions, and Jasmine's approach could be too unpredictable. "Business is about instincts," he told me, and while Rohan was right that often we do overemphasize traditional IQ-type skills or become overly enamored with someone's out-of-the-box thinking, it is just as much of a blindspot to dismiss those abilities completely. Not recognizing the value that they provide—especially when balanced with other types of intelligence—is just as much of a mistake as focusing too heavily on those strengths. Despite Rohan's evident charisma, I knew his cousins would never accede to his decision-making without a thorough analysis and discussion of their more data-driven ideas, and Rohan's tendency to dismiss their value would be catastrophic to family cohesion and unified leadership.

Finally, I met with Jasmine and hoped she would offer a fresh perspective. "You wouldn't think this would be related to our business at all," she told me, "but I remember being in church and feeling moved by the sermon ... and wondering: Why am I moved? It turned out that it was all about community and togetherness—and those were themes I realized were missing from our corporate culture. I was inspired to start a project to infuse a community feeling into our company, which took off like wildfire at the front-line level, ultimately reducing turnover and increasing employee satisfaction."

It was exactly the kind of creative thinking that sometimes gets overlooked. Similarly, Jasmine told me that reading about the battles between giant media companies and upstart streaming services reminded her of the dynamic between giant grocery chains and specialty markets, and that she'd been able to apply some lessons from one industry to the other—again, a set of unique insights that others weren't seeing. Even better, Jasmine understood that she didn't have all the necessary skills to lead. She acknowledged that she lacked the gravitas to negotiate with tough partners, and that she didn't have a good handle on reading financial statements. "But, to be honest, I find all of that stuff super boring, so I'd rather just let others do it."

While Jasmine did not suffer from the same kind of overreliance on one particular type of intellectual strength that plagued her cousins, she had a different kind of blindspot at the intersection of intellect and emotion, concerning knowledge acquisition. She knew what she didn't know—but she didn't care. This blindspot—failing to realize that as a leader you need to invest energy even in things you don't naturally find interesting—is worth a closer look.

Knowing What You Don't Know

We have seen Jasmine's knowledge-acquisition blindspot before. Recall Marcus from the introduction and his company, Aesthetics, which found itself flailing because Marcus wanted to do everything himself—yet there were certain areas that he underinvested in, like operations, because he was bored by them and didn't think they mattered.

Marcus's intelligence was off the charts in so many respects—his processing speed, his horsepower, his creativity, and even the street smarts he needed to build his company up from nothing. But his combination of arrogance to think he knew how to solve every problem his company faced, and his failure to invest in learning the things he needed to in order to deliver on that possibility, ended up being fatal for his leadership and for the company.

Marcus's intelligence not only wasn't enough to save him, but was in some ways what helped bring him down. Intelligence doesn't always win, because people who are overconfident in their intelligence can make assumptions and keep moving without slowing down to look at what they might be missing.

This was my blindspot, too, when I was in business. I gravitated toward the elements of the job that interested me but was prone to losing focus when it came to the things I didn't want to do. I would stay at thirty thousand feet even when I needed to be in the details.

Knowledge acquisition is the willingness and eagerness to learn even in areas of no interest when that's what the company needs, as well as the ability to tolerate and even thrive with the uncomfortable emotions that accompany the realization that there are things you do not know. The worry and anxiety—the nagging uncertainty—needs to push you to learn more, rather than pull you back to the domains where you are most comfortable. Leaders need to learn so much, across all functions of a company—finance, legal, operations, marketing, and more—and spending the time to understand those at the level needed to lead is not a trivial task. One can often look at a company's organizational chart to see where the CEO's interests lie. The functions that excite the leader will be extensively built out, while those that don't will be underresourced. In essence, avoiding this blindspot is about having an awareness of what you know and what you don't know, and acting appropriately in response. Are you confident in your knowledge yet still open to new ideas and information? Do you use anxiety and fear about your knowledge gaps as motivators to learn more, rather than running from the feelings and returning to what you find more comfortable? Do you have an established network of people who will tell you what you don't know?

There are times when this blindspot is intentional to some extent, as in Jasmine's case—when we can acknowledge the areas that don't interest us but still dismiss them, a kind of willful blindness. But there are other times when we *don't know what we don't know*—and that ends up being an even harder problem to solve.

Leaders make decisions. Using their existing knowledge, acquiring new information, applying their intellect, and exercising their judgment, they make choices as to how to solve problems. Ultimately, leaders are evaluated on the outcomes of their decisions. We have looked at how blindspots affect the types of *intellect* they rely on to make their decisions. But knowledge-acquisition blindspots can be about the types of *information* they rely on as they use their intellect to make those decisions.

The easiest way to explain is with a story. Mordecai was the CEO of a regional financial institution who wanted my colleagues and me to coach several of the company's senior executives. As I worked with Mordecai, I was struck by the way he would wander the halls, striking up warm conversations with virtually every employee, no matter their level of seniority. "What are you working on?" he would ask, or "What's exciting (or frustrating) you about your job lately?" At first, I thought he was just being friendly, but then I realized he was not only genuinely interested but using these conversations to gather information that might not otherwise filter up to him as CEO. He also had a vast external network of people he routinely reached out to, quizzing them on what they were worried about, on economic trends, and more.

Being the CEO often means giving up direct access to levels deep in the company. Everyone from front-line tellers to backroom data scientists would end up giving Mordecai their views on their work and on the world—helping him figure out what he didn't know that he didn't know, and through this new information he developed insights and uncovered new opportunities.

I was already beginning to understand this when he took me out to dinner. Before we had even ordered drinks, he was telling me how worried he was about how financial technology (fintech) startups were going to disrupt banking. He started moving around the salt and pepper shakers, the sugar bowl, and the glasses to show me how different aspects of banking could be peeled off by fintech companies, seriously cutting into his bank's margins. At first, I was merely curious about the story that he was weaving and amused at how he was telling it. But then it dawned on me: he knew I worked with Silicon Valley startups, and he was seeing if I was going to jump in and give him some intel on the fintech world. He was engaging me to find out what I knew, what I'd heard, and whether there was information he was missing—the same thing he was doing in the hallways with employees, all in the spirit of collecting as much knowledge as he could, trying to better understand the world.

Mordecai was natural, and his conversations were engaging—and purposeful. He was a master at using his intellect to learn new things and figure out how to improve his business. In the same spirit, he wanted me and my colleagues to coach his executives to mitigate their own blindspots and help them constantly be open to acquiring knowledge. He knew how best to use me, and I suspected it was similar for all the consultants he brought in. He didn't expect me to have answers. Rather, he would throw out ideas and prompt me to react, just like he did at dinner. He knew that there was always more to know. He surrounded himself with experts who spoke their minds, and he encouraged them to do so. As accomplished as Mordecai was, he continually grew in the role. He was determined never to let himself fall into what I call the Blind Zone.

We can think of knowledge acquisition as existing in a two-by-two matrix (see table 5-1). We all have things we know, things we don't know, and things we should know.

We spend much of our time living in the Comfort Zone, where we are knowledgeable and possess expertise. The blindspot here is failing to understand there is much more *beyond* the Comfort Zone. We must allow ourselves to venture there, where we need the emotional regulation to manage the feelings that can come from exploring new areas of knowledge. If a leader can't tolerate feeling anxiety over what they don't know, they become unwilling to move past their existing expertise and they dismiss the value of new information.

TABLE 5-1

Knowledge acquisition

The Comfort Zone	**The Anxiety Zone**
You *know* what you *know*	You *know* what you *don't know*
The Terror Zone	**The Blind Zone**
You *don't know* what you *should know*	You *don't know* what you *don't know*

In the Anxiety Zone—when we know what we don't know, and it worries us—anxiety can be a positive force to motivate us to learn new things, but blindspots occur if we don't see how to manage emotionally through the fear. Instead, we can become overwhelmed, lose confidence, and start to doubt our decisions. This is where impostor syndrome emerges, when someone worries they don't have what it takes and fears they are going to be "exposed" as a fraud. Anxiety over our limitations being revealed can lead us to make poorer, risk-averse choices.

In the Terror Zone, blindspots occur when we are surprised by something we don't know but realize we should know. Rather than being aware of our terror—owning it—and seeking help, we get paralyzed by the fear and perform poorly. When I was an entrepreneur, in one of our first, casual meetings with an adviser as we were beginning to explore selling our company, I was asked, "What is your exit plan?" I had never been involved in entrepreneurship before starting my company; I was not even familiar with the concept of an exit plan. My first instinct was to look for the red exit sign near the door—were they asking about fire safety? I froze, and didn't say anything at all, recognizing that this must be something I should know, and not wanting to be exposed for being ignorant. In hindsight, of course, it would have been just fine to say, "This is my first and only company; I don't think I have an exit plan, but can you explain to me what you're trying to understand?" We run into problems when we don't know what we don't know, so we find ourselves blind to the need to take steps to address the gaps. Those moments when reality exposes us can take us by surprise.

When we don't seek to learn more about the holes in our knowledge and let them remain a mystery, we are in the Blind Zone, suffering from a blindspot by definition as we fail to see that there is knowledge we could be possessing. Rather than succumbing to this, we should act like Mordecai, always looking for outsiders with a range of perspectives to explain what's missing and help us get a better grasp on a situation.

The Paradox of "Strategic Thinking"

Back at the family jam business, Rohan knew I was getting ready to report back to Patricia when he called me and asked to talk. I had to give him credit: he had the good sense to know that this was not a clear decision, and that I might be struggling with it. He told me that he didn't want to denigrate any of his cousins and didn't even want to advocate specifically for himself—he said he trusted that the family would make the best choice, and that he was okay with the decision however it turned out. But he told me he wanted to make sure the board was going to be focused not just on the person they were choosing but on their ideas, and he felt that now—in a retail world perhaps shifting more than ever—was a time to prioritize strategic thinking above all else. Rohan insisted it shouldn't matter who the strategy comes from, but that it was the right strategy.

I think he was taken aback when I responded with what might have sounded to him like a naive question from an experienced consultant like me.

"I agree with you, but I just want to ask: What, to you, does strategic thinking mean?"

It's a question I'd often thought about asking clients, but I'd never before had the direct opportunity to do so. Strategic thinking is a term that is hugely prized by many people in business, in ways I didn't fully appreciate when I first started coaching—but it is also a vague concept that I think many have tremendous trouble defining. In practice, after twenty years of thinking about this issue, what I've realized is that strategic thinking lives at the intersection of intellect and traits. It is a special type of problem-solving that draws on all four types of intelligence as well as the traits of curiosity, comfort with ambiguity, and an openness to new experiences and ideas. The blindspot here is failing to see that strategic thinking requires more than just raw intelligence.

The way people can get enamored with strategic thinking sometimes surprises me. I realized early on in my coaching career how much it mattered to some. In a draft report for one of my first clients, I wrote that he was "a tactical thinker," and when I showed the executive those words, he begged me to remove them before his superiors had the opportunity to see the document. "It's a career killer, if I get labeled as anything that sounds like the opposite of strategic," he told me, even as I insisted it was a compliment (he was a tremendous operator). I changed the wording at his request—the only time I ever did that in my career—and began to think about what it really means to say that someone is strategic. Is it a separate type of intellect, or a certain combination of the ones already discussed?

Even beyond the definition, I don't think most people have a good handle on who in an organization is actually thinking strategically. The most striking example I can recall is the time I was coaching a division president, tasked with grooming his successor. He complained, repeatedly, that his second-in-command was "not a strategic thinker at all." Meanwhile, to me, the division president doing the complaining seemed like the least strategic thinker I had ever encountered. He was all about his own revenue targets and not tuned in at all to the higher-level strategy discussions I had been hearing from the CEO. I'm not saying he should have been concerned with everything else, but to call himself strategic—and to criticize his direct report for not being strategic—seemed like a poor evaluation of his own skills.

There are a lot of scholarly articles defining strategy and strategic thinking, and some of them are quite interesting.[3] But it's not always easy to translate the academic research into evaluating whether or not the person sitting in front of you is being strategic. I believe it does end up coming down to a mix of the four types of intellect plus selected traits—curiosity, comfort with ambiguity, and openness—that together create exceptional insight.

There is also an element of strategic thinking—or at least the perception of strategic thinking—that connects to emotions. I have relied on an operational definition: people are generally seen as strategic thinkers if they worry about what their boss is worried about. This means that you are thinking more broadly than about your own world and effectively reading your boss and what keeps them up at night. The best explanation I've been given of corporate strategy is that it is like placing bets in the game of roulette. You have a limited number of chips and need to decide where and when you should put them on the table—what initiatives, people, and projects are to be focused on in the short term, and in what long-term objectives the company should invest its resources. If you are thinking about those same bets in a different way than your boss is and trying to add value to make your boss successful—bringing them useful information or ideas that address the issues that perplex them—then you get labeled by your boss and others as a "strategic thinker."

If you can identify the blindspots in your boss's thinking and intelligence, you should take the opportunity to jump in and add value—and you'll ride that strategic thinker label to your next step up in the organization. For instance, if your boss is creative, be the data hound they need. If they have the raw horsepower to digest and synthesize data, be the person who looks outside the box for new ideas. If they have a blindspot when it comes to making quick decisions, harness your processing speed to come up with answers on the fly that can make your boss feel like you've got them covered.

I saw this play out in practice while coaching Nessa, an executive vice president and the top human resources executive at a cosmetics company. While she was already leading her department, she didn't have a C-level title. She wanted to be the chief people officer, recognized for the full value she was providing. She was given the feedback that she wasn't "strategic enough" and called me for help. She honestly didn't know if she was strategic or not—her blindspot was not knowing what strategic thinking looked like and how highly prized it was at the company—but felt the concern was holding back her career, and she wanted to know what to do. Nessa explained to me that she had been rewarded in her career by getting things done—that she was all about the "What else?"—and was handling far more work than others might have been able to in the role. She was seen by her superiors as dependable, no-nonsense, and efficient—in intelligence terms, blessed with horsepower and processing speed, but lacking creativity and street smarts.

I asked her if she ever thought about the "Why?" of the business, and she was a little stumped. I explained that she needed to lean into certain traits—her curiosity, her comfort with ambiguity, her openness to new ideas—and see if that affected her thinking. We played out a particular scenario. The big issue she was dealing with at the time was how to return people to work in a post-Covid-19 world, and this was of course an area that the top human resources executive at the company should have been intimately involved in. When pressed, Nessa admitted that she was mostly taking orders, and then figuring out the best ways to execute on others' plans. She had ideas—she was, in fact, a strategic thinker when pushed—but she had never seen herself as empowered to own an issue from a strategic perspective as opposed to just finding ways to execute.

This was a communication issue and, really, an identity blindspot just as much as an intellect one. She needed help from me to redefine her role in her mind, embrace a part of her job that she wasn't seeing, and then communicate how "strategic" she was to the people who mattered. Only then could she get the recognition that she thought she deserved. We brainstormed some ideas for her to demonstrate her strategic thinking to the senior leaders. She ended up gathering her team and trying to get as full a picture of the return-to-work issue as she could, analyzing it from all directions, thinking through the implications of a range of different decisions, and preparing a white paper with recommendations that she presented to the CEO and his senior leadership team. By owning the issue—taking charge of the strategy, demonstrating a real understanding, and giving her boss answers and ideas that he wasn't otherwise hearing—she had the potential to change the way she was seen at the company.

A few months later, after the white paper and other moments she took to fully own the company's HR-related decisions, Nessa was told that she was "growing in the role" and got the promotion to CPO.

Sometimes different kinds of intellect are already within us, but we need to slow down and ask ourselves the right questions. For Nessa, she needed to spend less time asking "What else?" (horsepower) and more time asking "Why not?" (creativity).

As Rohan and I talked about the strategy for his family's company transition to the sixth generation, we both started to realize that all four of the contenders were in a position to bring different—and perhaps equally valuable—ideas to the table, and that more important than who was going to lead would be that all of their voices were heard and reflected in the company's choices. If only, I started to wonder, we could combine the strengths of each of the four into one super-CEO who would effectively bring all four types of intelligence to the job as well as the strategic thinking that requires all four intelligences and a comfort in all elements of knowledge acquisition.

The Family That Plays Together . . .

When I made my recommendation to Patricia and the board, I led with the unique opportunity that the company had as a family business. In the previous chapter on emotional blindspots, I wrote about how co-CEO situations rarely work, unless there are preexisting bonds that tie the leaders together and create an underlying sense of trust. Here, unusually, the company did have that sense of trust, with Ethan, Leila, Jasmine, and Rohan all cousins who got along quite well with each other and who were bonded by family name and storied ancestors who had created and perpetuated a living legacy for generations to come. In fact, the more I thought about it, the more I realized that this emotional strength could help create a solution that would compensate for the intellect blindspots possessed by each of them.

What if there could be a governance structure with all four of them as co-CEOs, each taking on different operational responsibilities?

Scott had been ready to step down as chairman of the board, but as we discussed this potential structure, he and Patricia had an idea. Scott's strengths as a leader had been in his development of Ethan, Leila, Jasmine, and Rohan as leaders in their own right, and in his ability to build strong teams within the company. He could give up his board seat and come back to serve as a senior executive with no real title or authority, but tasked with developing the four cousins as co-CEOs, coleaders who could form a strong, interdependent, mutually accountable leadership team, with the emotional bonds and family life experience to resist both their individual tendencies toward expressing ambition and their natural desires for individual power and authority. Scott's role could be as a facilitator and trainer, running meetings to make sure that each of the four were able to express their viewpoints. This way, they could grow to understand and appreciate each other's strengths, and the company would profit from the range of different intellectual approaches.

Patricia could take over as board chair and retain ultimate decision-making authority if the four co-CEOs were unable to agree on a decision, and Scott could aim to slowly fade out, giving the co-CEOs the tools over time to run the meetings themselves and either become a productive and effective team or see if one of the four could be elevated to CEO.

The board agreed to give the unorthodox structure a try, and a year later, when I checked back in (and ordered a new case of raspberry jam), things seemed to be going quite well.

. . .

Understanding Your Own Intellect

How can you avoid falling prey to an intellect blindspot? If you have been described as arrogant, overconfident, or intimidating, you may already have one. At the same time, if you've been told you're not strategic enough, or perhaps "too creative," said as a negative, then you almost certainly have room to improve.

Awareness

First, in reading this chapter, did you identify with Ethan, Leila, Jasmine, or Rohan? Your answer is neither good nor bad. The real question is whether you understand and respect that there are different types of intellect and don't think your way is necessarily the best or only approach. You need to try to understand your strengths, and then ensure that you aren't being held back by arrogance over your own intellectual abilities. Do you surround yourself with people who think differently than you? Do you enjoy those differences? If the answer is yes, then you are less prone to an intellect blindspot.

The next thing to examine is your curiosity and whether you are open to knowledge acquisition or in danger of a blindspot in that respect. Good leaders need to be open to new experiences, motivated to put in the effort and time to learn new things, interested in becoming knowledgeable even in areas that may be inherently uninteresting to them, and aware of what is unknown to themselves and others. Have you been told you are curious? Do you ask enough questions? Are you often wondering about what you don't know and what else you need to know?

How comfortable are you in areas of anxiety or terror? Are you aware of how you feel when you discover you don't know something? Are you defensive or open? Do you hide the truth or are you transparent?

Do you understand strategic thinking and how to apply it in practice? Do you know what your boss is worried about, and can you fill in those gaps? Do you approach situations with curiosity and openness to new information, or do you shy away from risks that may expose you as an impostor?

If all of this feels like a mystery to you, don't worry—you may well be one of those rare, balanced people who possess all four types of intellect and are not overly weighted in one direction or another. But you should ask people in your life how they see you in terms of intelligence—if they start saying you're "the smartest one in the room," you should know by now that this isn't always a good thing!

A failure to appreciate that leadership requires including all four types of intellect in decision-making—or an overemphasis on one while ignoring the others—means you are suffering from an intellect blindspot.

Action

Your first action should involve ensuring that you are surrounded by people with all types of intellect. Who in your life represents each type of thinking, and can you convene those people as a working group of sorts to bounce ideas off of or to talk through options that may not come to mind as easily for you? Within a corporate structure, it may be possible to build a team—much like Ethan, Leila, Jasmine, and Rohan—that can float throughout the company and tackle different issues with a variety of intellectual approaches.

Next, if you are like Nessa and your default (pretty common) is to think "What else?" and worry about how to execute, how can you make sure you are thinking strategically as much as possible and demonstrating that thinking to others in your organization? Are there things you can do to stretch those strategic thinking muscles and show off your ability to fill in the gaps where your boss is looking for knowledge or ideas?

When speaking up in meetings, can you slow yourself down and stretch your thinking into a series of "Why?" questions?

On the other hand, if you are strong in creativity or street smarts, can you force yourself to do the hard work of analyzing data and backing up your instincts? Can you try to impose more method to your madness and drill down to understand your own instinctual thinking and be able to explain it better to others?

No matter what your style, can you seek out mentors who think differently?

These steps should all help you move beyond your intellectual comfort zone and avoid blindspots in this area. In the next chapter, we look at the final blindspot, *behavior*. More than any of the other areas, behavior is something we can—and must—control. But having said that, it's not always easy. We can examine our behavioral blindspots and try to develop tools to correct them before they sabotage our ability to lead.

CHAPTER 6

BEHAVIOR

ARE YOU MASTERING THREE KEY AREAS OF BEHAVIOR THE WAY A LEADER SHOULD?

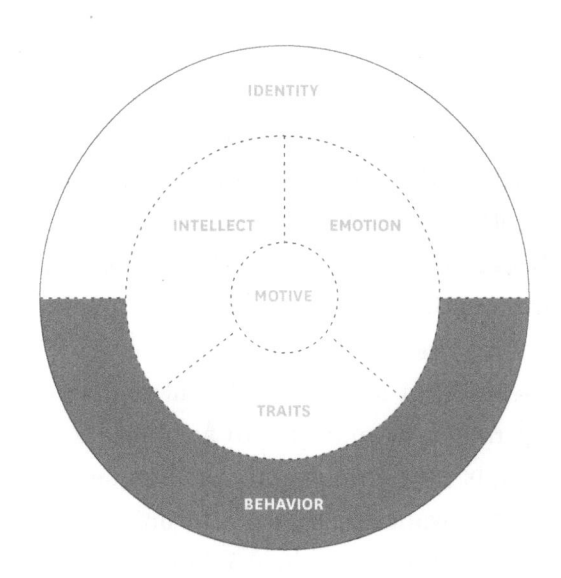

Back to the outer layer of awareness, our final blindspot is behavior. *Like identity, behavior can be more straightforward to change than the blindspots that emerge from deeper within us—but still, of course, it requires deliberate sustained awareness. In a sense, our behavior is*

everything that others experience from us. Behavior comes last in this book because it is in many ways the "output" of the other five blindspots. Our emotions, our intellect, our motives, our traits, and our identity all inform our behavior, so it can be challenging at times to isolate this element. But focusing on how we actually show up in the world—our behavior—can often make the biggest difference in our success. This chapter is a bit different, because I've already described behaviors associated with each of the other elements; here, we look at three complex leadership behaviors that many executives are blind to the importance of: communication, influence, and prioritization.

I received a call from the head of a private equity fund that had recently invested in an online marketplace, ConnX. ConnX was led by cofounders Gene and Lan, who had terrific reputations in the industry. "We love them both," the chairman told me. "But we're worried that Gene has gotten a little bit too caught up in the company's success. One of the reasons we invested in this company is because of its scrappy culture, and Gene just . . . doesn't seem so scrappy anymore."

I'll admit that my first reaction was to wonder if the chairman was being fair to Gene. After all, we hear about founders who lived for years on cheap ramen, crammed into apartments with sixteen of their closest friends. Is it a problem if once they see the fruit of their labor, some founders want to enjoy it a little bit? Not seeming scrappy enough when your company is valued at hundreds of millions of dollars and you're getting prepared to go public doesn't feel like such an urgent problem.

Yet when I started talking to employees, I understood the chairman's concerns better. Gene had apparently started taking a chauffeured limousine to work, showing up in tailored suits, and commandeering one of the office restrooms as his own "private bathroom." He wasn't just enjoying his newfound wealth; he was flaunting it, rubbing his staff the wrong way and affecting company morale. He had been "one of the guys," working late into the night, doing everything he could to get the business off the ground. And now he seemed taken with himself, unapproachable, and a poor fit with the culture the company was trying to maintain.

When I talked to Gene about it, he was apologetic, but not particularly open to change. "I suffered for a long time," he told me, "and if anything, I should be seen by my employees as a role model. If they work hard, they can reap the benefits, too."

"But they *are* working hard," I pushed back.

"Probably, but not for as long as I've been."

I told the board I could work with Gene to try to convince him to change his behavior—but I wanted to know how much I should push. "Are you looking to counsel him out," I asked, "or is he a critical member of the team?"

It was unanimous that Gene was an incredibly valued contributor, and they had brought me in because they were desperate not to lose him. "Especially on the board, he's crucial," the chairman told me. "He's our most articulate voice for ethics and fairness, the one who pushes us, again and again, to make sure we're doing the best thing for our customers and fulfilling the company's vision and mission. We need his perspective in the room—which is why it's so frustrating that he's behaving like this. We want to preserve what makes Gene great, and fix what's gone wrong."

Gene had so much insight into how the company needed to act—but his blindspot regarding his own behavior and its impact meant he didn't understand that he had changed in a way that was hurting how he was being perceived in the company.

The Behavioral Foundations of Leadership

Behavior is such an important blindspot to understand because our behavior is what others in the world experience of us. Our internal thoughts and feelings can be hidden from view—people may not recognize whatever is going on inside our heads—but our behavior is visible to all, and ultimately how the other five blindspot types show up in the world. Our sheepish introduction when asked what we do demonstrates our identity, our name-dropping as we try to impress gives away our motive, our calm nodding and shrugging of our shoulders might show our agreeableness trait, our rapid-fire questioning can show our processing speed (intellect), and the tone of our voice can reflect our frustration (emotion).

There are of course infinite ways that elements of our behavior can become blindspots, but there are three foundational behavioral blindspots that I see again and again, tripping up leaders in devastating ways, and in ways they can absolutely correct for. The blindspots in this chapter emerge from leaders leaning too heavily on their inherent behaviors and failing to understand that there is a wider array of options to select from. As we have seen before, defaulting to what feels comfortable and familiar can keep you from realizing there are better choices. And while this concern applies to everything we do, it is nearly impossible to be an effective leader if you fail on these three counts:

- *Communication.* Are you blind to how you are communicating through your words and your actions? Do you know what good communication looks like? There are specific behaviors associated with being an effective communicator. You need to be attentive to feedback in the moment, telling you to alter your communication style; aware of what your nonverbal behaviors are communicating to others; and adept at shifting your communication style, in different venues and for different audiences, away from what might be your default style.

- *Influence.* Are you blind to how you are attempting to influence the people under, above, and around you to get things done? Do you understand the different types of appeals you can be making, and are you consciously utilizing them in optimal ways rather than sticking to what you know best? The higher you rise in an organization, the more you need to rely on others to accomplish tasks and the more sophisticated you need to be in getting others to act on your behalf. Beyond direct reports, you need to influence people throughout the organization to get cross-functional initiatives across the goal line, and you need to influence up the hierarchy to get resources and to get obstacles removed to accomplish your goals. Do you know your default influence style? Do you know how to match an influence style with the situation and the personality of the person(s) you need to influence?

- *Prioritization.* Are you blind to what your role demands? Leaders are quite often—and certainly at the C-level—the only ones in their respective positions, but all too often they haven't thought through the activities that only the person in that role can do. The CEO, for instance, is the person who must be setting corporate strategy. If you are a CEO and you are not spending significant time on strategy, you are failing in your role. Yet many leaders spend their time doing what they like to do or what they think they are good at or what the previous person in the role did. If leaders aren't clear about prioritizing what they should be doing, they are at risk of doing others' jobs or letting what they should be doing fall through the cracks.

As a leader, you are not just a person but a tool of your organization who needs to be deployed in a range of different ways. Your behaviors—how you communicate, how you influence others, and how you prioritize your time—are the ways your company gets the highest and best use of you, and how you maximize your value.

We'll look at these three potential behavioral blindspots in turn.

Communication

Not just the words you say. When you think about how you communicate, almost surely the first thing you focus on are the words you speak. Of course, what you are telling your team, your customers, the public, your board, and any other stakeholders is important. But words are not the only form of communication. Tone communicates so much. Actions communicate. Body language communicates. I once worked with Tanya, the CEO of an intense, serious technology firm where the culture very much could have been a 24/7, work-at-all-costs, no-time-for-personal-life nightmare for her employees. Tanya's competitors did operate that way, quickly burning out talented engineers and having to spend incredible energy and expense on recruiting new ones to churn through.

Tanya's overt messaging was perhaps not so different from that of some of those other companies (expectations were high), but it was well known within the office that Tanya was a serious triathlete who worked out intensely, and that every day between 8:00 and 10:00 in the morning, Tanya was unreachable. She didn't apologize for it or try to explain it; she just blocked off her calendar and went to the gym. The act of doing so—and doing so in a way that everyone else knew about it—gave the rest of her team permission to do the same. They trusted that if their work got done, Tanya wasn't going to hound them about every minute on their calendars, and they could block off the times they needed in order to deal with the things that were priorities in their own lives. They trusted that work didn't need to take their freedom away completely. Tanya's act of making something outside of work a priority effectively communicated, without words, that placing boundaries around work and maintaining personal commitments to health and self-improvement were valued attributes. Far from suffering from a blindspot, Tanya was fully aware of the implications of her actions and what those actions were saying to her team.

At ConnX, Gene was communicating something quite different, and his failure to see this was a blindspot. His nonverbal behaviors—the suits, the limo, the private bathroom—affected the team. Rather than reinforcing the desired culture—humility, camaraderie, and equality—he was sending the message that these attributes didn't apply to him. *That stuff is for you, not me.* This was particularly frustrating to his cofounder, Lan, whose communication skills were a strength. Lan was so personally aligned to the values of ConnX that her messages, whether in large forums or smaller groups, built a consistent sense that what she said could be trusted. When the company received negative media attention for a situation with a provider on its platform, Lan could have said that bad things happen, or that it wasn't ConnX's fault. Instead, she stepped up and took responsibility, communicating to the team that accountability was a critical corporate value.

Gene believed in the same values as Lan, and the board insisted that in the boardroom Gene was the most articulate advocate for those values, but he had somehow separated his beliefs from his personal actions. He was giving himself a pass to do whatever he wanted. No matter how much I worked with him, he wasn't able to see that his own behavior mattered as much as the board and I knew it did. "No one cares how I'm getting to work," he would tell me, even as I presented him with interview transcripts that insisted the employees were very much paying attention.

I call this the "fishbowl effect" of being a senior executive. Gene's issue is a blindspot for plenty of leaders who spend years trying to build their companies, desperate for any crumb of attention, whether from industry peers or media. On the long and bumpy road toward success, they're used to being ignored. But when the enterprise you lead suddenly becomes a publicly recognized sensation, people start paying attention, and how you behave has a real effect on culture and morale.

This is also a problem for leaders who say, "It isn't about me. It's about the results I get." While this demonstrates humility, which is a wonderful trait, it misses the reality that everyone pays attention to what the people at the top are *doing*, not just what they're saying. This can cut against the typical advice people hear to "be yourself" in the workplace. Yes, there is something to be said for authenticity, but authenticity only works if your authentic self happens to behave consistent with corporate values. Lan could be herself because she was so well-aligned with the values of the company. But the authentic Gene and his captivation with markers of success wasn't what the company needed him to be. His blindspot was in failing to see that. There was also perhaps a motive blindspot in play for Gene, as he was unaware that achieving the material manifestations of success was very much a driver of his behavior.

In a short time, Gene found himself pushed into a less visible role focused on ancillary aspects of the company's business—its social-impact work and some foreign investments the company was exploring—with only a few direct reports. The board hoped this would solve the problem, allowing the company to harness Gene's strengths without his communication blindspot getting in the way.

Unfortunately, it wasn't that easy. A few months later, the board called me again.

I was told that where Gene had been adding tremendous value in the past—speaking truth at the board meetings and asserting the company's ethical obligations and responsibilities to its customers and the broader tech community—he was now being quiet and barely contributing. "We thought we solved the problem," the chair told me, "but now we have a new problem—a sour cofounder—and we don't know if Gene even wants to be here anymore."

Gene said he still cared very much about the company and wanted to be valuable. "I'm annoyed I was pushed to the side," he admitted, "and so maybe I've been taking that out on the board." He hadn't intentionally shut down at the meetings, but he wasn't paying enough attention to his communication to notice. This was *another*, different communication blindspot. Again he was behaving on instinct without sufficient reflection. He was letting his emotions dictate his behavior instead of remaining fully conscious and purposeful. Clearly this was also an emotion blindspot for Gene, as he was not aware of his emotions and failed to regulate them appropriately.

It's worth noting that the board was also suffering from a communication blindspot. By removing Gene from his central role, they had sent a very strong, unintentional signal that they did not value his contributions—when in fact they still valued him very much. Once they were clear with him that his voice was still needed and important, and once Gene could come to terms with his new role, he was able to find his voice again and continue to be a strong contributor. To that end, the board addressed their blindspot by encouraging Gene to write some of the company's public-facing statements, where he could assert company values. And given this new responsibility, Gene reengaged, especially as his statements received positive public attention.

Intent versus impact. Gene did not intend to send a signal with his lavish behavior, nor to sulk at the board meetings once his role was changed, and the board did not intend to communicate that they didn't value his contributions. But intent is an internal feeling that others don't always see. At least in a business context, intent doesn't matter as much as a behavior's impact. Executives with communication blindspots end up feeling like they haven't been heard, because what they think they are communicating is different from what others are taking in. This can erode trust and bring an entire company to the point of crisis. This is such a common part of the communication behavior blindspot. When I share with executives a complaint from someone interviewed for their 360-degree report, I so often hear, "That's not what I said," or the somewhat more self-aware "That's not what I meant."

Good communication demands more than good intentions. It's a social skill that demands the ability to sense how others will perceive what you are saying and doing, and even better, the ability to communicate that you are open to receiving feedback on your communication. People are seen as good leaders when they communicate in ways that make others socially safe and comfortable. These abilities are innate for some leaders but can also be learned, by focusing on developing four communication skills to help you overcome or avoid a communication blindspot:

- *Active listening.* When you are listening, are you *really* listening? Or are you thinking of how you'll respond to what you think you've heard? People can be quite good at seeing when someone isn't really paying attention to them. Do you use nonverbal cues like nodding, smiling, leaning forward, or making eye contact? Do you use verbal "encouragers" in conversation, such as "Yes, I understand" or "Tell me more," or make sounds of approval like "uh, huh"? Active listeners also paraphrase ("I hear you telling me . . .") and focus on the emotional elements of what their conversation partner is saying ("It sounds like you are frustrated . . ."). They summarize to move the conversation to the next topic ("I will definitely look into your concerns about the new product launch happening too quickly, and without enough involvement from the leadership team. I wanted to also touch on something else today . . .").

- *Balance.* Good communication is not just about listening and reflecting. You want to be a true participant in the conversation, fully engaged, contributing your own thoughts and asking good questions. At the same time, you want to make sure that you are not taking up too much airtime. You need to find the right balance between speaking and listening, and between making declarative statements, asking questions, and reflecting what the other person is saying.

- *Nonverbal cues.* Think about the volume and tone of your voice, your gestures, and even the setting of the communication. Are you in a place where the other party may feel intimidated, like in your office, or are you in a neutral location where they can feel like an equal partner? How are you dressed compared with your conversation partner? Are you rushed, seeming like you have somewhere else to be?

- *Metacommunication.* This is an often overlooked tool in the leadership toolbox. Metacommunication means communicating *about* the communication. It can mean starting a tough conversation by acknowledging what is to come ("We're going to have a difficult conversation, and I am going to do my best to make it productive for you"). It can also mean stopping when a conversation has gone awry and trying to change course midstream ("Whoa, let's stop for a moment. I'm sorry this conversation has begun to affect our relationship. Let's see if I can push restart and get us back on a productive course"). Being aware of when things are proceeding poorly and having the sophistication to stop and move to the meta level to get things back on track can be a terrific way to preserve trust at a moment when it might be in danger of being compromised.

For difficult conversations in particular, there is a hidden structure that can increase the likelihood of success. I often walk clients through a framework—Difficult Communication in Five Acts—that can help overcome the communication blindspots that are particularly prone to occur when conversations are challenging. This is a sequence; one shouldn't progress to the next act until the previous one has been completed.

Zach was a client who struggled with communication like this. During our engagement, he happened to be looking for a new public relations firm, so I referred him to a friend of mine for an introductory call. "Zach got right down to business," my friend told me afterward, "coming at me with all kinds of questions about what would happen if we didn't deliver what we promised, asking me what I thought the biggest challenges of the project would be, and trying to negotiate the fee before we even got started. These were all legitimate questions, but we never got into who we are, why he wanted to work with us, and trying to establish a little bit of rapport. I felt attacked and on the defensive—and this was just a get-to-know-you call."

My friend wasn't sure what to do. "I think we could do great work for him . . . but I don't know if I want to!"

Meanwhile, Zach reported that the call went great: "We got all the issues out on the table. They answered all my concerns. I'm just waiting to hear back with a contract."

Relationships are critical, and so is a bit of goal-setting before you jump into the hard stuff. You cannot take a shortcut through the acts below. Each one must be fully accomplished before you move to the next.

- *Act one: Build rapport.* Create a bond to have a productive discussion, agreeing to mutually commit to a successful outcome. Creating the bond can be as simple as using "small talk" to discover areas of mutuality—where you've lived, favorite hobbies, music, etc. *Act one goal: A feeling of goodwill and mutual respect.* (Do not proceed to act two until this goal is achieved.)

- *Act two: Identify objectives and reveal facts.* Use active listening and engaged inquiry to get all the facts onto the table, and identify areas of agreement and disagreement without diving into the specifics just yet. *Act two goal: Both participants have articulated their objectives, and agreed-upon facts have been established.* (Do not move to act three until this goal is achieved.)

- *Act three: Allow for conflict and challenge.* Be comfortable with conflict emerging, and don't allow emotional blindspots to derail the conversation. You can negotiate and discuss while staying focused on the issues at hand—and not impugn the person or strain the relationship. *Act three goal: Maintain a positive working relationship as areas of conflict are explored.* (Move to act four once you have identified all areas of conflict.)

- *Act four: Achieve resolution.* Find common ground where it exists, reach agreement where you can, and identify the issues that can't be resolved at this time. *Act four goal: Mutual agreement on issues that have been resolved and identification of unresolved issues.* (Once act four goals have been achieved, you can move on to act five.)

- *Act five: Move to follow-up actions.* Develop a mutually acceptable plan for next steps and a timeline for how long they should take.

Too often, just like with Zach, leaders jump right to act three, without laying the groundwork to make sure the conversation will be a success. No surprise, in many of these cases the meeting quickly deteriorates and any opportunity for a positive outcome is made impossible.

Influence

Making your case. Oleg, the director of engineering at an aircraft firm, reached out to me directly. "I know I could be more effective in my job," he said, "but I'm not sure how." He was a rising star at the company, young and ambitious, but he was clashing with the CEO and didn't know how to fix the problem. "I spend weeks putting together these presentations," Oleg told me, "dozens of slides, all the data, everything the executive team needs to know about what the engineering team is doing. And before we even get to the third slide, the CEO stops me and starts asking questions we're either going to cover ten slides later or are extraneous to the presentation. The top engineers are in the room with me, and I'm embarrassed in front of them, ashamed that I can't even get through our presentation, and that the CEO has so little respect for me that he's willing to disregard the work I've put in. When I ask him how I can make the presentations better, he doesn't have any answers for me. I don't know what to do."

I asked Oleg to walk me through one of his presentations, as if I were the CEO, and it was clear that Oleg was well-prepared and conscientious. The material was comprehensive and clear, persuasive and thorough. Yet it clearly wasn't what the CEO wanted. So I talked to the CEO to get his take. "Oleg's great," he told me. "But I want three minutes from him first about the most important issues that need decisions. He tells me you can't make decisions about what engines to build in three minutes, as if I don't know that. What he doesn't realize is that my job isn't to see all his work, like I'm a teacher correcting his exam. I just need him to tell me the problems and challenges; his recommendations and why; how certain he is; what could go wrong; what he still isn't sure about. If I want details, I'll ask for them."

I brought that message back to Oleg, who laughed. "Yes, he says that. But the one time I went super-high-level, he pushed back and wanted me to walk him through the engineering specs. I didn't have them in front of me, and he ended up rejecting our plan. He said I didn't seem confident enough in my choice, whatever that meant. I can't win."

Confident. That word was a tip-off about the blindspot here. Oleg—like many engineers—was driven by data. To him, rational arguments were the way—the only way—to make his case. But the CEO wasn't just interested in Oleg's logic. He was also assessing Oleg and his team. Oleg was failing to understand that he wasn't just solving an engineering problem. He was also solving a motivational problem, an emotional problem, a relationship problem, and more. His blindspot was not realizing there is more than one way to influence someone. He was sticking to his comfortable data-driven approach rather than adjusting to reflect the kind of appeal that the CEO would more eagerly respond to.

Understanding what motivates others. Oleg believed that the only thing that was important was whether he was *right*. And, sure, being right is important, but people don't necessarily follow you only because you have the right answer. I often see executives focus exclusively on data, believing that as long as they can make a case with numbers, they have nothing to worry about—a glaring blindspot.

The higher you are in an organization, the harder the answers are. There isn't always a *right* answer, and the answer may be dependent on many elements that are unknown, undiscoverable, or constantly changing. You need more than logic to get others to trust you, follow you, and stay loyal. The *rational* argument—"do it because the data says so"—isn't the only type of influence, and it isn't always the best one. The interpersonal influence blindspot is about failing to recognize that there are many other ways to influence people, and about failing to realize that often you should be choosing more than one influence style so that your overall approach can make the greatest positive impact given the individuals and the circumstances at hand.

We can think about nine types of influence, shown in table 6-1.

TABLE 6-1

Nine types of influence

Authority (self)	"Do it because I say so."
Authority (third party)	"Do it because the CEO wants it done."
Inspirational	"Do it because it is important for us" or "Do it because it's our mission."
Values	"Do it for the greater good" or "Do it because it's the right thing to do."
Personal	"Do it for me."
Relational	"Do it for our relationship."
Cultural norms	"Do it to be part of the group."
Igniting internal desire in others	"Do it because [a reason you have identified is important to the other party, appealing perhaps to their motives, intellect, identity, or one of the other self-awareness areas in the book]."
Rational	"Do it because the facts say we should."

These choices exclude one additional tactic that may cross your mind, which is less about using your own influence and more about appealing to someone else's personal interests: horse trading. I'll give you more money, for instance, or I'll give you less work, more vacation time, a free lunch, etc.

But the blindspots I'm talking about here go back to Oleg and his problem satisfying the CEO. There are styles we all default to. Some of us instinctively present rational arguments, others look to leverage their authority, and others may find themselves automatically appealing to values. The influence blindspot is failing to realize that your default style is not the only one, and that you can and should choose to deploy different styles as needed.

Take Emma, a client whose company needed to make significant workforce cuts. As the CFO, Emma needed to get her division leaders to trim staff, but no one was stepping up. "Do it for the good of the company," she kept saying, but no one was moved to commit. Unable to adjust to a different kind of appeal, Emma had a blindspot as to her alternatives and stuck with the one type of influence that made sense to her.

Fortunately, after Emma's repeated failures to get anyone to sacrifice more of their team members, one of Emma's colleagues stood up, took a deep breath, and announced: "I will do this for the team, and go further with my reduction, but I'm going to come back to each of you one day with a request for something my team needs, and I want you all to remember this moment when I do."

This was fundamentally a relational appeal: I will do this for you, but I expect you to respect the importance of our mutual relationship and do something for me in the future. It took a person with a solid understanding of interpersonal influence—no blindspot there—to make that offer.

Similarly, think about leaders asking their team to come in over the weekend to finish a piece of critical work. There are many ways to phrase that request, and the right way likely depends on factors idiosyncratic to the person and the task—but the best way is not necessarily going to be the first one that comes to mind, or the same for every individual. "Come in because the CEO needs you to" and "Come in because that's what we do at this firm" and "Come in because it's the right thing to do" all feel like different types of requests, and if you stick to the one you feel most comfortable with, whether or not it moves the person you're asking, you likely have an influence blindspot that needs to be addressed.

Getting influence right. It was the final day of a week-long leadership training with six senior executives from various industries. They didn't know each other coming in, but after seven days of intense exercises and learning, they had grown quite close. I asked each person which of their fellow participants they had learned the most about leadership from, and five of them gave the same answer: the Colonel.

It was the same answer I would have given. In this group of extraordinarily accomplished individuals, the Colonel—a former military officer, slight in stature and soft in volume, lacking the physical presence or natural charisma you might expect from a masterful influencer and yet possessing some of the best interpersonal instincts

I'd ever seen—stood out from the first session. As I watched from behind a one-way mirror while the leaders discussed the issues and problems we'd presented them with, the Colonel barely spoke, at least at first. He mostly listened, jumping in only to ensure that everyone was being heard, making sure that each person got their turn and wasn't being steamrolled by the loudest in the group. He was building relationships with each person in the room by inquiring about their ideas. Each felt valued by him.

By the end of the first day, he'd been pulled into the role of group facilitator, drawing others out and asking open-ended, penetrating questions that kept them talking. He would summarize the group perspective, productively moving the discussion along; he rarely offered his own opinions, but the rest of the group couldn't help but look to him for direction and maybe even approval, hoping he would nod his head or give them a smile. While the other leaders respectfully but vigorously vied for airtime and attempted to direct group activities, he never competed, always remaining committed to the team and its results.

His exchanges were warm but brief, and he waited to speak until discussions were almost fully complete, even then saying only as much as was necessary. The dominant "type A" leaders around him, all of whom came into the week certain they would end up in charge of the group, hung on his every word.

"I learned over time that when you withhold your opinion until the end, it ensures that you listen and seek information. By not showing your hand in advance, it increases your autonomy and authority," he told me. "In the military, when I would state my feelings early on in a discussion, my subordinates would stop communicating their ideas. This decreased our effectiveness as a group. As the leader, I knew I had the power to control the discussion or make the decision, but waiting as long as possible got me the most information and made everyone else feel fully heard."

The Colonel's behavior was a masterclass in overcoming or avoiding an influence blindspot. Everything he did guaranteed better outcomes, including listening first, ensuring every voice was heard, and building relationships so that when he finally did offer his own perspective, he would be listened to. He could tell that the other leaders were going to be moved more by this approach than by him asserting his authority in a room full of people who all thought they should be the one in charge.

Not every leader needs to adopt the same style as the Colonel, but every leader ought to be just as deliberate when it comes to their behavior. Once you understand your default instincts, you can adjust when it seems like another approach might be more effective. Good leaders understand how to shift into every style in the mix of nine, constantly evaluating their approach and adjusting depending on whom they're trying to influence and what they're trying to influence them to do.

Inevitably, people will be more skilled in some kinds of appeals than others, and knowing where you do best can make a real difference. Very tactically, understanding ourselves can play into how we decide to deliver messages. First, we can choose whom we decide to influence, knowing that some people will be natural influence spreaders and convey our ideas further along. Imagine, for instance, in the example of trying to get people to come in over the weekend, that there is one team member everyone else looks up to. Getting that person on board first might be the right tactic, knowing if she announces she'll be in on Sunday, others will follow.

Second, we can work through others who might be more effective than we will be. In that same weekend-work example, maybe we want to designate the influential employee to be the "team leader" for the weekend assignment and charge her with the task of getting everyone to agree to come in, instead of attempting to use our own influence to do it.

Third, we can control the stage and the pace for our messaging. We might want to start talking about the need for weekend work months in advance of when it will be necessary, or maybe it would be better to frame it as a last-minute emergency. We can also choose to deliver the message in a scheduled one-on-one conversation, in a casual walk around the office, within small informal groups, in formal group meetings, in all-staff gatherings, or through written formal (memo) or informal (email) communications.

Some executives are ineffective in large groups, where they may come across too stilted and formal, even if they are warm and relatable one-on-one. Others are the opposite. Leaders should play to their strengths as well as seek out opportunities to improve in the areas where they struggle.

The influence blindspot afflicts both those who fail to be intentional about the tactic they're using and those who rely on only those tactics from the nine that they're most comfortable with in spite of contextual cues that those tactics may not be working. Some may not realize that there are choices to be made and other paths you could go down, beyond the one that comes most naturally.

This was clearly Oleg's issue at the aircraft company. He kept foisting his rational appeal on a CEO who was clearly driven more by the confidence of an inspirational appeal ("Do this because I know it's the best") or an authority appeal ("Do this because you've trusted me to make the right engineering decisions").

During our work together, Oleg and I also realized that he had an opportunity to influence the rest of the executive team and hope that they might then come to his defense if the CEO started to bristle during the meetings.

Together, we came up with a range of behavioral strategies to draw on different interpersonal influence options. What if Oleg socialized his ideas with a few trusted members of the executive team before the meeting, giving them a preview and asking them if they had any questions or concerns, which he could then address in advance and incorporate into the three-minute presentation he would prepare for the CEO? If he could convince some of them, one-on-one, even before they walked into the room, that could help.

He could also respond directly to the CEO's motivations by providing answers to the CEO's key expressed questions (the problems, the challenges, the unknowns, his confidence in the outcome) on the first presentation slide. He could also draw on relational appeals, trying to strengthen his bond with the CEO outside of these meetings, so that he would be more likely to get the benefit of the doubt in the room. Oleg arranged for a monthly coffee with the CEO—which the CEO was glad to put on his calendar—so that they could get to know each other better and build rapport that would serve to help Oleg when trying to make his case in the room.

By broadening his thinking, Oleg landed on some relatively easy behaviors that erased his blindspot and changed his results. With more of his ideas getting approved, he found himself back on the fast track at the company—eventually promoted to vice president—and trusted by the entire executive team because they felt he was relying on them and listening to their opinions.

Prioritization

When there's too much to do. Yara, the CEO of a thriving computer hardware business, sighed. Her chief product officer, Milos (the third person in the role in three years), was exiting, and she wanted my help to make sure the next one would stick. "I liked Milos," she told me, "and he had a lot of terrific ideas. But he had never been in a role so senior and needed a lot of my support—so maybe it's a good thing that he's leaving."

I was happy to help assess future candidates but suggested that we might want to first take a look at what was making this particular role so difficult to fill. I had worked with Yara for several years, and her company had done extremely well. She was an excellent leader, overflowing with competence and integrity, and the struggle to find a long-term chief product officer was an outlier; for the most part, everything Yara touched had turned to gold. In fact, I had done very little coaching of Yara directly—she simply hadn't needed it. Most of my work for her company had been with others on her leadership team, helping them to fulfill the promise she saw in them and round out their skill sets.

Yara had started her career as a product engineer and had filled the head product role at other companies. It was notable that the job she was having trouble filling was the one she understood most closely. As I talked to Yara's product team, it became clear that this was no coincidence.

Yara's product team felt quite fortunate that she spent far more time dealing with the product side of the business than any other. But it was a double-edged sword. When I spoke to the outgoing chief product officer, Milos, he said he liked Yara, and the company, but the job wasn't as fulfilling as he'd hoped. Yara had told me that Milos needed her support; Milos painted a different picture. Yara had seemed reluctant to give him the freedom to make his own decisions, he said. She was in many ways doing his job. She constantly stepped in to guide his thinking. She met with even the lowest-level members of the product team, leaving Milos a bit frustrated and resentful. His new job was a lateral move, not a promotion, to a place where he hoped he'd have more autonomy.

The rest of Yara's leadership team, meanwhile, had been feeling Yara's absence as she tended to the product team. "She's available if I need her," one of her leaders told me. "But I feel like I'm always the one who has to seek her out." The company was falling behind its competitors because, too often, Yara didn't have the bandwidth to focus on the big picture. At times, she was slow to make decisions in areas where she wasn't expert, and at other times she would quickly make an ill-informed choice because she wasn't that interested. The other leaders never knew which Yara they would get.

Yara wasn't shocked to hear some of this, though she did push back on the idea that some of her decisions hadn't been the right ones. But as far as too much of her attention being on the product side, she was defensive. "Of course I'm spending more time dealing with the product," she said. "The company lives or dies right now on the quality of our product, and I haven't had a completely strategic leader there, so what choice have I had?" For her, it was a catch-22. She *had* to focus on product because there had been one crisis in leadership after another.

But focusing so much on product meant the business would suffer, which she would attribute to the problems with product, making her double down on her focus there.

She had too much on her plate—but it could all be fixed if we could find her an effective CPO. Still, there was a different way to look at things, one that exposed a blindspot in how Yara was prioritizing her time and energy.

Understanding what your role requires. Most roles at a company are typically well-defined. People devote their time and energy to what their predecessors have done, or to what their supervisors tell them to do. There are preset boundaries around the function, established meetings and objectives, people to manage, and things to get done. Roles shift to favor what feels urgent, what people like to do, what they're good at, and what they believe fits their professional identity, but in general, there is not that much flexibility over what the day-to-day—or at least the week-to-week—should look like.

This changes as you get toward the top of an organization. The higher one rises, as I've said before, the more freedom there tends to be in deciding how to spend time. In entrepreneurial ventures, especially early in their growth stages, almost every job requires active thought as far as what needs to be done. As the first CFO, CMO, CTO, or otherwise, one has no established guidelines, no preset meetings, no handbook for the role. This has its benefits—you get to shape the job to fit your vision, and you can work on what is mission critical for company survival and forward momentum. But at the same time, those working in established businesses struggle to escape the structure of their roles, structure that often restricts ingenuity and causes executives to focus too narrowly, sometimes at the expense of what is best for the overall enterprise.

Many leaders, both in entrepreneurial businesses and in established companies, don't spend enough time thinking about what *only* someone in their role can and must do. Fifteen years ago, the

CEO of Procter & Gamble, A.G. Lafley, wrote an article in *Harvard Business Review* titled, "What Only the CEO Can Do."[1] He identified four distinct roles: defining and interpreting what is meaningful to outside stakeholders, deciding what business the company is in and what business it is not in, balancing focus on the present with investment in the future, and shaping the values of the organization.

More granularly, I would make the case that there are five things that *only* a CEO can do:

- Select the senior team

- Have the final say on corporate priorities

- Make the strategic decisions about what resources to deploy in the short and long term

- Own the culture

- Own certain external relationships—the board, key customers, key public officials, key stakeholders and investors

These responsibilities are not optional. If the CEO does not do any of these tasks, the tasks will not get done effectively; they cannot be delegated. At the same time, leaders of functions have their own equivalent questions to answer: who should be on their senior team; what should the function's priorities be; how do we balance short-term and long-term work; what is the culture of the division, and what are the expectations of the team; which stakeholders need personal attention and cannot be delegated down (as CMO, for instance, you should be meeting with other companies' brand officers and not sending a lower-level director)?

The blindspot here is about failing to see these things as essential and instead spending your time elsewhere. Leaders need to do what only they are in a position to do; only then can they figure out what else to focus on. Deciding what you do as a leader is different from the identity question tackled in chapter 1. This isn't about the role you see yourself playing or your personal definition of success. It's not about working on the things you see yourself as an expert in and ignoring the rest. It *is* about taking the time to think about what your role demands and making sure your behavior and prioritization match those needs. This is most distinct for the CEO, because aside from the board telling you to show up for board meetings, no one is telling you what to do with your time.

After one firm got funding, its CEO told me, "I don't know what to do anymore. I watch for emails that say someone is having a problem, and then I try to help them, but beyond that, I just don't know how to fill my time."

This was a blindspot. He wasn't aware that there were things that only the CEO should be doing, so those things never got done. He was not an effective CEO, at least not until we worked together to figure out what he should actually have been doing.

The five CEO tasks bulleted above are necessary, and everything else is extra. Once these bases are covered, of course a CEO with a passion for design can engage in that process and jump in on whatever pet projects they choose. But if those projects encroach on the time that must be spent doing the required tasks, then there is a prioritization blindspot, and it needs to be addressed.

It was clear after talking to Yara and her team that Yara was investing far too much time and energy into the product group, and it was distracting her from the core CEO roles that were left unfilled. She couldn't find a long-term chief product officer because she was acting as the CPO herself. The people she was hiring felt stifled by her micromanagement and her absorption of their responsibilities. Yara would argue that she needed to step in; they would argue that she was stepping on their toes, taking over the role, and causing significant inefficiency. They'd leave, and she'd be obligated to continue focusing on that group, reinforcing a vicious cycle.

This is not to say Yara didn't have the right, as CEO, to get involved in areas where she had unique expertise, skills, and intellect. But once you're a CEO, there is a limit to it. If the CEO can get involved and be efficient and productive with their advice, moving the needle in a positive direction, that is great. But overstepping without seeing that you've done so is a dangerous blindspot—especially when communication isn't clear and the people whose roles you might be venturing too close to aren't fully aware and fully on board with the plan.

It was eye-opening for Yara to realize that her priorities had become a blindspot. She wasn't intending to sideline her CPO, but she realized that this was why she hadn't been able to find the right person to fill the role. She was having a hard time letting go of her area of expertise, partially because she hadn't fully understood the unique role of the CEO and hadn't fully bought into how her unique gifts could be realized through embracing the priorities of the position.

Effective prioritization means effective communication of your involvement in projects and activities. You can avoid a prioritization blindspot by being clear with yourself and then with your team about:

- What you own (the five areas listed above, at the very least)

- Where you jointly share accountability with another senior leader

- Where you will delegate and supervise, ensuring the accountability of others

- Where you will monitor—making others accountable to delegate and supervise, but remaining in the background if needed

- What you will ignore and leave to others

Role clarity. Yara's situation illustrates how prioritization can become a blindspot when it turns into role confusion, but that isn't the only way the prioritization blindspot can manifest itself. Veera and her brother, Zahir, had started a marketing agency that grew from just the two of them to nearly three hundred employees. As co-CEOs, they had split the job according to their strengths and interests and filled in gaps as needed. Zahir was clearly focused on analytics, and

Veera took on the culture as the business expanded. She designed in-depth interview, orientation, and onboarding processes. Once those were established, she jumped to other areas of interest, but it was hard to figure out the full scope of her job.

And if it was hard for me, no wonder it was hard for her team. She had brought me in for 360-degree evaluations of the entire leadership team, in advance of an investment round. Hers was glowing in many respects, but I also heard from multiple people, "She's great, but I don't really know what she does!" This was fine when Veera and Zahir were fully in control, but with outside investors coming in, the concern was that if Veera's role wasn't clearer, she could be pushed out or sidelined by new board members.

She wasn't surprised by the feedback, but she did become defensive about it. "Why should I need to justify what I do?" she asked. But by the end of our meetings, she realized it was a blindspot. If she wanted to stay as a co-CEO, she needed to see her schedule the way an outsider would. Eyes open, she had to prioritize her activities around things that a CEO should do and not just indulge her passions. Veera spent some time intentionally crafting a portfolio of activities—owning culture, owning the management of the senior team, owning key external relationships—that were easier to put into a "co-CEO" bucket than were the seemingly random mix of activities she was doing before. She was able to shift her passions into a more formalized set of roles that allowed her to properly prioritize and behave as a CEO.

Managing Your Own Behavior

How can you correct for any behavioral blindspots—or, a lack of awareness of all of the aspects involved in one or more of the three complex behaviors discussed, resulting in a lack of sophistication in their expression? First, it's important to understand how you are actually behaving—and then you can look at ways to address the behavior and make sure you are doing everything you can to succeed. We can look at the three categories of behavioral blindspots again and focus on gaining awareness and the actions you can take to course correct.

Communication

Awareness. The best way to understand your own communication behaviors is to listen to how you communicate, from as objective a perspective as possible. The next time you are giving a talk or engaging in some kind of public communication (where it wouldn't be unusual to have it recorded), record it, and then watch it back carefully. Yes, it may feel uncomfortable watching and listening to yourself, but it's the fastest, best way to see what others are receiving from you—the words, the tone, the body language. Ask yourself, did you achieve what you hoped for, and do you think it had the intended impact? Watch it once with the sound off, to get an appreciation for your body language, your expression, and your gestures. Are they communicating something different from the words?

You can also use online tools to analyze your communication. Some use artificial intelligence to evaluate how often someone is asking questions or the tone of their voice. It may be worth experimenting with some tools, just to get additional perspectives. When I worked with one entrepreneur with an identity blindspot, he told me he thought he spoke during meetings perhaps 20 percent to 30 percent of the time. But I tracked it, and it was close to 80 percent. That is a clear communication blindspot. Ask the people in your life about how you communicate. Do they think you communicate effectively?

Action. Armed with data and impressions, what do you need to change or work on? The best action step for communication-related blindspots is creating transparency. Put your issues out in the open and ask others to hold you accountable. Assign someone in a meeting to prompt you when you've been talking too much, or to quietly hold up a finger to signal that you should smile more, or lower your volume, or whatever it is you're working on. Ask for their support. Move more often to the metacommunication level, acknowledging the conversation during the conversation, to figure out a path to a productive end.

Influence

Awareness. First, look backward. What are the most recent influence situations where you needed to convince an individual or group to do something? How did you do it, or why, perhaps, didn't you succeed? If you look at five or ten examples from recent history, you will probably find patterns and be able to identify a default influence style that you typically use. Reflect on how some of these situations could have been approached differently and what other appeals you might have tried from the nine types of influence. For instance, if you ordered your team to stay late one evening and complete a report, relying on authority, what could it have looked like if you appealed to the relationship instead and asked them to "Take one for the team," or promised them that another day you'd let them out early to compensate? Perhaps try to create a cultural norm in the company—"Wednesdays are going to be our late night for a while; it's just how we do things here."

Sometimes I ask senior leaders to take a stack of 3-by-5-inch index cards and put the name of a direct report on the front of each one. Under their name, list some things that motivate them. Then, on the back, given what motivates each person, write which of the influence appeals might make the most sense to use with them. For instance, if you know someone is motivated by being a team player, then you might want to use a relational approach—"Do it for the team."

Action. Push yourself to experiment with the types of influence you don't ordinarily default to using. If you typically try to motivate through personal appeals ("Do it for me"), try exerting authority ("This is the rule now") and see what happens. Or try creating a new group norm. It will almost surely be that some of these approaches feel more natural than others, but, especially in low-stakes situations, you can try things out and see if the response you get is predictable or unexpected. Make sure you are appealing in different ways to different people, thinking about *their* motivations and not just your own. We get stuck in the styles that are most comfortable for us without always thinking about what will have the greatest effect on our teams.

Prioritization

Awareness. Here, I recommend a calendar audit. Look back over the last calendar quarter. This isn't just about looking at your meeting schedule but also about documenting where you put your attention. What were the priorities for the quarter, and what problems were you trying to solve when you were attending to the five tasks *only* you can do? How well does it align to what someone in your role ought to be doing? If 40 percent of your time is being spent on 5 percent of your responsibilities, then something isn't matching up. And if there's a core element of your job that isn't getting any attention at all, then that's worth noting.

I often employ a spreadsheet as a prioritization tool for clients. I ask them to list all of their activities in a given time period, their priority (low, medium, high), the recent trend of how much time and energy is spent on the activity, their self-perceived competence, the business impact, how much they love the activity, and how much effort is needed. Tracking activity for a week or two can provide a much better sense of what you are actually doing, as opposed to what you think you are doing.

Action. Once you know what you're doing, map it against the demands of your role. There will always be pet projects that you should take on, and areas where you are superskilled or in which you are highly interested and want to make sure you have time for, but the core jobs *must* be covered first.

Reflect on where you've underinvested and make a concerted effort to change. Spend time exploring the areas you might be ignoring and see if that helps to improve overall effectiveness or uncovers something about the business that you might have been missing. Architect an ideal calendar—if you were investing time in the right ways—and try to move your actual calendar in that direction.

Taken together, these tips can help you behave like a leader and address any hidden behavioral blindspots. In the conclusion, we put it all together. Now that you've come a long way toward understanding your blindspots in each of the six areas, how does it all combine, and how do you embark on real change that can take your career to the next level?

CONCLUSION

ADDRESSING YOUR OWN BLINDSPOTS

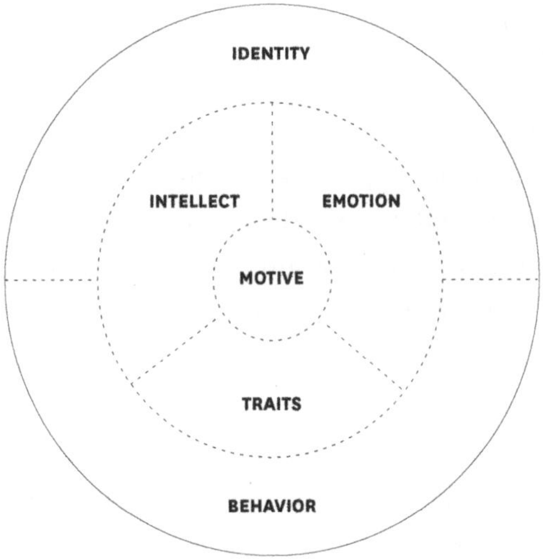
IDENTITY
INTELLECT
EMOTION
MOTIVE
TRAITS
BEHAVIOR

"You know why I'm here," I said to Angela, a member of the senior leadership team at Luxueux, a national upscale retailer, once we were through with pleasantries and moving to the substantive part of our meeting. The publicly traded company had endured a decade of flat sales and income, so the old CEO, Leslie, was replaced by a new one, Jack, who was brought in from outside. Jack wanted an evaluation of each of the senior leaders to determine whom to keep. Angela was one of those senior leaders.

"I've never been through a process like this," Angela said. "I'm excited to dive in and learn more about myself."

It was savvy of Jack to embark on these evaluations right away. *I waited too long to exit senior team members I had doubts about from the start* is one of the most common regrets I hear from CEOs reflecting on their entry. As we just saw in chapter 6, on *behavior*, hiring the senior team is something only the CEO can do. Figuring out the roles, who would work well with him, and who would augment his strengths and compensate for his weaknesses were all critical tasks for Jack—as they would be for any new CEO.

"I'm glad you're open to it," I said to Angela. "We can start with some background."

"Well, I grew up on the product side," she said, "beginning as a buyer, and then going deeper into the manufacturing process and working closely with our suppliers around the world."

Angela was underselling herself. Her role as executive vice president in charge of suppliers and manufacturing was a critical one—and she'd risen incredibly quickly, the youngest member of the leadership team by almost a decade. Angela exuded command and confidence; that's why it was no surprise to me that she had made it to senior leadership in record time.

"I was fortunate to have a wonderful mentor in Leslie, and she really took me under her wing. But it's been great to get to know Jack as well."

I could hear in Angela's voice—just a subtle indication—that she was not confident about her relationship with Jack, who had confided in me that his initial impression of Angela was that she was struggling with self-doubt and was not sure she belonged on the executive leadership team. That was the big question he wanted me to address with her: *Why should I keep you in executive leadership if it doesn't seem like you think you deserve to be there?*

There's a version of my conversation with Angela where it could have been easy—*Jack is worried that you're not right for the role*, I would have said, and Angela would have neatly declared, *Oh, that's just because I'm not a confident person. I guess that's a trait issue we can work on*, or *I still don't see myself as a corporate executive. Can you help me revise my identity?*

But that would have been extremely unusual. People rarely have the self-awareness to know their own issues or, as we've learned throughout this book, to see their blindspots.

Instead, we must unearth them. Angela started out with exactly the right attitude—instantly charming despite the stakes of our meeting, warm, engaging, and charismatic. In the first few minutes, we'd established that she lived three blocks away from my cousin, and that we both loved the hiking trail at a nearby park. We were bonding from the start. Her role meant that she needed to be able to make stakeholders eager to cooperate with her, and I could see those skills on display right away. I could easily imagine her walking right into a factory, shaking hands with everyone from the foreman to the line workers, making sure they knew and felt motivated by the fact that they were all critical parts of the Luxueux team.

But she also knew that things had not started off perfectly with her new CEO, Jack, even if she couldn't yet identify why. Most of us can sense when something isn't right, but we struggle more with identifying the actual problem—though I hope you will struggle less now that you're nearing the end of this book. What the six blindspot areas provide is a template for evaluating your sense that things are off, the sinking feelings. Knowing the six areas can help you isolate which blindspot areas you need to look into and what is actually going on beneath the surface. It can be painful to admit when things aren't perfect and to dive deeper instead of looking externally for reasons that don't have anything to do with you, but the best thing you can do to find your blindspots and get past them is never to hide. Instead, even if it goes against your instincts, you must expand your curiosity about yourself and about how you approach the world, and ask—and answer—the hard questions.

One indirect question that gets leaders to begin to reflect on their leadership characteristics: *Who has been an influential leader in your life?*

I tell people they can give me positive examples or negative ones; leaders they want to emulate or people they hope to be nothing like. How they answer this question provides good insight into the traits they value, the type of intellect that they best relate to, their deeper motives, or other areas that might be prone to blindspots. Sometimes people tell me about early supervisors, leaders at companies where they started their careers. Others go even further back and tell me about their very first role models for leadership: parents, grandparents, teachers, coaches.

"I guess the first person I think of is my mother," Angela said when I posed the question to her, and then—surprising us both—she teared up and couldn't speak. "Sorry," she started, but I wanted her to stay with the feeling and keep going. You have to be comfortable with strong emotions to get at the truths deep inside of you. Emotion is often the key to something real and fundamental, the fastest way to motive.

I looked in Angela's eyes and could tell that she was deciding if I was someone to trust or whether this kind of reveal might be used against her with Jack. "I guess I just miss her," Angela started to say, but I wasn't going to let her move on.

"Tell me more," I said.

Blindspotting Begins with Awareness

While we all have blindspots, oftentimes we can ignore them. Human beings are naturally flexible and resilient, and if you are stumbling a bit, you will most likely find your way to an effective solution. You may find straightforward ways to compensate for the blindspot you don't even know you have—for instance, relying on colleagues who can complement your skills and gaps—but sometimes we get stuck.

If you are not progressing as you would like to—feeling frustrated, receiving adverse feedback, failing to move toward a goal—then a personal blindspot is most likely impairing your ability to move forward, and the whole premise of this book is that there are tools you can use to address this. If you've read this far, then you are curious and eager to understand how to both identify and overcome blindspots to improve your career, your effectiveness, and your happiness.

In the introduction, I wrote about how most self-help books are present on the "help" but erroneously absent on the "self." I've focused more on the latter throughout this book to get you to understand blindspots—the self. Now we turn directly to the help part and focus on overcoming your blindspots. I want this last chapter to be as actionable as possible. To do that, we'll first walk through Angela's growth plan, and then I'll show you exactly how to apply the principles to your own life and supercharge your leadership.

Unlike clients who ask for my help, Angela knew I was there to evaluate her for the CEO. Those engagements can be quite uncomfortable. Often, it encourages the person to control what they present. A big part of my job is simply to help people open up and engage. Of course, that's not the *entire* job, and a big part of this book has been trying to give you the tools so you can coach yourself even if you don't have someone like me there to help.

The challenge in being a coach is knowing what to listen for; what is extraneous information; what is at the core of the problem. Without a framework like the self-awareness model in this book, coaches—and you—are left to intuition. That intuition can be quite biased, and that's why there are bad coaches as well as good ones. Conversations—whether the ones I have with executives like Angela, or the ones you can have inside your own head—meander. In that rambling approach, you can miss clues or get stuck in irrelevant rabbit holes.

This book provides you with a model and the language to shape your exploratory process into something more deliberate and effective. You can train yourself to think productively about your blindspots and ask the right questions so that you know when you're dealing with an identity blindspot, or a motive blindspot, and aren't merely lost in the confusing place where what you're doing isn't working but you don't know why. You can become more self-aware. In that spirit, as I explain Angela's struggles, see if you can pick out her blindspots before I reveal them, and then I'll show you how she was able to overcome them and thrive.

I had a sense when she teared up about her mother that pushing her to continue was going to reveal something profound and helpful.

"She was amazing," Angela continued, "and yet she was held back by the people around her from ever achieving what she could have. She was so dynamic and competent. She had come to this country from South Korea when she was just a kid. She learned English and went to college at night while she worked two jobs. She passed away when I was in high school. And while I'm sure she would have found her way if she hadn't died so young, a big part of her story is that the world never took her seriously. She was so capable and aspired to so much, but I think we hadn't gotten there yet as a society, giving strong women the opportunity to reach their potential, and so she was held back."

Angela started to tear up once more. "There I go again."

"Why do you think this is affecting you so strongly as you talk about it?" I asked her.

"I don't know, I guess I still really miss her, and maybe I'm angry, too."

"It feels like it's still so present for you."

"Hmm. I never really thought about it." I gave her a moment to reflect, and Angela shrugged. "I guess I'm always kind of worried that what happened to her will happen to me, and I won't be taken seriously as a leader. I'm afraid I'll get ignored like she was."

I pointed out to Angela that she was the youngest person on the leadership team and had risen so quickly. "You haven't been blocked at all—you've been on the fast track ever since the beginning."

"Maybe, but it doesn't always feel that way."

In a later meeting, I walked Angela through her 360-degree feedback. So much of what people had to say was positive—Angela was strong, smart, competent, and emotionally available—but there were a few comments that struck a different chord.

"She's uncompromising at times," one person said, "and can suddenly switch from being a warm and caring colleague to a cold and calculating opponent. You don't always know which Angela you're going to get, and so it's hard to always trust her."

"She's clearly ambitious," said another, "but it's kind of too much. It's very clear that she wants to make it to the top, and it feels like she's in too much of a hurry to get there."

"What do you make of this?" I asked her. "Do you ever sense that in yourself?"

Angela thought about it for a few moments. "I think I know who might have said those things, and I think it's because there have been times when it seemed like there were people standing in my way, and I do get defensive sometimes."

"So you felt like they were holding you back?"

"Potentially, sure. And I'm not going to argue about the ambition point, but I feel like you have to push, or you're never going to get what you deserve."

"Does that remind you of anything we talked about last time?"

Angela sighed. "I never thought about it before, but I guess maybe it does come back to my mother."

I nodded and let her continue. "I feel so strongly that she was blocked—when she shouldn't have been—that maybe I do get particularly irritated when I sense that it's happening to me, too, and feel like it's something I have to constantly pay attention to. It's not intentional—"

"And that's kind of the point," I interjected. "This isn't a conscious thing you're trying to do, but you have these feelings deep inside that you're not thinking about, and they're driving your behavior in these situations."

Angela was not aware of how cold she could be to colleagues, how she was overreacting to perceived slights, and how nakedly obvious her ambition appeared at times.

There was another category of comments in her review that hinted at Jack's initial impression of Angela. "She's quite competent as a leader," one colleague said, "but it sometimes seems like she doesn't think she deserves a seat at the table."

"She's young to be such a senior leader," someone else said. "She's earned it, yet sometimes she doesn't realize that everybody's fine with her needing to learn something. Heck, we all are learning."

Angela's Blindspots Revealed

It should be no surprise after reading her story that Angela was dealing with a *trait blindspot*—ambition—connected to the underlying motive of overcoming her mother's unfulfilled professional potential. Angela's ambition—ambition being a good thing in its proper dose, but not when you are blind to how it is showing itself in the workplace—was being supercharged by the pressure of a *motive blindspot*, so when she was blocked, she ended up acting like she was fighting her mother's fights as well as her own and overcompensating. Her colleagues saw and felt this, but neither they nor Angela understood its subconscious source. This was showing itself quite starkly in her behavior—she was sometimes the helpful colleague, but other times a contentious fighter.

It was also creating an *emotion blindspot* for her. When Angela was blocked from realizing her objectives, she wasn't in control of how she was expressing her feelings. Without realizing it, she was agitated and difficult, cold and uncompromising.

But these weren't the only blindspots Angela was facing. Despite her outsize ambition, she found herself sometimes feeling like an imposter in the boardroom. Even though Angela believed her mother had been held back, and she was angry about that, there was also a part of her that was unsure. On a conscious level, she knew she belonged as a leader, but subconsciously she couldn't help but wonder if maybe those in charge were right that her mother didn't have what it took. And if they were right about her mother, then maybe she didn't have what it took either. Maybe she didn't really belong at the big table; maybe she was a pretender.

This was an *identity blindspot*, and it showed even in our first conversation when she undersold her role in a way she didn't need to and jumped right to acknowledging the mentorship she had received from the previous CEO. Angela had reached the executive level, but still saw herself as someone who needed the support and mentorship of someone else, and not as someone who could stand on her own. Jack picked up on this identity issue and was now unsure as well if she was fit for the role.

Together, these four blindspots—a trait one manifested in her ambition; a motive one driven by her mother's experience; an emotion one that showed up as sudden shifts to agitation and coldness; and an identity one in her self-doubt—stood a good chance of derailing Angela's career. Jack had doubts based on her identity blindspot, and first impressions matter—it was going to be hard to change his mind. At the same time, colleagues questioned her fit due to her trait and motive blindspots.

It should be noted: her motive was clearly leading to negative behavior; indeed, it is only when our blindspots cause problems that they become something we need to address. In other words, a trait like ambition can be a good thing, until it isn't. There was a helpful side to Angela's ambition. One junior colleague described how Angela had pushed the company to recognize and promote her and how Angela was a terrific teacher and mentor. Her ambition, when channeled properly, was a huge strength. When it tipped over into emotional and calculating behavior, without her being aware of it, only then did it become a blindspot.

As we walked through the other blindspot categories, now that Angela was on the lookout, we found another. She came to the realization that when she was fatigued, it was harder for her to control her instincts, and she knew that she would sometimes give in to her default quickness of thinking and processing, talking over people, interrupting them, and generally barreling forth from one concept to the next (*intellect blindspot*).

Angela also felt like she lost focus on choosing the right influence styles when she was tired (*behavior blindspot*). She would stop trying to work out the best approach for a particular individual and would instead try to use her own authority—*just do it because I need you to*—to move people to perform. She did believe that she was good at prioritizing as a leader and understood how to communicate effectively. And when she wasn't fatigued, she felt she had a much better handle on herself and control over all of her blindspot areas. Oftentimes, blindspots are not whole-person, all-the-time problems but, rather, situational. We are fine when things are going well—but as soon as we are stressed in a new way, a blindspot emerges.

Once we were able to name Angela's blindspots, we could move to the next stage and figure out how to manage them more effectively.

Developing a Change Plan

In our next session together, Angela and I made a plan for overcoming the blindspots. First, we set objectives to address Angela's identity blindspot (recall that identity and behavior are the easiest to change since they are closest to the surface of our consciousness—so it often makes sense to put those first and create early wins). Next, we would see if that change could have a knock-on effect and reduce the intensity of her motive, trait, and emotion blindspots. The behavior she was currently exhibiting was that she was showing up to meetings with self-doubt, not acting as strongly as she could.

Objective 1: Act as a stronger leader at meetings

The focus here was on the literal actions Angela could take to project confidence and command. We talked about how she could walk into the room with more confidence, where she should sit, how much she should participate, and what her participation ought to look like as far as asking questions or offering opinions. "I want to show everyone that I'm thinking about agenda items that aren't even in my domain, because I want to be seen as an enterprise-level leader who belongs here," she told me.

We talked about triggers—were there things that made her feel like she didn't belong? She mentioned that she would notice if people didn't follow up right away on something she said, and get agitated if she saw someone raise an eyebrow—*Why is she talking*? So we worked on consciously ignoring those triggers, making sure she leaned in at the table and continued to engage even when she thought people might not be taking her ideas as seriously as she hoped.

We made a plan for Angela to journal after every big meeting, writing down how much she contributed and whether she was able to avoid being triggered by other people's responses. Journaling is a deeply useful tool to self-monitor and keep yourself on track. I told her to pay attention to when a meeting was hard or when she failed to live up to her objective, so that we could see what was preventing her from executing on the objective and we could brainstorm new solutions.

This focused, specific work enabled her to more fully believe that she was a leader who belonged. She adopted a persona at the senior executive team meetings—*be it until you are it*—of someone with the quiet self-assurance that she was a leader. *I belong here*, she told herself, *because I am a senior leader who will make a difference for this company. My competence put me here, and while I have plenty to learn, I don't need to fight my peers or be fearful that someone will deny me my due.*

When walking into meetings, she decided to rely on a short phrase— "step into the role"—to remind her of the mission. Catchphrases like this, as silly as they might seem, can be powerful tools to control our behavior. Angela wanted a way to remind herself that it was okay for her to be there even if she didn't have the same amount of experience as some of her colleagues.

We then moved onto a second objective, based on the coldness that some of her team had been perceiving from her.

Objective 2: Be less emotional when handling pushback from colleagues

Here, we again needed to identify triggers and come up with a plan to consciously cope with them. Angela noticed that she would feel tightness in her neck when people started to criticize her, maybe a shiver up her spine or a feeling of tension in her jaw. Her words would start to get clipped, and she would stop smiling. With this new awareness, she thought she would be able to catch herself and not be so quick to become agitated and respond coldly. For this objective, she decided an accountability partner could help her. She confided in her number two that she was working on being more positive in tough situations and asked her to watch for when people were criticizing her and give Angela a signal so she could control her response. Through journaling, Angela figured out which team members tended to trigger her the most, and she made a concerted effort to act warmer toward those individuals and not fall into her usual traps.

The accountability partner was a bonus ally for Angela, but it's not always realistic to confide in someone at work. Sometimes a coach can help; other times it might be someone at home you report to at the end of the day. If there is no one to help you, then you can use journaling to track your behaviors, with a special focus on journaling immediately after interactions so that the memories are fresh.

Having recognized that fatigue was her Achilles' heel when trying to control her emotions, we instituted a number of changes that would keep her as fresh and relaxed as possible. She looked at her schedule and made sure she had downtime before taxing meetings or before interacting with taxing people. She made sure she exercised and got enough sleep. And when she traveled across multiple time zones, she made sure she had a couple of easy days before any difficult ones.

Putting this plan into action, Angela felt more confident, and she was able to more fully satisfy her motive and address her blindspot. *I am successful, and will continue to be successful,* she told herself.

No one can stop me, like they stopped my mother, so I don't need to worry about that.

Note that Angela's plan didn't remove the situations from her work life. People were still going to criticize her. She would still have moments of feeling unworthy. It just meant she was more aware of what was happening and could react in a more positive way in the moment. Colleagues suddenly didn't seem as threatening, and thus Angela's emotion blindspots could fade into the background along with the motive one. She didn't need to resort to being cold and calculating, because she wasn't feeling threatened. And, feeling fewer threats, she didn't have to concentrate so much on her own ambition in ways that were destructive. Instead, she could find coping mechanisms around whatever seemed to be blocking her. *I can regulate my emotions and ensure that I am behaving with my usual warmth and cooperation,* she told herself. *I know what the fearful emotion feels like, and I can regulate it when it appears.*

"You completely freed me up from the burden I didn't even know I was carrying," Angela told me as we finished our sessions. "It's so weird that I was reacting to people in my life like they were the same people who held back my mother. I didn't realize those feelings were causing me to put people in categories—supporters or blockers—and affecting how I treated them."

Change Isn't Always the End of the Story

Angela made tremendous—and visible—progress during the time we worked together. But even though I thought she was demonstrating her leadership abilities to Jack, the Luxueux CEO, he hadn't shaken his first impression. It was clear that she was being marginalized and her career at the company had flatlined. Had we not addressed her blindspots, I believe this would have continued. It would have been harder for her to find her next job and keep her career momentum going.

To Jack's credit, he recognized Angela's ability to improve, and armed with good reviews from Jack and others, she was able to leave on her own terms. As it turned out, Tameka, Luxueux's former COO who'd left the company when Jack came on, had become the CEO of a competing brand, and her first hire was Angela as her chief operating officer, a tremendous promotion and vote of confidence.

Under Tameka's mentorship, Angela continued to grow as a leader. Except that, unfortunately, it turned out that Tameka had her own blindspots. I had continued to work with Angela, and it became apparent to me through our conversations that Tameka was not long for the CEO role. The private equity firm that owned the business was pushing for faster growth than Tameka was equipped to deliver. It appeared to be a trait blindspot: Tameka was far too cautious for the situation, and the private equity firm began to talk directly to Angela and other senior leaders, looking for a replacement CEO. This would have been a tremendous opportunity for Angela, but she was unable to capitalize because of her own additional trait blindspot that emerged: she had placed Tameka in a "supporter" camp—and was loyal to a fault.

I don't mean to dismiss loyalty as a valuable trait, but there are absolutely times when our loyalty can blind us, just as it blinded Brendan when it came to his friend Miguel in chapter 3, on *traits*. Because Tameka had brought Angela with her, and had taken her under her wing, Angela could not appreciate that Tameka was failing to hit targets, underperforming as a leader, and losing market share rapidly. Angela was failing to use her considerable analytical skills to realize what was happening. "She'll figure it out," Angela kept telling me, and she refused to engage in a more aggressive growth strategy.

Angela had spent her career dividing the world—on a subconscious level—into people who supported her and people who blocked her, and while we had already worked on neutralizing her emotional response to the blockers, we hadn't addressed the idea that even the good guys can have problems, and you don't want to be blind to the flaws of the people who like you.

"I guess I have rose-colored glasses where Tameka is concerned," Angela told me, yet the result became inevitable. Tameka was fired, and Angela was pushed out with her. Angela's next role was a lateral step, but we continued to work together and she admitted that she had let her loyalty to Tameka blind her view of the situation. When the next opportunity came up—to jump into the CEO role of a smaller but quickly growing luxury accessories brand—Angela was ready. She got the job and achieved tremendous success, guiding the company to an IPO before stepping back to become a mentor to female entrepreneurs for a startup accelerator.

Building Your Own Change Plan

I have presented you with a great deal of material. There are in fact more than sixty blindspots we've covered. They are listed in the appendix, and you are encouraged to go through them, one by one, to consider how any one of them may apply to you. Most of the blindspots will not be relevant to a particular person at a particular time—probably just one or two primarily, and maybe three to five all together. The key is figuring out the handful that matter to *you*, ensuring you have the awareness to pursue meaningful change.

That word—*change*—is the crux of it all, and it's not as simple as it seems. As I've said throughout this book, I think you can change. Certainly, you can change the outside layer—your identity and behavior—even if you don't change the inner layers. Changes in behavior and in identity alone can create marked improvements in how you are perceived and how others relate to you. This can result in significantly different outcomes in your leadership journey. If you can go even deeper and detect blindspots in your traits, emotions, intellect, and motives, and then adjust to minimize them, you can make even more-profound change.

Here is how you can do it.

Start by answering a few bigger-picture questions. As you reflect on the prompts below, think about what resonated with you as you read the chapters, and what you've learned about yourself.

We start with the big questions of the book:

> Who are you? You are made up of your identities.
>
> Why do you do what you do? Your motives.
>
> What is the makeup of your personality? Your traits, emotions, and intellect.
>
> How do you show up in the world? Your behaviors.
>
> Then, we focus on awareness.

Do you have an identity blindspot? Recall—these are the stories that you write about yourself; how you describe yourself; what you would put on your name tag; what you would say to someone you meet for the first time.

We all have a limited number of core identities, and we are aware of most of them. You just need to figure out which of your identities, connected to work, are acting outside your conscious awareness. *How well does your identity fit your current role? Are there parts of your identity that are unfulfilled by your role? Are there parts of your identity in conflict with your role? In what ways would your identity need to change to fit your next career role?*

Do you want to make any changes?

Do you have a motive blindspot? *What drives you? What do you gravitate to and away from? How would you describe your balance of needs for achievement, power, and affiliation?* See if you can figure out the one or two motives that show up when you are feeling strong emotion. These are probably the motives that are tripping you up. *Are you aware of how your drives make you successful? Do any of your motives cause you difficulties at work? Can you adjust them to be less problematic?*

Do you want to make any changes?

Do you have a trait blindspot? Psychologists have identified a lot of traits, but we can focus on the traits where you know (or others tell you) that you are at an extreme end. These are the traits that you are prone to overuse, meaning that you rely on them at times when they are not helpful to you and may in fact cause you problems. *Are you aware of any supertraits that serve you well? When do they become overused and problematic? When you think about your job and your role, which of your traits contribute to your success and which can become problematic? Do you have any trait gaps that make you less successful in your role?*

Do you want to make any changes?

Do you have an emotion blindspot? *What is your self-assessment of your awareness of emotions? In what ways is your emotional awareness a strength or a deficit? Are there any emotions that surprise you—that you are confused by in the moment—or any that you have trouble regulating, and that you regret after the fact? These emotions may be your emotion blindspots.*

Do you want to make any changes?

Do you have an intellect blindspot? *What is your intellectual strength? Speed of processing? Horsepower? Creativity? Street smarts and business acumen? Do you have any weaknesses or gaps in any of the four types? Are there times when you overuse your strength?*

Do you want to make any changes?

Do you have a behavior blindspot? *How well do your actual behaviors at work fit what is needed by your role? How well are you doing what only you can and should be doing in your role? What aspects of your role are you particularly effective at? In which aspects are you deficient?*

How strategic are you with your interpersonal influence? How many of the types of influence do you routinely employ? How aware are you of your communication effectiveness?

Do you want to make any changes?

Finally, we move to action, using Angela's change plan as a model. Angela's change plan followed these steps:

1. ***Problem:*** What is the challenge you are currently facing?

    - For Angela, it was that the new CEO wasn't sure if she belonged on the senior leadership team.

2. ***Awareness:*** What blindspots are present?

    - Review the blindspots (see the appendix) and try to identify the issues at play.

3. ***Target behavior:*** What is the problematic behavior that needs to change?

    - In Angela's case, there were two: (1) she was showing uncertainty as a leader, making people wonder if she really belonged; and (2) she was getting agitated when she didn't get full support from her peers, withdrawing her normal warmth and becoming cold.

4. ***Trigger:*** What makes these behaviors occur?

    - It was at executive team meetings or during other difficult interactions when Angela was most in need of a change plan.

5. ***New behavior:*** What would be a better behavioral response?

    - Angela wanted to (1) act like she belonged at the table and (2) not react to pushback in a defensive way but instead be thoughtful, ask questions, and remain warm and friendly.

6. *Change plan:* When and where will you aim to deploy the new behavior?

    - Angela and I identified which meetings and interactions (three to four per week) to focus on.

7. *Prompt:* How will you trigger your change?

    - Angela put reminders on her schedule: "Act like you belong!" "Stay focused!"

8. *Accountability:* Is there someone who can hold you to your commitment to change?

    - Angela had her colleague to confide in, and I was also there to hold her accountable at our regular meetings.

9. *Timeline:* How long do you plan to work on this?

    - Angela decided to focus on this for six months.

10. *Review and revise:* How often will you revisit and adjust the plan?

    - Angela decided to give it an initial evaluation after two weeks and then check in with herself and her accountability partners once a month.

It's a good bet that after reading this book and going through these exercises, you will naturally start to notice the blindspots of the people around you. We can often recognize issues in others that are more challenging to see in ourselves. You should now have the vocabulary to articulate what is bothering you about others, and eventually, with practice and focus, it should be easier to spot blindspots in yourself. I'd also urge you to go back to those other leadership books you've read over the years to see if they can produce greater impact now that you have a better understanding of how to apply the "help" to the "self." So many of the leadership insights that others have formulated can be far more meaningful once we understand ourselves and have done the hard work of self-awareness—this is precisely why I focused so much on the self. Getting that right is the only way to make meaningful change.

Lastly, remember that this isn't a onetime exercise. Just as circumstances change, the blindspots that affect us change as well. Characteristics that only helped us in the past can become blindspots that affect us in the future. I urge you to revisit the tools in this book as you encounter new bumps in the road, and I hope they can keep you on track throughout the rest of your career. I wish you the very best of luck as you keep improving your leadership skills.

APPENDIX

BLINDSPOT CHECKLIST

1. Where are your **identity** blindspots?

    Which of the entrepreneurial and general business identities best describe how you see yourself?

    How well do those identities fit with your current role and future roles you aspire to?

    Do you overindex on any of those identities to the extent that it limits your options?

    - **Entrepreneurial identities**
        - Innovator
        - Business builder
        - Leader
    - **General business identities**
        - Subject-matter expert
        - Loyal follower
        - Tactical operator/executer
        - Leader

What are your personal identities (in addition to the suggested list below)?

How well do each of those identities fit with your current role and future roles you aspire to?

Do you overindex on any of those identities to the extent that it limits your options?

- **Personal blindspots**
  - Impostor syndrome
  - Independent thinker
  - Rule follower
  - Unworthy
  - Entitled
  - Rebel
  - Peacemaker

2. Where are your **motive** blindspots?

   Which of the entrepreneurial and general business motives best describe what drives you?

   How well do those motives fit with your current role and future roles you aspire to?

   Do you overindex on any of those motives to the extent that it limits your options?

   - **Entrepreneurial motives**
     - Need to change the world
     - Need for fame
     - Need for money

- **General business motives**
  - Need for achievement
  - Need for affiliation
  - Need for power

What are your personal motives (in addition to the suggested list below)?

How well do those motives fit with your current role and future roles you aspire to?

Do you overindex on any of those motives to the extent that it limits your options?

- **Personal motives**
  - Need for approval
  - Need to prove significance
  - Need for affection
  - Need to win
  - Need to avoid conflict

3. Where are your **trait** blindspots?

Which of the Big Five, entrepreneurial, and general business traits best describe you?

How well do those traits fit with your current role and future roles you aspire to?

Do you overindex on any of those traits to the extent that it limits your options?

- **Big Five traits**
  - Extroversion
  - Openness to experience

- Accommodation
- Conscientiousness
- Neuroticism

- **Entrepreneurial traits**
  - Resilience
  - Perseverance
  - Confidence
  - Bias to action
  - Owner mindset
  - Comfort with risk
  - Abundance mentality
  - Vision
  - Passion

- **General business traits**
  - Self-awareness
  - Respect
  - Compassion
  - Vision
  - Learning agility
  - Collaboration
  - Influence
  - Integrity
  - Courage

- Gratitude
- Resilience

4. Where are your **emotion** blindspots?

   Is your emotional bandwidth limited to the extent that you have difficulty identifying and describing emotions?

   How aware are you of what you are feeling in the moment or shortly after?

   What emotions do you have difficulty managing? What situations trigger emotions that are difficult to manage?

   How skilled are you in recognizing others' emotions?

   How skilled are you at predicting downstream outcomes of your and others' emotions?

   - **Emotional bandwidth**
   - **Emotional self-awareness**
   - **Emotional self-regulation**
   - **Empathy/awareness of others' emotions**
   - **Awareness of downstream impact of emotions**

5. Where are your **intellect** blindspots?

   Which of the intellectual abilities best describe your strengths and your gaps?

   How well do those intellectual strengths fit with your current role and future roles you aspire to?

   Do you overindex on any of those strengths to the extent that it limits your options?

- Horsepower
- Processing speed
- Creative intellect
- Street smarts/business acumen

Do you have strategies to mitigate what you don't know?

- **Know what you know—comfort zone**
- **Know what you don't know—anxiety zone**
- **Don't know what you should know—terror zone**
- **Don't know what you don't know—blind zone**

6. Where are your **behavior** blindspots?

   What are your communication gaps that limit your effectiveness?

   How effective are you at utilizing a broad skill set of influence strategies?

   How well do the priorities of your role match where you are spending your time and energy?

   - **Communicate**
   - **Influence**
   - **Prioritize**

NOTES

Introduction

1. Dan Pilat and Dr. Sekoul Krastev, "Why Do We Fail to Accurately Gauge Our Own Abilities?" The Decision Lab, 2021, https://thedecisionlab.com/biases/dunning-kruger-effect.

2. Ben Horowitz, *The Hard Thing About Hard Things: Building a Business When There Are No Easy Answers* (New York: Harper Business, 2014).

Chapter 2

1. Abraham H. Maslow, "A Theory of Human Motivation," *Psychological Review* 50, no. 4 (1943): 370, https://psychclassics.yorku.ca/Maslow/motivation.htm.

2. David C. McClelland, *Human Motivation* (Cambridge, UK: Cambridge University Press, 1985).

Chapter 3

1. Annabelle G.Y. Lim, "Big Five Personality Traits: The 5-Factor Model of Personality," SimplyPsychology, December 20, 2023, https://www.simplypsychology.org/big-five-personality.html.

2. See, for instance, Micela Leis and Stephanie Wormington, "12 Essential Qualities of Effective Leadership," Center for Creative Leadership, July 3, 2024, https://www.ccl.org/articles/leading-effectively-articles/characteristics-good-leader/; and Brian Downard, "101 Best Leadership Skills, Traits & Qualities—the Complete List," https://briandownard.com/leadership-skills-list/.

Chapter 4

1. See https://www.danielgoleman.info/.

Chapter 5

1. Kendra Cherry, "Alfred Binet and the History of IQ Testing," *Verywell Mind*, March 13, 2023, https://www.verywellmind.com/history-of-intelligence-testing-2795581.

2. Reza Pishghadam et al., "Intelligence, Emotional Intelligence, and Emo-Sensory Intelligence: Which One Is a Better Predictor of University Students'

Academic Success?" *Frontiers in Psychology* 13 (2022), https://www.frontiersin.org/journals/psychology/articles/10.3389/fpsyg.2022.995988/full.

3. See, for instance, Eric Van den Steen, "Strategy and Strategic Thinking," Harvard Business School Technical Note 721-431, January 2021, https://www.hbs.edu/faculty/Pages/item.aspx?num=59508; and Marc Asobee, "Exploring the Importance of Strategic Thinking to Strategic Planning in the Strategic Management Process," *Journal of Business and Management Sciences* 9, no. 2 (2021): 68, https://www.researchgate.net/publication/352019936_Exploring_the_Importance_of_Strategic_Thinking_to_Strategic_Planning_in_the_Strategic_Management_Process.

Chapter 6

1. A.G. Lafley, "What Only the CEO Can Do," *Harvard Business Review*, May 2009, https://hbr.org/2009/05/what-only-the-ceo-can-do.

INDEX

achievement motive, 52, 63, 76
active listening, 171–172
affiliation motive, 52, 54–56, 63, 76
agreeableness, 82–84, 98–100, 104
anxiety
   emotional blindspots and, 133
   motive blindspots and, 61–63
Anxiety Zone, 152–153, 160
approval motive, 57

bandwidth, emotional, 114, 134–135, 183, 217
behavioral blindspots, 6–7, 14, 162, 163–192, 202, 209–210
   checklist on, 218
   communication and, 166, 167–175, 189–190
   correcting, 188–192
   influence and, 166–167, 175–182, 190–191
   leadership and, 165–188
   others' motives and, 176–178
   prioritization and, 167, 182–188, 191–192
behaviors
   change plans for, 207–212
   definition of, 163–164
   examining for identity, 35–37
   identity changes and, 39–42
   leadership and, 165–188
   managing your own, 188–192
belonging needs, 51
Big Five traits, 88–89, 96, 215–216
blindspots
   addressing your, 193–212
   becoming aware of, 196–200
   behavior, 6–7, 163–192
   change plans for, 202–205
   checklist on, 213–219
   compensating for, 196–200
   defining, 3–5
   emotion, 7–8, 107–136
   identity, 6–7, 19, 21–47
   intellect, 7–8, 137–162
   motive, 8, 49–79
   noting in others, 211–212
   traits, 7–8, 81–106
Blind Zone, 152, 153
body language, 168, 172
brand identity, 32–35
business builder identity, 28, 29–30

Center for Creative Leadership, 17, 93
Comfort Zone, 152
communication
   behavioral blindspots with, 166, 167–175, 189–190
   beyond words, 167–171
   difficult, 173–175

communication (*continued*)
   influence and, 178–182
   intent versus impact in, 171–175
   prioritization and, 187
conscientiousness, 88, 89, 104
creative intelligence, 142–143, 148–149, 161
culture issues, 132–133
   behavioral blindspots and, 169
   leadership and, 185

Difficult Communication in Five Acts framework, 173–175
Dunning-Kruger effect, 5

emotional blindspots, 6, 7–8, 13, 16, 18, 107–136, 200, 209
   awareness of, 134–135
   changing, 117–120, 130–131, 136, 204–205
   checklist for, 217
   connections and, 123–127
   culture issues and, 132–133
   emotional mastery and, 112–116, 127–132
   information overlooked through, 120–123
Emotional Intelligence (Goleman), 113
emotional quotient (EQ), 113–114
emotions, 3–4
   awareness of others', 115, 117–120, 217
   awareness of your, 114–115
   bandwidth with, 114, 134–135, 183, 217
   changing, 136
   comfort with, 196
   as data, 120–123
   effects of on others, 112–113, 115–116
   fear of, 122–123
   identity changes and, 29–30
   ignoring, 124–127
   knowledge acquisition and, 150

   mastery of, 112–116, 127–132
   motive blindspots and, 70–71, 77
   pushback and, 199–200, 204–205
   self-regulation of, 115
   strategic thinking and, 155–156
entrepreneurs
   identity blindspots of, 27–30, 213
   motive blindspots of, 214–215
   self-awareness in, 10–12
   trait blindspots of, 93–94
   traits of, 93–95, 216
EQ. *See* emotional quotient (EQ)
established companies
   role/identity misalignments in, 28–29
   trait blindspots and, 93–94
extroversion, 88, 89–91, 92, 104

fame, desire for, 53
feedback
   on communication, 171–175
   on emotional blindspots, 134–135
   on motives, 71
   success, blindspots, and, 11–14
   on traits, 104
fishbowl effect, 169
founder identity, 28, 29–30

Goleman, Daniel, 113

The Hard Thing About Hard Things (Horowitz), 17
hierarchy of human needs, 51
Horowitz, Ben, 17
horsepower intelligence, 142, 146

identity, 208
   changing, 46–47
   deciding you want to change, 35–39
   definition of, 23
   evolving your, 39–42

INDEX

finding yours, at work, 32–35
mapping, 45–46
misalignment around, 26–32
personal, 29, 31–32
power of, 23–26
role misalignment with, 27–32, 37–39
traits and, 103–104
identity blindspots, 6–7, 12, 16, 21–47, 200–201
change plans for, 202–203
checklist on, 213–214
common, 27–32
in entrepreneurs, 27–30
finding your, 44–47
finding your work identity and, 32–35
misalignments as, 26–27
power of identity and, 23–26
impostor identity, 29, 31–32, 194–196, 200–201
independence motive, 57
independent thinker identity, 29, 32
influence, 166–167, 175–182, 190–191
getting it right, 178–182
types of, 177–178
innovator identity, 28, 29–30
inspirational influence, 177–178, 181–182
integrity motive, 71–74
intellect
defining, 141–144
leadership and, 137–140, 145–149
perspective and, 144–145
types of intelligence and, 142–143, 145–149
understanding your, 159–162
intellect blindspots, 7–8, 14, 18, 137–162, 201, 209
awareness and, 145–149, 159–161
changing, 161–162
checklist on, 217–218
common types of, 158–159
defining intelligence and, 141–144
identifying, 145–148

knowledge acquisition and, 149–153
perspective and, 144–145
strategic thinking and, 154–158
intelligence. *See* intellect
intent, communication and, 171–175
introductions
identity clues in, 24–25
motive clues in, 69
IQ tests, 141–142

knowledge-acquisition blindspot, 149–153, 160

Lafley, A.G., 185
leaders and leadership, 16–17
behavioral foundations of, 165–188
choices for, 14–15
emotional mastery and, 116–120
emotional vulnerability and, 3–4, 107–108, 121–123
identity/role misalignment in, 27–32, 33–35
intellect and, 137–140, 144
in meetings, 202–203
personality and, 2–3
reflecting on characteristics for, 196
role requirements for, 184–187
self-awareness and, 16–19
"Swiss cheese," 12
traits and, 92–94
listening, active, 171–172
loyalty, 82–84, 98–100, 206–207
fear-driven, 110

Maslow, Abraham, 51
McClelland, David, 52
metacommunication, 172–173
money, as motive, 52, 53–54
motive blindspots, 6, 8, 47, 49–79, 208–209
affiliation motive and, 54–56
balancing motives and, 56–61

INDEX

motive blindspots (*continued*)
  behavior blindspots and, 170
  checklist on, 214–215
  emotions indicating, 70–71
  finding your, 76–79
  leveraging for success, 71–74
  name-dropping and, 9–10, 12–13
  personal motives and, 68–70
  stress and, 61–63
motives
  balancing, 56–61
  behavioral blindspots and, 176–178
  in business, 51–54, 215
  changing, 78–79
  definition of, 49
  hierarchy of needs and, 51–52
  influence and, 190–191
  leveraging for success, 71–74
  personal, 56–57, 68–70, 215
  street smarts and, 143
  universal, 51–52, 56

needs, hierarchy of human, 51
neuroticism, 88, 89, 103–104

openness to experience, 88, 89, 96, 104, 215

peacemaker identity, 29, 31–32
Perception Gap, 4–5
persistence, 69–70, 82–84, 96
personal identities, 29, 31–32, 214
personal influence, 177–178
personality. *See also* traits
  awareness model on, 5–8
  leadership ability and, 2–3
  stability of, 19
personality tests, 88
personal motives, 56–57
physiological needs, 51
power motive, 52, 63, 76
prioritization, 167, 182–188, 191–192

role clarity and, 187–188
role requirements and, 184–187
processing speed intelligence, 142, 144–145, 146–147
professional development, 15
  blindspot awareness and, 197–198
  identity changes and, 30–32, 35–42
  trait blindspots and, 98–100
purpose, 51–54, 152, 170

rational influence, 177–178, 181–182
rebel identity, 29, 31–32
relational influence, 177–178
relationships
  affiliation motive and, 56–61
  communication and, 173–174
  emotional blindspots and, 113–114, 119–120
  intellectual blindspots and, 151–152
RHR International, 17, 70–71
roles
  awareness of functions in, 45–46
  behavioral blindspots and, 184–187
  changing identity for, 35–37, 39–44
  clarity around, 187–188
  emotional misalignment with, 123–127, 136
  identity misalignments with, 27–32, 37–39
  motive alignment with, 79
  prioritization and, 167, 191–192
  stepping into, 203
  trait misalignment with, 89–91, 98–100, 105–106
  understanding requirements of, 184–187

safety needs, 51
self-actualization needs, 51, 95–100

INDEX

self-assessment, 4-5, 134-135
self-awareness, 11-14, 19
  of blindspots, 3-4
  blindspotting and, 196-200
  of emotional blindspots, 134-135
  flaws in, 4-5
  identity blindspots and, 45-46
  of intellectual blindspots, 159-161
  model for, 5-8
  of motives, 57-61, 73-74, 76-79
  of personal emotions, 114-115
self-awareness model, 6-8
self-confidence, 13, 96, 200
  behavioral blindspots and, 175-176
  intellect and, 149-150
self-doubt, 194-196
self-regulation, emotional, 115, 217
  skills
  emotional, 119-120, 126
  overestimating our own, 4-5
  traits versus, 84-85
states, traits versus, 84-85
strategic thinking, 154-158, 160, 161
street smarts, 143, 146, 147-148, 161
  strategic thinking and, 154-158
strengths. *See also* traits
  intellectual, 143-144
  weakness from investing too much in, 82-86
stress
  change and, 202
  emotional self-regulation and, 114, 115
  motive blindspots and, 61-63
  trait-based, 90-91
subject-matter expert identity, 28
success
  blindspots built on, 11-14, 19
  emotional intelligence and, 108
  leveraging motive for, 71-74
  luck and, 11-12
  motives and, 77-78
  trait blindspots and, 82-87
succession planning, 50-51

teams
  behavior blindspots and, 168-169, 178-181
  emotional blindspots and, 113-120
  influence and, 190, 191
  intellect blindspots and, 159
  trait blindspot compensation with, 91-92
Terror Zone, 152, 153, 160
timelines, for change, 211
time management, prioritization and, 182-188
trait blindspots, 6, 7-8, 13, 16, 79, 81-106
  addressing, 200, 209
  checklist for, 215-217
  development of, 84-87
  in entrepreneurs, 93-94
  leadership traits and, 92-95
  role misalignment and, 89-92
  self-awareness and, 95-100, 103-104
traits
  awareness of, 103-104
  Big Five, 88-89, 96, 215-216
  changing, 95-102
  definition of, 81
  leadership and, 90-94, 130-131
  persistence, 69-70
  skills versus states and, 84-85
  stability of, 85
  weakness from investing too much in, 82-86
trust
  behavior blindspots and, 169, 171, 173, 176
  emotional blindspots and, 110, 124-126
  identity blindspots and, 34-35, 40
  motive blindspots and, 71, 72-73

validation motive, 74–75
values, influence based on, 177–178
verbal encouragers, 172
vision, 13
   behavior blindspots and, 165, 184
   entrepreneurs and, 1, 8, 10, 13, 216
   execution and, 10, 91
   identity based on, 26–27, 30
   leadership and, 93, 94, 95
   motive and, 66, 75
vocal tone, 168, 172
vulnerability, 3–4, 107–108, 121–122

"What Only the CEO Can Do" (Lafley), 185

ACKNOWLEDGMENTS

I never planned to write a book. But as Covid-19 stretched into its second year I realized: I've had an unusual career, and if I could synthesize what I've learned over the years, it could probably help others. I should write it down. Over the next few months my writing evolved from being an exercise to keep my brain engaged to being something I became convinced could become a book. I hope you agree.

Before I express my gratitude to those who joined me on the book journey, I want to acknowledge my clients—psychotherapy and business—who trusted me to join them on their own journeys. My struggles to understand and help with their questions, concerns, pains, and joys are the source of the ideas in this book.

Psychology professors and mentors saw some promise in me and shaped me through their challenging, guiding, and modeling. Nelson Jones, Dick and Jean Hoerl, and Jeff Dolgan, your voices and presence will be with me forever.

To Ted and Martha Wirecki and Mitch Berdie—business partners and dear friends—our mutual respect and trust permitted me to grow and learn from my many mistakes. Thank you for allowing me to join you on our wild ride.

Julie Wolf, Joanne Starek, Chris Treadwell, and Leigh Allen, you opened the world of business consulting for me. I still smile thinking about how you gently chided me one day for being "too much of a psychologist" and another for being "too much of a businessperson." I don't think I ever got fully comfortable with the *consultant* identity.

Shaifali Prakash, our work together discovering how to translate psychological principles into actionable advice to help venture capital firms and portfolio company leaders has been a creative highlight of my career. And without the trust and confidence of a16z we wouldn't have had the opportunity.

How do you get a book published when you know nothing about the book business, and no one is asking you to write a book? This book simply wouldn't have progressed without early guidance from Dave Nixa, Jeff Hacker, and Rob Geller, and without critically constructive comments on and support of the first draft manuscript from Steve Baskin, Sean Slovenski, Tom Brook, John Waldstein, Norma Fiedotin, Julie Wolf, and Rick Breden and the Behavioral Essentials team.

And without serendipity it wouldn't have seen the light of day. Thank you to Joan Drucker Winstein, who introduced me to Steve Hanselman, who generously passed my book proposal on to Roger Freet, at Folio, who put this project in the hands of the terrific team at Harvard Business Review Press, led by my editor, Scott Berinato, who immediately saw the potential of this book to impact people's careers and lives. I am incredibly thankful for his hard work and valuable insights, along with support from the rest of the team at HBRP, including Stephani Finks for the delightful cover design, and Julie Devoll, Felicia Sinusas, Alexandra Kephart, Sally Ashworth, Jon Shipley, Lindsey Dietrich, and Jordan Concannon, who are helping the book get out to the world.

Finally, a profound thanks to the incomparable Jeremy Blachman, my writing partner, who took my writing, my ideas, and my stories and orchestrated them, made them sing, and helped me transform them into a book I could be proud of. You are supremely talented, a true craftsman, and now a treasured friend.

ABOUT THE AUTHOR

MARTIN DUBIN is a clinical psychologist, serial entrepreneur, business coach, and adviser to C-suite executives and Silicon Valley entrepreneurs. He has founded several companies, including a multimillion-dollar health care company where he also served as CEO. A former partner at talent firm RHR International, he worked directly with hundreds of C-suite senior executives from *Fortune* 500 companies and with Silicon Valley venture capital firms and their portfolio companies.

With a doctorate in clinical psychology from the University of Denver, Dubin began his career in private practice as a psychotherapist. He continued this practice for over a decade before moving to the business world as a founder and entrepreneur. He built a company with over 250 employees, ultimately driving its sale to *Fortune* 50 health insurer Anthem Blue Cross Blue Shield, where he worked as a senior vice president for three years. Dubin then launched the third act of his career, bringing his training in psychology and his business experience to the coaching space. His experience as an entrepreneur won him consultation contracts with portfolio companies of Andreessen Horowitz and Sequoia, both venture capital firms.

Dubin's work as a clinical psychologist taught him to think deeply about why people do what they do. That, combined with his business experience has enabled him to provide his coaching clients with actionable advice directed at both personal and professional success. His clientele has spanned industries and work roles across the globe.

ABOUT THE AUTHOR

Dubin has held faculty appointments at the Center for Creative Leadership in Colorado Springs and the University of Denver's Graduate School of Professional Psychology. He has also been a member of the American Psychological Association and a board member and chair of the Ethics Committee of the Colorado Psychological Association.

He lives in Colorado and New Mexico, where he enjoys skiing and hiking in the mountains and the desert and continues his work with clients, both individually and in corporate settings. His work on blindspots has informed not just this book but also a test to discover any individual's blindspots. Find him at martindubin.com.

Uncover your blindspots with the Blindspotting Assessment.

You've read all about blindspots—now it's time to see yours.

Taking the **Blindspotting Assessment** is your next step. This science-backed tool gives you a clear, data-driven view of the blindspots that may be holding you back—so you can start making better decisions, lead with greater clarity, and move beyond the patterns that limit your potential.

Grounded in clinical psychology and psychometric principles, the Blindspotting Assessment goes beneath the surface to reveal the hidden patterns shaping your decisions, leadership effectiveness, and professional performance. Using the **Blindspotting Self-Awareness Model,** the assessment identifies your potential blindspots across key areas and provides actionable steps to help you address them.

Scan the QR code to visit blindspotting.com to take the Blindspotting Assessment and move toward awareness and action.